Soils in Archaeology

Soils in Archaeology

Landscape Evolution and Human Occupation

Edited by Vance T. Holliday

SMITHSONIAN INSTITUTION PRESS

Washington and London

Designer: Susan Cook

This text is published from disk files prepared by the contributors and the volume editor, who assume full responsibility for the contents and form.

Library of Congress Cataloging-in-Publication Data

Soils in archaeology : landscape evolution and human occupation / edited by Vance T. Holliday.

   p. cm.

   Proceedings of the first annual Fryxell Symposium held in Phoenix in April 1988 and sponsored by the Society for American Archaeology.
   Includes bibliographical references.
   ISBN 1-56098-111-3 (cloth); 1-56098-308-6 (paper)
   1. Soil science in archaeology—Congresses. I. Holliday, Vance T. II. Society for American Archaeology. III. Fryxell Symposium (1st : 1988 : Phoenix, Ariz.)
CC79.S6S67 1992
930.1'028—dc20   91-13686
                  CIP

British Library Cataloguing-in-Publication Data is available.

Printed in the United States of America.
97 96 95   5 4 3

Contents

CONTENTS

List of Contributors

E. ARTHUR BETTIS III,
Iowa Department of Natural Resources, Geological Survey Bureau, 123 N.
Capital St., Iowa City, Iowa 52242

C. REID FERRING,
Institute of Applied Sciences, P.O. Box 13078, University of North Texas,
Denton, Texas 76203

BRUCE G. GLADFELTER,
Department of Geography, MC/183, University of Illinois at Chicago, Chicago,
Illinois 60680

PAUL GOLDBERG,
Institute of Archaeology, Hebrew University, Jerusalem, Israel 91905

VANCE T. HOLLIDAY,
Department of Geography, Science Hall, University of Wisconsin, Madison,
Wisconsin 53706

ROLFE D. MANDEL,
Department of Geography and Geology, University of Nebraska at Omaha,
Omaha, Nebraska 68182

JONATHAN A. SANDOR,
Department of Agronomy, Iowa State University, Ames, Iowa 50011

JULIE K. STEIN,
Department of Anthropology, DH-05, University of Washington, Seattle,
Washington 98195

VANCE T. HOLLIDAY

Foreword

The papers in this collection represent the proceedings of a symposium sponsored by the Society for American Archaeology (SAA) at the annual meetings in Phoenix in April 1988—the First Annual Fryxell Symposium. I was invited by the Fryxell Committee of the SAA to organize and chair this symposium within the broad area of "Earth Sciences in Archaeology," to complement the general theme of the 1988 Fryxell Award (given to David M. Hopkins). The topic I selected for the symposium was "Soils, Landscape Evolution, and Human Occupation"; the title has been changed only slightly for this volume.

To my knowledge, there are no edited volumes that deal with the broad spectrum of soil science applications in archaeology. There are some single-author books on soil science in archaeology (Cornwall 1958; Limbrey 1975) and a coauthored volume on soil micromorphology and archaeology (Courty et al. 1989). In addition, volumes on soil resistivity and archaeology (Carr 1982) and chemical analyses in archaeology include soil chemistry (e.g., Brothwell and Higgs 1970; Lambert 1984) and artificially modified soils (e.g., Eidt 1984; Groenman-van Waateringe and Robinson 1988). Indeed, soil chemistry and the study of human-influenced soils are probably the best-known applications of soil science in archaeological research. For the Fryxell Symposium, however, I wanted to cover a broader spectrum of soil science applications. This includes soil chemistry, which remains an important area of research, particularly for determining the presence or absence of human occupation and detecting agricultural practices. But another important area of soil science I also include is pedology (the study of soil genesis and morphology) and specifically soil geomorphology (the study of relationships between soils and landscapes). In addition to supporting and recording human occupations, soils are integral parts of the landscape and reflect the passage of time for stable surfaces. This consideration of soils—as intimate components of the landscape—is an approach less commonly employed or understood in archaeological contexts. In my view, however, such an approach can make significant contributions to archaeological research. The collection of essays presented here makes clear that other geoarchaeologists share this view. Moreover, it is encouraging to see that talented individuals with training and academic ties in a variety of disciplines (archaeology, physical geography, Quaternary geology, and pedology) are contributing to such studies.

The essays in this volume discuss the use of soils for reconstructing past landscapes and landscape evolution, for use in estimating the age of surfaces and depositional episodes, and for providing physical and chemical indicators of human occupation. The first four chapters in this volume focus on soil geomorphology in archaeology; specifically they deal with soils for reconstructing landscapes and site settings and the use of soils as age indicators. In Chapter 1, Reid Ferring discusses the archaeological implications of soils and soil geomorphology in alluvial settings. There is relatively little information in the pedologic literature on soils in alluvial settings, yet such areas are of obvious archaeological significance. Furthermore, the frequent additions of sediment and the usually high water tables make floodplain settings unique on the pedological landscape. Ferring's paper, therefore, presents a pedosedimentological framework for reconstructing alluvial landscapes from an archaeological perspective and for interpreting archaeological materials found in such settings. Rolfe Mandel, in Chapter 2, complements Ferring's work by presenting several case studies involving the use of soils for reconstructing complex alluvial histories and assessing archaeological site distributions. In particular, his paper illustrates the geoarchaeological utility of soils as stratigraphic markers and correlation tools, as relative and numerical age indicators (the latter by means of radiocarbon dating soil humates), and as unconformities denoting landscape stability. These interpretations are then used for interpreting archaeological site visibility and for predicting site locations and ages.

The next two chapters focus on the geoarchaeological significance of time and pedogenesis. In Chapter 3, I discuss some fundamental geoarchaeological considerations in the interpretation of buried soils and the reconstruction of associated landscapes. Buried soils are indicative of landscapes that were essentially stable surfaces for substantial amounts of time. Archaeological assemblages can, therefore, accumulate over time on such surfaces and can represent multiple occupations. Understanding such situations is crucial to proper interpretation of the archaeological record associated with buried soils. Chapter 4, by Art Bettis, presents a model for identifying alluvium of different ages based on pedogenic and other weathering characteristics. The essay is a specific illustration of how soil geomorphic research can be applied to provide valuable baseline information for the prediction, evaluation, and interpretation of archaeological site distribution in alluvial settings.

The second group of four essays in this collection deals with the archaeological significance of particular attributes of soils and includes both soil geomorphology and soil chemistry. In Chapter 5, Paul Goldberg reviews the wide variety of geoarchaeologically significant information that can be gleaned from soil thin sections. Thin section analysis, in pedology in general as well as in geoarchaeology, is often viewed as an "ancillary" study. But it should be considered as complementary to the more traditional "macromorphological" field and laboratory studies, providing equally important information at a different scale. A case study of soil and sediment investigations for archaeological purposes is presented by Bruce Gladfelter in Chapter 6. Gladfelter focuses on the problems of identifying pedologic features in aggrading alluvial settings and specifically on the difficulties of differentiating deposits of lacustrine and groundwater carbonate from pedogenic carbonate accumulation. Calcium carbonate is ubiquitous in soils and sediments in dry environments and sorting out the genesis of zones of carbonate accumulation is a recurring problem; correct identification is critical to the interpretation of landscape evolution and paleoenvironments. Julie Stein, in Chapter 7, deals with a common component of archaeological soils and sediments, reviewing the processes that introduce and alter organic matter in a site. She demonstrates how an understanding of these processes is crucial to an understanding of archaeological site formation processes, local landscape evolution, and, in a specific application, radiocarbon ages on organic soils and sediments. In the final essay in the volume, Jon Sandor reviews several of his research projects on the detection and interpretation of agricultural activity, one of the widest applications of soil science in archaeology. Agriculture has profound, but often subtle effects on soils, and Sandor discusses his approach to detecting changes in the soils and changes in the landscape resulting from agricultural practices in two regions where such activity was especially significant in prehistoric economies.

Included at the end of the volume is a glossary of selected soil science terms. Because of the potentially broad audience for this collection of essays, we decided to include a glossary of some terms, largely from pedology and soil micromorphology, that appear in this volume. Also included are some terms commonly used in soil description and classification, soil geomorphology, and soil geoarchaeology.

I extend my thanks and appreciation to the 1987 Fryxell Committee and the SAA for the opportunity to arrange the symposium. The task was especially enjoyable because it allowed me to call on and work with a number of colleagues whose research I have followed and admired. I thank everyone who participated in the symposium and contributed to this volume for your considerable time and efforts, and for your cooperation and patience. All authors reviewed manuscripts and I thank everyone for their help in this regard. I thank symposium participants Joe Schuldenrein (GeoArch Consultants, Inc.) and John Jacob (Texas A&M University), who were unable to submit manuscripts but provided considerable help with reviews. I also thank William R. Farrand (University of Michigan), Angela R. Linse (University of Washington), and the late John Treacy (University of Wisconsin) for providing very helpful reviews of several manuscripts.

REFERENCES

Brothwell, D. R., and E. S. Higgs (editors)
   1970   *Science in Archaeology.* Thames and Hudson, London.

Carr, Christopher G.
   1982   *Handbook on Soil Resistivity Surveying.* Center for American Archaeology Press, Evanston, Illinois.

Cornwall, I. W.
   1958   *Soils for the Archaeologist.* Phoenix House, London.

Courty, Marie-Agnès, Paul Goldberg, and Richard MacPhail
   1989   *Soils and Micromorphology in Archaeology.* Cambridge University Press, London.

Eidt, Robert C.
   1984   *Advances in Abandoned Settlement Analysis: Application to Prehistoric Anthrosols in Colombia, South America.* The Center for Latin America, University of Wisconsin-Milwaukee, Milwaukee.

Groenman-van Waateringe, W., and M. Robinson (editors)
   1988   *Man-Made Soils.* BAR International Series 410, Osney Mead, England.

Lambert, Joseph B. (editor)
   1984   *Archaeological Chemistry—III.* American Chemical Society, Advances in Chemistry Series, no. 205, Washington, D.C.

Limbrey, Susan
   1975   *Soil Science in Archaeology.* Academic Press, London.

1

C. REID FERRING

Alluvial Pedology and Geoarchaeological Research

As in other geomorphic settings, soils that form in alluvial valleys provide evidence for the age and geomorphic/environmental contexts of archaeological sites. Alluvial soils data are also useful for reconstructing site formation histories. The use of pedology in archaeological research in alluvial valleys is, therefore, an important component of geoarchaeological research. The objective of this chapter is to explicate the geoarchaeological significance of soils analysis in alluvial valleys. To accomplish this, I discuss first soil formation in alluvial valleys. I then evaluate applications of pedology to archaeological research in alluvial settings, emphasizing stratigraphy, paleoenvironmental reconstructions, the prediction of archaeological site locations, and the study of site formation processes. The discussion is illustrated with examples from North America, especially the Southern Plains.

An implicit theme of the chapter is that geoarchaeological research in alluvial valleys (or any other landscape setting) must be a fully interdisciplinary effort to maximize our understanding of archaeological records and their contexts. Soils analysis needs augmentation from geomorphology, radiometric dating, and independent biotic evidence of past environments. Because soils form only on relatively stable land

1

surfaces (Holliday, this volume), alluvial soils are largely a consequence of patterns of alluvial sedimentation. Thus, study of alluvial soils cannot be divorced from study of alluvial depositional histories. Spatial and temporal variation of alluvial soils has been used extensively as an aid to reconstructing Quaternary alluvial geologic histories (Morrison 1978) and to reconstructing Quaternary environments. But alluvial pedology can benefit from archaeology as well. Archaeologists routinely attempt to date sites and to reconstruct the paleoenvironments of site occupations. Resulting chronometric and paleoenvironmental data enhance pedologists' study of soil formation factors. In many cases, artifacts in a soil parent material can provide evidence of soil formation. For example pedogenic carbonates adhering to artifacts provide a good minimum age for calcic horizon development (Malde 1988). Artifacts buried along an otherwise imprecise paleosurface can provide evidence of soil welding (Ruhe and Olsen 1980) or prolonged faunalturbation (Johnson 1989).

Interdisciplinary applications of pedology to archaeological research are broadly treated in the several essays in this volume. The objective of this paper is to focus on pedology vis a vis study of archaeological sites in alluvial valleys. The concentration of sites in alluvial valleys and the valuable records of past environments that are contained in alluvial geologic histories are sufficient reasons to improve geoarchaeological research methods in alluvial settings. Soils analysis is one means to accomplish this goal.

ALLUVIAL SOIL FORMATION

For the discussions in this essay, alluvial soils are defined by their parent material: they are soils that form in alluvial sediments. Included are soils that are still forming at the surface and soils that are buried and are no longer forming. Two major classes of alluvial soils are floodplain soils and terrace soils (Gerrard 1987). Floodplain soils are surficial soils that form on floodplains and are subject to incremental additions of new alluvial parent material. Surficial terrace soils are not flooded, except by rare, large magnitude floods (Baker et al. 1983). Soils formed in alluvial fan sediments are not considered here, although these are often important in archaeological research (see Bettis and Littke 1987; Butzer 1977).

Factors of soil formation in alluvial settings are those described by Jenny (1941) for soils in general. Jenny's factors are time, parent material, topography, climate, and organisms. These factors, and the pedologic methods outlined by Jenny are premised on a clear distinction between geologic and soil-forming processes: "Accordingly, natural phenomena such as volcanic eruptions, depositions of loess, and sedimentation in lakes and rivers are not soil-forming processes. They build up parent material and are classified as geologic phenomena" (Jenny 1941:55). Jenny notes that this distinction is arbitrary, yet necessary in order to isolate parent material and time as independent factors of soil formation. Episodic deposition of alluvial sediment during floods results in complex soil profiles, analogous to profiles that formed in aggrading loess or dune sands. In these aggradational settings, the degree of soil profile development is inversely proportionate to rates of sediment deposition. Rapid sedimentation inhibits development of soils, while relative geomorphic stability promotes development of soil horizons.

Fluvial sedimentation is subject to change at several scales. Flooding, resulting in incremental additions of sediment to the floodplain, is usually a low magnitude, high frequency component of depositional variation (Knox 1983). Internal stream dynamics characteristic of most fluvial systems, such as channel migration, channel cut-off, or meander belt avulsion impose larger scale spatial variability in sedimentation (Allen 1965). Low frequency, larger scale processes are climatically or tectonically induced, producing changes in stream gradients or stream discharge, with accompanying geomorphic responses such as rapid channel adjustments, valley alluviation or valley incision (floodplain abandonment with concomitant terrace formation).

Short-term spatial differences in alluviation are best documented for meandering streams (Allen 1965; Lewin 1978). On the floodplain of a meandering stream, spatial differences in patterns of sedimentation result in different environments for soil formation. The interrelationship between sedimentation and floodplain soil formation leads to problems in the description of alluvial soils and in the discrimination of sedimentary from pedogenic features in alluvial sections. To accommodate this situation, Kraus and Bown (1988) have proposed the term *pedofacies* for spatial variation in alluvial sedimentary facies and associated floodplain soils. While this term is intuitively satisfactory for conveying the complexity of sedimentation and pedogenesis on floodplains, it remains important to discriminate between deposition of parent material and post-depositional or syndepositional soil formation, especially in geoarchaeological studies. The term *soil facies* (Morrison 1978; Birkeland 1984:326) is conceptually the same, and is used in this paper.

Floodplain Soils

Within a given river basin, incremental addition of alluvium to floodplains, at different rates in different sedimentary environments (Ferring 1986a), is probably the chief factor that defines properties of floodplain soils (McClelland et al. 1950; Gerrard 1981:106–116). Near channels, in levee or splay environments, rapid deposition can preclude soil formation (Gray 1984; Guccione et al. 1988), or will result in formation of Fluvents or Fluvaquents (Soil Survey Staff 1975:181). These soils usually exhibit irregular decreases in organic carbon with depth, and often exhibit depositional layering, including superposed organic-rich finer strata resembling buried A horizons. Clay bands, or clay lamellae, sometimes form below the A-horizons of sandy soils (Soil Survey Staff 1975:25; Dijkerman et al. 1967). More commonly found in eolian sands, these are sometimes misinterpreted as sedimentary structures in alluvial sections. That they can form under floodplains within a few decades was demonstrated by Webb (1939). Clay lamellae are also features of terrace soils (Anderson and Schuldenrein 1983).

Farther from channels, where rates of sedimentation are slower, different soil forming environments are present. Depending on the rate of sedimentation, cumulative soil profiles often develop on floodplains. Here, the term cumulative soil is used in the genetic sense of Birkeland (1984:184). The taxonomic term *cumulic* denotes an overthickened soil that results from deposition of parent material concurrently with pedogenesis; the term *pachic* denotes an overthickened soil with no visible evidence of added parent material at the surface (Soil Survey Staff 1975:87). Jenny (1962) described cumulative soils as "inverted" soil profiles, since the deeper horizons have undergone the most pedogenic alteration. Profiles of cumulative floodplain soils have overthickened A-horizons (Birkeland 1984:185). Organic matter in these soils includes that which is inherited with parent material (usually adsorbed to clays) and that which accumulates in situ. Radiocarbon dating of humate fractions from floodplain soils entails risks of dating inherited organics, thereby obtaining anomalous old ages for the soil horizon. A safer approach is to date the accumulation of parent material with charcoal samples, and use these ages to help interpret humate ages from the soil profile (Haas et al. 1986).

Because of frequent flooding and/or high water tables, floodplain soils are often gleyed (Hayward and Fenwick 1983; Walker and Coventry 1976). Seasonal drying of clay-rich floodplain soils often results in silt coats on crack surfaces (Brammer 1971). Structure develops rapidly in clay-rich floodplain soils as well (White 1966), even in A-horizons.

Flooding and groundwater processes also complicate translocation and precipitation of calcium carbonate in floodplain soils. Rates of calcic horizon development in arid environments are generally assessed for soils formed on stable surfaces (Gile et al. 1981). These approaches are suitable for terrace soils yet require modification for aggradational settings. Leeder (1973) has proposed a model for accumulation of carbonates in floodplain soils in arid lands that incorporates rates of sedimentation. In mesic environments, where calcic soils are not dominant, calcic horizons form by the redistribution of primary (inherited or allogenic) carbonate (Machette 1985).

Stream Dynamics and Floodplain Soils

Spatial variation in soils is increased further by larger scale geomorphic change on floodplains caused by channel migration and meander belt avulsion. Since these processes are significant at the scale of the late Quaternary, they are relevant to the study of archaeological records in alluvial settings.

Channel cut-off and lateral channel migration cause changes in sedimentation that may be rapid or slow, with varying sedimentary results (Walker and Cant 1984). In the direction of channel migration, sediments will grade upward from floodbasin to levee facies, while in former channel positions the vertical sequence will grade from lateral accretion to vertical accretion deposits. The contacts between these facies are defined by the rate of channel migration. These rates also are partial controls on soil formation in different positions relative to the channel.

Along meander belts, relatively rapid rates of deposition promote development of an alluvial ridge (Allen 1965). Near channels, rapid sedimentation inhibits soil development compared to locations away from the meander belt where sedimentation rates are slower (Guccione et al. 1988; Gray 1984). Following avulsion, the old meander belt ridge is elevated above the floodplain (Figure 1-1). Soils will form on this relatively stable surface until valley alluviation has raised the flanking portions of the floodplain. Along the new meander belt, the pre-avulsion surface soils are rapidly buried by levee and splay sediments.

Because avulsion may occur at intervals of hundreds to a few thousand years (Bridge and Leeder 1979), the sedimentary-pedogenic effects

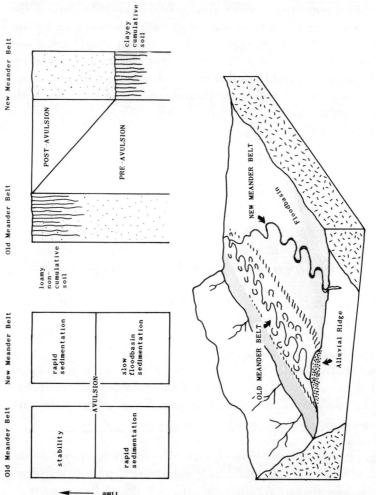

Figure 1-1. Floodplain depositional geomorphology and model of soil formation processes. Important local factors in floodplain soil formation are rates of deposition and sedimentary environment. Rapid geomorphic change associated with meander belt avulsion generates different sedimentary-soils records without necessary changes in climate. Floodplain diagram modified after Walker and Cant (1984).

of avulsion are significant to archaeological investigations (Ferring 1986a). As shown in the hypothetical case, different sequences of sediments, and different soil profiles are formed in floodplain reaches where avulsion has occurred. Archaeological sites in these separate locations should exhibit marked differences in natural stratigraphy and soils, even if the sites are of the same age. To compare site formation in these settings, and to avoid erroneous temporal or environmental interpretation, these larger scale floodplain sedimentary processes must be defined first.

Terrace Soils

Alluvial terraces are formed when a floodplain is abandoned through valley incision, thereby isolating the terrace surface from flooding. Subsequently, soils form on terraces under the influence of the factors of Jenny (1941), without the added complexity noted above for soils formed on floodplains.

In general, soils on successively higher terraces should exhibit increasingly stronger profile development (Walker and Coventry 1976). Terrace soil chronosequences can be defined on the basis of Bt horizon properties (Birkeland 1984:203–218; Walker and Green 1976; McFadden and Hendricks 1985), stages of calcic horizon development (Gile et al. 1981), base saturation trends (Parsons and Herriman 1970) or multiple properties and indices of soil development (Ponti 1985; Rockwell et al. 1985). The hydrologic and geochemical conditions for soil formation on terraces are obviously distinct from those of floodplains. In deeper horizons, rapid oxidation of reduced iron and manganese, and rapid oxidation of organic material usually occurs (Hayward and Fenwick 1983). Bedrock benches under terrace alluvium can maintain perched water tables that complicate diagenetic and weathering processes. For example, over limestone bedrock benches, calcic horizons in terrace soils can be pedogenic, or may have formed by calcite precipitation from groundwater (Machette 1985; Ferring 1986b).

Of particular significance to North American archaeology are terraces and terrace soils that formed during the Holocene. Alluvial terrace soil chronosequences can be established on a Holocene time scale, as shown by an example from a small watershed in Wisconsin (McDowell 1983; Table 1-1). Differences in these Holocene terrace soils are poten-

7

TABLE 1-1

Age and Characteristics of Holocene Terrace Soils from a Small Drainage in Wisconsin

Terrace	Period of Alluviation (year B.P.)	Soil Types	Characteristic Soil Properties
E	9000–7800	Typic argiaquolls	Bt horizon, high chroma
D	5700–5000	Haplaquepts, Hapludolls	Bw horizon, patchy argillans
C	4500–4000	Typic udifluvents, Terric medisaprists	A/C, O/A/C profiles
B	3000–2000	Typic udifluvents	A/C profiles

Source: Data from McDowell (1983).

tially important evidence for site prediction and also for assessment of site formation processes.

Terrace soils can exhibit marked lateral variation because of spatial differences in parent material inherited from the antecedent floodplain (Holliday 1987a). This variation makes it difficult to correlate soils along terraces and to establish terrace soil chronosequences (Vreeken 1984). Terrace soils may have inherited clay-rich A-horizons with moderate or strong structure from the antecedent floodplain soil. Upon oxidation and loss of organics, these convert to B-horizons (Parsons and Herriman 1970; Birkeland 1984:11) and can resemble much older argillic horizons.

Younger exogenic sediments may partially cover terraces. Possible types of exogenic sediments are: eolian (Sellards 1923; Corless and Ruhe 1955; Follmer 1985), colluvial (Boison and Patton 1985) or alluvial fan deposits (Butzer 1977). Soils formed in these younger exogenic parent materials are often difficult to distinguish from older, buried soils formed in alluvium. For example, soils formed in thin loess mantles are difficult to separate from underlying terrace soils in the lower Mississippi Valley (Miller et al. 1984:10–14). These soil complexes are called "welded soils" (Ruhe and Olsen 1980). Even more complex alluvial soil sequences are generated when terraces are buried by renewed valley alluviation (Birkeland 1984:203; Vreeken 1984).

Overall, terrace soils initially carry sedimentary-pedogenic "signatures" of the abandoned floodplain. With time however, terrace soils develop profiles that reflect continued weathering in relatively stable settings, usually without periodic flooding and addition of sediment. Many archaeological sites are found on terraces, and it is essential to understand terrace soils in the course of analyzing archaeological sites in these settings.

ALLUVIAL PEDOLOGY AND GEOARCHAEOLOGY

Alluvial pedology is important to archaeology for several reasons. First is the simple abundance of archaeological sites in alluvial valleys relative to other settings. This concentration of sites is made more important by the fact that much archaeological research is concentrated in river valleys, both by choice and through reservoir construction and associated cultural resources management (CRM) projects. Second, geologic records in alluvial settings are complex, and soils are an important means of defining and correlating stratigraphic units and making paleoenvironmental reconstructions. Third, analysis of alluvial soils can contribute to geoarchaeological research at several scales: within sites, among sites, and in studies of regional scope. As described below, alluvial pedology can help in the study of site formation processes, local and regional environmental reconstruction, archaeological stratigraphy, and prediction of archaeological site locations in river valleys.

The study of alluvial soils can make contributions to archaeological research only if factors of alluvial soil formation, as outlined earlier, are linked to empirically relevant aspects of the archaeological record and its context. I will explicate this contingent significance of alluvial soils for archaeological research by briefly discussing the factors mentioned above, and by indicating their relationship to archaeological problems, using examples from the soils and archaeological literature. My emphasis is on alluvial soils as they relate to chronology, environment, and archaeological site formation.

Soils, Alluvial Stratigraphy, and Archaeology

Soils are among the most important stratigraphic markers used in Quaternary research, and are certainly the most important in alluvial stratigraphy (Morrison 1978; Birkeland 1984:325–339; Evans 1982). Buried soils commonly define contacts between mappable alluvial sedimentary units (allostratigraphic units) while surface soils are useful in mapping

9

and correlating terraces. Beyond the scope of this discussion are complex relationships among soils, sedimentary units, and sequences of burial or exhumation of soils (Vreeken 1984), although such relationships are clearly relevant to study of alluvial stratigraphy in archaeological research.

Although laboratory data are often needed to fully establish many time-dependent soil properties (e.g., clay, carbonate or sesquioxide content, base saturation, thickness/abundance of clay films), field recognition of age-related soils properties is important to archaeological studies on alluvial terraces (e.g., Gardner and Donahue 1985). Along the South Platte River in Colorado, Holliday (1987b) integrated terrace morphostratigraphy with a soils chronosequence that is relevant to the prediction of the stratigraphic position of Paleoindian and younger sites. While lateral variations in parent material resulted in differences in soil development on terraces, the soil chronosequence will assist extensions of archaeological surveys of these late Quaternary surfaces.

In arid lands, soils scientists use calcic and argillic horizons in late Quaternary alluvial soils to establish soils chronosequences (Gile et al. 1981; McFadden 1988; McFadden and Tinsley 1985). In these areas, accurate mapping of soils would enable prediction of terrace sites of given ages. Alluvial soil stratigraphy in mesic regions offers the same potentials, albeit with different types of soils (e.g., Follmer 1983; Gooding 1971).

Soil-stratigraphic studies focused on buried alluvial soils are less common than for surface terrace soils (Birkeland 1984:203), especially for Holocene settings. This is because Holocene soils are usually weakly developed and soils that formed over similar intervals before burial, but at different times, will be hard to distinguish among separate localities without independent age controls (Birkeland 1984: 334). Nonetheless, buried soils are significant to archaeology because most North American sites are of Holocene age and because burial and superpositioning in alluvial settings is conducive to better preservation of archaeological records (see Mandel, this volume). The archaeologist's need to establish alluvial stratigraphic frameworks has clearly encouraged pedologists working with archaeologists to document Holocene soils-stratigraphy (Bettis this volume).

In the Southern Plains of the United States (Figure 1-2), similar patterns of late Holocene alluviation and floodplain stability make possible regional correlations of late Holocene episodes of soil formation (Figure 1-3). In this region alluvial terraces are almost all Pleistocene in age

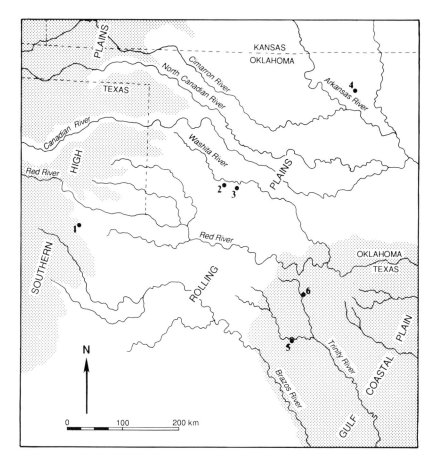

Figure 1-2. Map of the Southern Plains of the United States with locations of sites discussed in text: 1, Quitaque Creek; 2, Carnegie Canyon; 3, Delaware Canyon; 4, Little Caney; 5, West Fork Trinity River; 6, Site 41CO141.

(Ferring in press). Holocene terraces are present in the Red River Valley, but for other major valleys and their tributaries, late Pleistocene and Holocene alluvium is below floodplains. Thus, archaeological sites of any age can occur on terraces, and buried sites in alluvium are almost all below floodplains.

Most Southern Plains valleys were deeply incised at the end of the Pleistocene, and filled during the Holocene. Hence, Holocene alluvial fills are thick, and there are few exposures of early to middle Holocene sediments. Comparison of many dated alluvial sections, of which a few

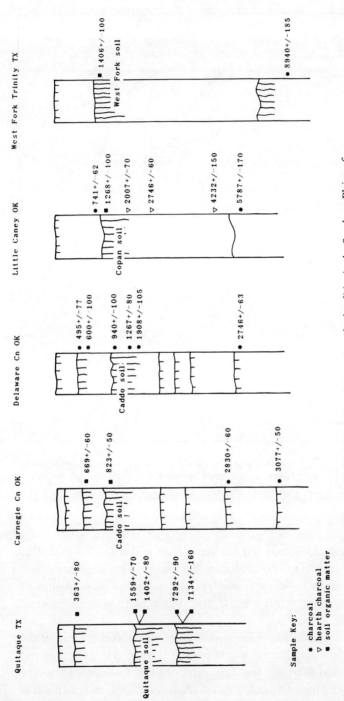

Figure 1-3. Holocene soils-stratigraphic sections for localities in the Southern Plains of the United States (not to scale). Surface of each section is floodplain. Radiocarbon ages are all in years before present, calibrated after Stuiver and Reimer (1986). Data are from: Quitaque (Baumgardner and Caran 1986), Carnegie Canyon (Hall 1987), Delaware Canyon (Ferring 1986c), Little Caney (Artz and Reid 1984), West Fork Trinity (Ferring 1986b, in press). See Figure 1-2 for locations of sections and text for discussion.

12

are shown in Figure 1-3, shows evidence of a late Holocene episode of floodplain stability and soil formation roughly between 2000 and 1000 B.P. This soil is identified in north central Oklahoma (Hall 1977; Artz and Reid 1984), in southwestern Oklahoma (Pheasant 1982; Ferring 1986c; Hall and Lintz 1984; Hall 1987; Ferring and Hall 1987) and in north central Texas (Ferring 1986b, in press). In the Rolling Plains of Texas a buried soil of the same age, herein informally named the Quitaque soil, has been described and dated at several localities (Gustavson 1986). In the Southern Plains, formation of these late Holocene floodplain soils was terminated by alluviation and burial between 800 and 1200 years B.P.

The buried facies of these soils almost always exhibit overthickened A-horizons. In southwestern Oklahoma, the Caddo soil is cumulative, as shown by concordant radiocarbon ages on charcoal and humates from the upper part of the soil (Ferring in press). At Delaware Canyon an unburied facies of the soil is more developed than the buried facies (Figure 1-4). The Copan soil also exhibits geomorphically controlled unburied facies with moderate B-horizon development (Artz and Reid 1984).

Weakly developed A-C soils commonly occur above and below these thick soils (Figure 1-4). Because of local, nonsynchronous alluvial events, these weak soils cannot be reliably correlated. By contrast, the Caddo, Copan, Quitaque and West Fork soils are useful stratigraphic markers in late Holocene alluvial sections. They can be used to identify stratigraphic positioning of late Archaic, Plains Woodland, and Late Prehistoric archaeological sites (Artz 1985; Ferring 1986c, in press; Hall 1988). Because these soils denote slow alluvial deposition for up to 1,000 years, the soil parent material usually has higher site densities than the alluvium above or below (Ferring 1986a). On the other hand, local differences in the time at which these soils were buried, and the importance of geomorphic and not temporal controls on their morphology argue against regionwide, formal correlations. Use of local names for these soils should be maintained.

Holocene alluvial soil-stratigraphic frameworks have been developed in several other regions of North America, and are useful in correlating and predicting archaeological sites. These include examples from the Central Plains (Johnson and Martin 1987; Mandel, this volume) and the Midwest (Bettis and Littke 1987).

Alluvial soils have been used in description and stratigraphic correlation of Paleoindian sites over large portions of the Southwest and Great Plains regions (Haynes 1968, 1970; Reider 1980, 1982; Albanese

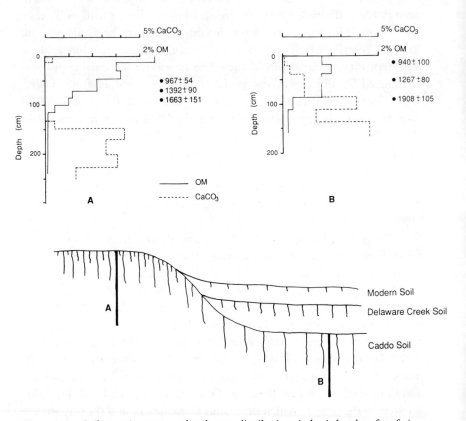

Figure 1-4. Soil organic matter and carbonate distributions in buried and surface facies of late Holocene Caddo soil from Delaware Canyon, Oklahoma. Note accumulation of organic matter and greater carbonate leaching in surface facies.

1986; Irwin–Williams et al. 1973). Many of these sites have Holocene deposits overlying the Paleoindian horizons. Buried soils and archaeological materials in these Holocene sections are used to correlate Archaic and Late Prehistoric sites in the same regions. Soil-stratigraphic studies of Paleoindian sites in the eastern United States are rare, but include analyses at Shawnee Minisink, a stratified Paleoindian–Early Archaic site in Pennsylvania, and at the Thunderbird site in Virginia (Foss 1977).

During archaeological surveys, soils can provide the best means to implement and modify site discovery strategies (Bettis, this volume). For regions where late Quaternary soil-stratigraphic frameworks have been developed, survey strategies can be designed that exploit available data to stratify the survey area, train crews with respect to the potential for buried or surficial site settings, and plan subsurface exploration. Even preliminary soil-stratigraphic frameworks should greatly improve archaeological surveys. These frameworks can later be refined through detailed fieldwork and radiometric dating, which are usually not possible in early stages of research, especially in contexts of CRM projects. Geomorphological and soils investigations, coupled with study of known sites in a new project area *should* be implemented before survey crews begin their work.

ALLUVIAL SOILS AND PALEOENVIRONMENTS

Alluvial soils can provide evidence for paleoenvironments (Ruhe 1970, 1983), and thus are valuable in the study of the environmental contexts of prehistoric occupations. In too many cases, unfortunately, direct evidence for paleoenvironments, such as pollen, snails or plant macrofossils, is poorly preserved in alluvial sediments. Under these circumstances, soils are especially important evidence for past environments.

Environmental reconstructions that are based on alluvial soils data complement archaeological research at local and regional scales. Local (habitat) reconstructions help define the original setting of a site. Soils that formed for a short interval prior to burial are well-suited for these purposes, since they are less likely to be affected by subsequent climate changes. For example, Reider (1982) used soils data to describe changing environments at the Agate Basin site in Wyoming that included Clovis, Folsom, and later Paleoindian occupations. Reider used A-horizon organic matter content, evidence for gleying, and a sequence of clay illuviation and carbonate leaching to define local changes in habitat at the site. Waters (1986) integrated soils analysis with alluvial geology to re-construct Holocene environments of site formation at Whitewater Draw, Arizona. Other instructive examples of site habitat reconstruction using soils data include Guccione et al. (1988) and Reider et al. (1987).

At a larger scale, alluvial soils are used to make climatic-environmental reconstructions that are relevant to regional studies of prehistoric settlement patterns. Holliday's (1987b) evaluation of late Pleistocene soils in eolian sediments on the Southern High Plains illus-trates how pedogenic data can be used in this regard. In most regions of the United States, surface terrace soils are used to help infer late Pleistocene environments. These must be used cautiously, because sur-face soil formation is influenced by all climatic-environmental changes since the parent material stopped accumulating (Birkeland 1984:329).

Buried Holocene soils are better suited for paleoclimatic recon-structions than terrace soils because they are less likely to be affected by postburial climate changes. Indeed, climatically induced episodes of floodplain stability (accompanied by pedogenesis) are investigated wide-ly as part of Holocene climatic reconstructions (Knox 1983). Because floodplain soil formation is affected directly by floodplain stability re-gardless of the cause, both local (Ferring 1986a) and downstream (Knox 1976) geomorphic controls must be evaluated *before* floodplain soils are attributed to climate change. At several Holocene archaeological lo-calities in the northern Great Plains, buried Holocene soils are claimed as evidence for dry mid-Holocene climates as originally proposed by Leopold and Miller (1954). These soils have argillic and calcic horizons (Albanese 1986; Reider 1980, 1982; Irwin-Williams et al. 1973).

ALLUVIAL SOILS AND SITE FORMATION

The study of site formation processes is an area of archaeological research that integrates methods from earth science and archaeology (Butzer 1982; Schiffer 1983). These inquiries, within and between sites, focus on differ-ential preservation of artifacts and features and on their differential spatial-stratigraphic physical associations. While cultural factors are nec-essary considerations (Schiffer 1987), the present discussions focus on how alluvial pedology can assist site formation analyses.

Specific soil forming processes have direct implications with re-spect to site formation. These include: organic matter accumulation-decay; addition, translocation or removal of salts; mineral oxidation-reduction; eluviation, illuviation, and shrinking-swelling of clays; and bioturbation. Geochemical soil forming processes generally result in deterioration of plant, shell, and bone remains through leaching, oxidation, and biogenic degradation. In contrast, translocation of salts can help preserve shell and bone in calcic horizons. Translocation of carbonates to deeper horizons will promote bone deterioration in the leached horizons. Changing redox conditions are often found in floodplain soils (Hayward and Fenwick 1983). Iron or manganese mottles or concretions attest to these changes, and signify probable oxidation of pollen and other organic materials. Eluviation of clay can make the eluviated horizon more prone to erosion, and illuviation can increase clay shrink-swell effects in the deeper horizons. Bioturbation, through the action of plants and animals is often greatest in a soil, because of root density and the availability of food in the A-horizon for burrowing organisms (Wood and Johnson 1978; Butzer 1982:110–114). Also, action of fossorial rodents (Johnson 1989), crayfish, amphibians or worms (Stein 1983) can translocate artifacts or selectively move finer sediments to the surface. Bioturbation may, on the other hand, beneficially result in burial of objects that were deposited on a stable surface (Darwin 1896:308–309).

Soils and Site Formation on Floodplains

Study of formation processes on floodplains requires coordinated analysis of sedimentary environments and soils. One of the most important factors in floodplain soil formation is the rate of alluviation. Rates of deposition are in themselves key factors in archaeological site formation processes (Ferring 1986a). Rates of matrix accumulation define potentials for: (a) superpositioning of artifacts associated with serial occupations, (b) differential preservation of organic materials, and, (c) differential physical disturbance of original associations among artifacts and features. Clearly, rates of sedimentation will correlate at some level, in a given environment, with soil development (Holliday, this volume). Study of these relationships begins with the general observation that a floodplain soil within a section of alluvium denotes a period of relatively slower sedimentation or even surface stability.

Within a particular environment, assessing the impact of floodplain soil-forming and sedimentary processes on archaeological sites involves consideration of several factors: (a) the chronology of sedimentation (parent material deposition) relative to nondeposition and floodplain stability, (b) the chronology of archaeological occupations relative to sedimentation *and* soil formation, (c) the texture of the soil parent material, (d) the length of time the soil formed and (e) the burial history of the soil.

The chronology of floodplain sedimentation (parent material deposition) relative to soil formation defines whether the resulting soil will develop as either a cumulative or a noncumulative soil. Cumulative soils (Birkeland 1984:184–189) formed as parent material aggraded, while noncumulative soils formed during periods of nondeposition. A more complex case would involve a cumulative soil forming during a period of levee sedimentation, followed by continued pedogenesis on the stabilized levee sediments after avulsion. Overall, however, site formation processes are different for archaeological materials associated with cumulative or noncumulative soils. As depicted in Figure 1-4, synpedogenic burial associated with cumulative soils protects artifacts from erosional disturbance, carnivore gnawing of bone, and active near–surface bioturbation. By contrast, rapid deposition, followed by flood plain stability and development of a noncumulative soil entails different site formation processes; in this case, the shallowly buried archaeological materials are subject to more intense, adverse modification effects. If stratified archaeological materials are present in a section with an overthickened A-horizon, it may be difficult to determine, because of site disturbance, if the artifacts were deposited in single or multiple occupation episodes. Refitting of artifacts (Villa 1982) or examination of vertical trends in spatial patterning (Ferring and Peter 1987) are means to assess this problem. For archaeological occupations that postdate deposition of the alluvial parent materials, greater pedoturbation and bioturbation is expected with noncumulative soils, owing to greater age than cumulative soils with similar thickness (Figure 1-4).

The timing of archaeological occupation relative to sedimentation and soil development determines the burial depth of the artifacts and features in a site, and their position relative to soil horizons (Figure 1-4). Again, the differences between cumulative and noncumulative soils are important. Rapid deposition of parent materials before and after occupation results in better primary context for artifacts. If a noncumulative soil forms in these sediments, the archaeological materials will be exposed longer to pedogenic effects. By contrast, artifacts and features within an overthickened cumulative soil (at the same depth as in a noncumulative soil) are subjected to a shorter interval of pedogenesis, but may have been exposed longer to pre-burial agents (erosion, carnivore scavenging).

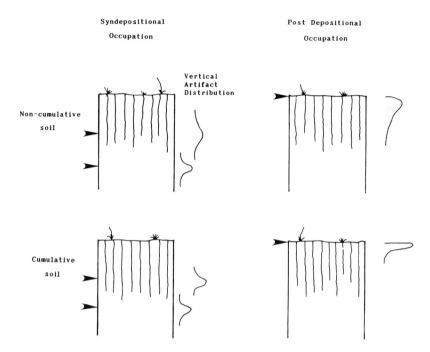

Figure 1-5. Diagram illustrating relationships between sedimentation, pedogenesis, and archaeological site modification. Model is for alluvial soils with overthickened A-horizons. Differences in site modification are results of different sequences of sedimentation and pedogenesis for cumulative and noncumulative soils.

Spatial and temporal variations in sedimentation can result in laterally continuous variations (soil facies) from cumulative to noncumulative alluvial soils. The relationships described here are ends of this continuum, and specific site histories must be evaluated accordingly. The main point for geoarchaeological investigations is that to understand preserved soils-stratigraphic positioning of archaeological materials, it is necessary to document patterns of pedogenesis and sedimentation, as shown in the following example.

At Delaware Canyon, Oklahoma, the cumulative Caddo soil exhibits buried and surface facies (Figure 1-4). Radiocarbon dating of soil parent material using charcoal samples provided control for deposition rates (Ferring 1986a,c). Along the valley axis, the cumulative Caddo soil was buried sometime between 900 and 600 B.P., and soil formation stopped. Along the valley margins, the Caddo soil was not buried and is

19

still forming. The buried cumulative facies of the Caddo soil exhibits higher carbonate content and little vertical change in organic matter (Figure 1-4). In this setting, bone was well preserved throughout the buried soil A-horizon. In contrast, the surface facies of the soil show evidence of continued organic matter accumulation and carbonate leaching after the valley axis facies were buried. Bone preservation in this section is good only in the lower part of the A-horizon because of leaching (Ferring 1986a). In contrast to the simple relationships shown in Figure 1-5, the surface facies of the Caddo soil here has gone through a cumulative/noncumulative sequence of soil formation.

Returning to discussion of factors in site formation, the texture of alluvial parent material influences the rate of soil formation (Birkeland 1984:179–181) and thus the rate of pedogenically controlled site modification. In coarser sediments, salts are leached more rapidly and to greater depths than in clayey sediments. In arid regions this will promote faster leaching of carbonates to deeper horizons (Gile et al. 1981; McFadden 1988), adversely affecting bone preservation for shallow buried archaeological sites. In clayey alluvium, Bt-horizons tend to develop more quickly and seasonal clay shrinking can hasten pedoturbation (Birkeland 1984:180; Brammer 1971). Because of greater surface area, clayey sediments also tend to have higher amounts of adsorbed organic matter (Birkeland 1984:246). In north central Texas, calcic horizons are common in Holocene soils formed in clay-silt rich alluvial parent materials, but are leached quickly from sandy alluvium (Ferring 1986b). Bone and shell are usually well preserved in the former and absent or poorly preserved in sandy alluvium.

Progressive soil formation processes that are factors in site formation continue, with additive effects, unless the soil is buried and soil formation ceases. Field and lab evidence for relative soil ages can be used to assess site formation histories at sites of varying age. Soil age evaluations must take into account textural variations in parent materials and possible climatic differences between periods of soil formation. Some of these considerations are illustrated by study of a late Holocene locality in north central Texas.

Geoarchaeological investigations at Site 41CO141 in north central Texas (Figure 1-2) revealed evidence of late Holocene fluvial sedimentation, pedogenesis, and archaeological site formation (Ferring 1987b). The site is situated on the eastern part of the Elm Fork Trinity River floodplain, and is exposed in a channel cut bank of the river. Borehole data show that the alluvium under the floodplain and above bedrock is

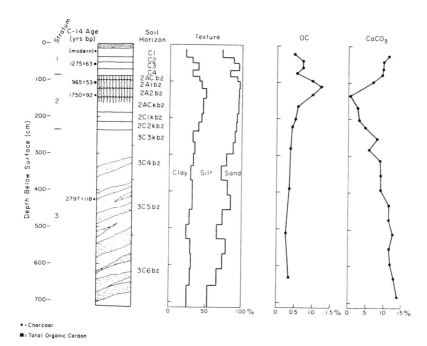

• : Charcoal
■ : Total Organic Carbon

Figure 1-6. Soil-stratigraphic column for site 41CO141, a late Holocene locality in north central Texas. Sedimentary facies include lateral accretion (stratum 3), floodbasin (stratum 2), and levee (stratum 1). Compare age of West Fork soil, here formed on stratum 2 parent material, to late Holocene soils in Figure 1-3.

ca. 12 meters thick. About 7 meters of late Holocene alluvium is exposed in the cutbank (Figure 1-6). Other exposures were made in backhoe trenches on the floodplain and in archaeological excavations above the cutbank. Study of these profiles revealed that the meander belt of the Trinity had shifted several times in the late Holocene.

The stratigraphy of the archaeological site includes the following units (Figure 1-6; Table 1-2):

   A. lateral accretion (point bar) facies, ca. 4.5 meters thick; these exhibit dipping beds of fine sands and silts, with preserved primary structures and abundant organic detritus; they grade upward into,

   B. fining upward clay and silt floodplain facies, ca. 1.5 meters thick; contains stratified late Archaic artifacts, hearths and faunas; a soil formed in the upper part of these sediments; the soil is buried by,

   C. recent coarsening upward silty levee facies, ca. 1 meter thick (these sediments were truncated by construction).

TABLE 1-2

Profile Data for Site 41C0141

Horizon	Depth	Color Dry	Color Moist	Texture[a]	Structure[b]	Boundary[c]	Comments
x	0–11						Disturbed zone
C1	11–34	10YR5/3	10YR4/3	L	m	cs	Thin beds
C2	34–50	10YR4/3	10YR3/3	STCL	m/1fgr	cs	Common burrows
C3	50–69	10YR5/2	10YR4/2	STCL	1fsab	cs	
C4	69–87	10YR4.5/3	10YR4/3	STCL	1fgr	ai	
2ACb2	87–98	10YR4/2	10YR3/2	STC	3msab	cs	Bioturbated
2Ab2	98–121	10YR3.5/1	10YR2/1	STC	3mag	gs	Few burrows
2A2b2	121–146	10YR3.5/2	10YR3/2	STC	3mag/1mpr	gs	Thin argillans
2ACkb2	146–187	10YR4/3	10YR3/2	STC	3mag/1mpr	gs	Comm. argillans Comm. carb. fila.
2Ckb2	187–213		10YR3/3	STC	2mag/1mpr	gs	Few carb. fila.
2Ck2b2	213–235		10YR3/3	STC	1fsab/1mpr	gs	Few carb. fila.
3Ck3b2	235–275		10YR3/3	STCL	1fsab/1mpr	ds	Few carb. fila.
3C4b2	275–335		10YR3/3	STCL	1fsab		Few carb. fila.
3C5b2	335–565		10YR4/2				Med. beds Massive silts; laminated
3C6b2	565–720+		10YR4/2				Fine sands, coarse silts

[a] L, loam; STCL, silty clay loam; STC, silty clay.
[b] grade: 1-weak, 2-moderate, 3-strong; class: f-fine, m-medium, c-coarse; type: gr-granular, sab-subangular blocky, ag-angular blocky, pr-prismatic, m-massive.
[c] Distinctness: a-abrupt, c-clear, g-gradual, d-diffuse; Topography: s-smooth, w-wavy, i-irregular.

The point bar facies mark the position of the late Holocene channel prior to late Archaic occupations. As the channel migrated away, presumably to the west, a gradual transition to slower overbank floodplain deposition occurred. As rates of deposition slowed, pedogenesis accompanied deposition, and the cumulic West Fork soil began to form in the floodplain facies parent material. Sometime after ca. 950 B.P. the meander belt was located on the western part of the valley. It subsequently avulsed to the east, and the channel began to migrate eastward, toward the archaeological site. Relatively rapid deposition of levee sediments buried the floodplain soil.

The buried West Fork soil, exposed at 41CO141 and many other localities in the upper Trinity Basin, is evidence of floodplain stability in the late Holocene (Ferring 1986b). The West Fork soil is vertic and calcareous because of the smectitic, calcareous clays from Cretaceous limestones, chalks, and marls in the valley (Ferring 1986b; Putnam et al. 1979).

At 41CO141, the West Fork soil exhibits an overthickened A-horizon (Figure 1-6; Table 1-2). The A-horizon has strong angular blocky and weak prismatic structure, despite its relatively brief period of formation (less than 1,200 years). This type of structure is characteristic of other West Fork pedons, and is the result of high clay content and frequent clay expansion and shrinking. Similarly, thin clay films are common in the A-horizon and upper C-horizon. The clay films are interpreted as stress argillans, resulting from clay expansion, although micromorphological studies have not been done on these soils.

Formation processes at 41CO141 have included cultural and natural factors (cf. Ferring and Peter 1987). Multiple occupations of the site were indicated by stratified assemblages of late Archaic artifacts, hearths, and faunas. Occupation of the site first took place after the sedimentary environment had gradually shifted from lateral accretion to vertical accretion (Figure 1-6). Faunal materials and spatial patterning of artifacts was excellent in the lower part of the site, because moderate rates of sedimentation hastened burial, and because calcareous alluvium improved bone preservation. Higher in the profile, bone deterioration and artifact displacement accompanied soil development. As the soil formed, primary carbonates were leached to the lower part of the A and upper part of the C-horizons, maintaining higher soil pH and enhancing bone preservation. Formation of the soil was arrested when the locality was buried by calcareous levee sediments.

Site Formation on Terraces

With respect to alluvial pedology, the study of archaeological site formation on terraces entails a shift in emphasis from the dynamic factors considered for floodplains to progressive modification processes associated with stable terrace surfaces. Prolonged soil development, erosion, and bioturbation alter not only archaeological records, but also the sedimentary and biotic evidence used to reconstruct environments for the archaeological occupations. To simplify the following discussions, I will not consider eolian or colluvial sediments on terraces, although these are clearly important and in some regions common contexts for archaeological sites.

For purposes of geoarchaeological study, archaeological sites associated with alluvial terraces can be classified as follows:

1. *Buried terrace site*—site that is clearly buried within alluvial terrace fill. These sites were occupied and then buried under the antecedent floodplain prior to terrace genesis.
2. *Surficial terrace site*—site that occurs on or near the terrace surface. The age of occupation relative to terrace genesis defines two types:
   a. *Antecedent site*—site that was occupied on the active, antecedent floodplain, shortly before terrace genesis.
   b. *Subsequent site*—site that was occupied after terrace genesis, on a stable terrace surface.

Buried terrace sites and antecedent surficial sites, because they were initially formed on floodplains, are subject to pedogenically related modification in proportion to their burial depth and to the age of the terrace. Initially in the same position as floodplain sites, these are affected by modification processes following development of the terrace due to changes in groundwater hydrology and from weathering and soil formation at the surface of the terrace. The age of the terrace, holding other soil formation factors constant, defines how long modification agents will affect the site. Burial depth is a principal control on the kind and intensity of pedogenic processes that will affect site modification (e.g., Funk and Wellman 1984). For pedocals, site burial depth defines the position of artifacts and bone with respect to calcic horizon development, which will influence bone preservation. For pedalfers, burial depth will determine whether the archaeological materials occur in the leached, eluviated soil horizons (prone to erosion and bioturbation) or in the clayey B-horizons where pedoturbation and oxidation may be more pronounced. Burial depth also defines the positioning of archaeological materials relative to water tables and the potential for oxidizing or reducing (gleying) preservation conditions.

Ferring and Peter (1987) analyzed site modification in late Holocene valley fill in Oklahoma. They studied a Late Archaic site, with artifacts ca. 50 cm below the terrace surface. Substantial bioturbation and pedoturbation caused vertical displacement of artifacts, and virtually all organic remains had deteriorated in less than 2500 years. At the Murray Springs Clovis site in Arizona, weathering and bioturbation resulted in deterioration of virtually all organic materials in the terrace camp areas, yet spatial patterning of lithic artifacts was preserved (Haynes 1981).

Antecedent and subsequent surficial sites may be difficult to distinguish without independent control over the age of the archaeological assemblages, the age of the terrace, or both. There are several reasons why it is important to make this distinction, and why soils analysis is important in the study of surficial terrace sites. Prehistoric peoples located their floodplain settlements based on prevailing locations of habitats; if these settlements are preserved as antecedent surficial terrace sites, the sediments, soils, and depositional geomorphic features surrounding the sites yield information on the original settlement setting. By contrast, when prehistoric peoples located settlements on existing terraces, they may have considered habitats on the terrace and adjacent floodplain. Therefore, for purposes of settlement pattern studies, the difference between antecedent and subsequent terrace sites is significant. Reconstructions of site habitats that use relict depositional geomorphic features such as channel scars or levees are probably valid for antecedent sites only. Analysis of subsequent sites should consider the terrace sediments, geomorphology, and soils as important elements of habitat analysis. Waters (1988) documented major shifts in Hohokam settlement locations along the Santa Cruz River, Arizona. Settlement locations on lower bajada surfaces (geomorphically equivalent to terraces in this case) shifted through time in response to environmental changes on the adjacent floodplain, as indicated by a series of buried cienega soils in the floodplain alluvium.

In other regions, and particularly for sites associated with horticultural economies and village settlements, terraces were often selected for habitation because of soil fertility and protection from flooding. Because these sites are generally less than 2000–3000 years old, they are almost always situated on terraces. For these sites, soils analysis can focus on modification processes that are associated with the stable surfaces, including those related to human activities (Eidt 1985).

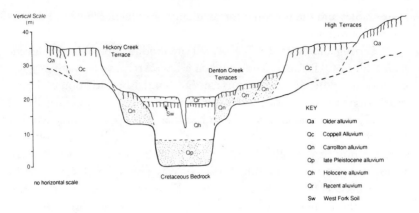

Figure 1-7. Diagrammatic geologic cross section of the Upper Trinity River Basin, Texas (from Ferring in press).

For sites associated with earlier cultures, however, soils analysis plays a potentially more important role in assessing site formation processes. Alluvial terraces along most drainages in the Southern Plains are Pleistocene; few examples of Holocene terraces have been identified. In the Upper Trinity River drainage basin, all terraces of the major streams and their tributaries are late Pleistocene or older (Ferring 1986b, in press). Younger Pleistocene and all of the Holocene alluvium is buried below the floodplains. Because of deep burial of prehistoric sites below the floodplains, and because of good visibility of sites on the terraces, the majority of recorded sites, ranging in age from Paleoindian to Historic, occur in terrace settings (Ferring 1987a). Therefore, all of these sites are subsequent surficial terrace sites. Site formation processes on the Trinity terraces are dominated by pedogenic effects.

Almost all sites above the Trinity floodplain are located on one of the Denton Creek terraces, or less commonly, on the Hickory Creek terrace (Figure 1-7). Site densities are much higher on the Denton Creek terraces, probably because of proximity to the floodplain and because of better drained, sandy soils. Among all terrace settings, however, the modification factors that dominate the character of preserved archaeological records in sites are soil properties and site age. The upper part of the Coppell Alluvium, the fill for the Hickory Creek terrace (Figure 1-7), is calcareous clay and silt. The strongly developed soil on this terrace (Figure 1-8), has been forming for much of the Late Quaternary.

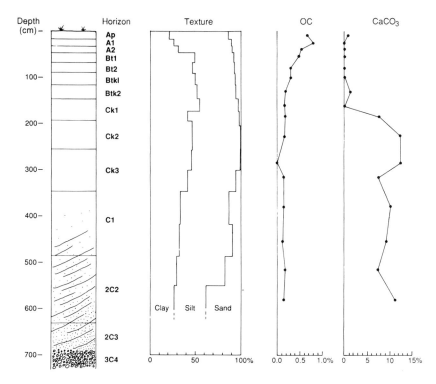

Figure 1-8. Soil Stratigraphic Profile for the Coppell Alluvium, Trinity River Basin, Texas. Alluvium forms fill of the Hickory Creek Terrace. Terrace surface is 12 meters above floodplain.

The soil at this locality is a Mollisol with calcareous B and C horizons. Large deep cracks form on these soils in summer due to the presence of shrink-swell clays and considerable mixing of sediment takes place seasonally. Sites that occur on this terrace show evidence of substantial pedoturbation, and even late Holocene sites with Archaic and Late Prehistoric occupations typically have mixed assemblages.

Parent materials for the Denton Creek terrace soils are almost uniformly sandy (Figure 1-8), and well-developed Alfisols have formed on them since middle to late Wisconsinan time. The profile shown in Figure 1-9 is representative of the soils formed on the lower Denton Creek terraces. The thick A-horizon is leached and usually heavily bioturbated. Substantial movement of sediment in the A-horizon by burrowing rodents, insects, and worms probably accounts for the presence of "buried"

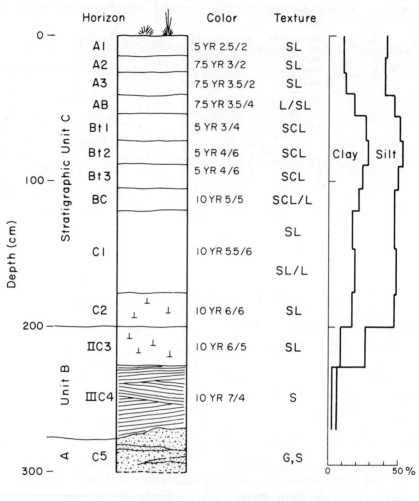

Figure 1-9. Soil stratigraphic profile of a Denton Creek terrace, Trinity River Basin, Texas. Fill for terrace is younger part of Carrollton alluvium. Terrace surface is ca. 4 meters above floodplain.

Archaic artifacts that have been used erroneously to date the alluvium (Crook and Harris 1957). As for the Hickory Creek terrace, sites of any age occur on the Denton Creek terraces and disturbance is proportionate to age.

Because of the antiquity of the Trinity River terraces, all sites on them are subsequent surficial sites. Neither geomorphic position nor soil development can be used to predict the age of sites, and progressive site modification is controlled mainly by soil formation processes.

In other regions of the United States, Holocene terraces are common contexts for archaeological sites. Where Holocene terraces are present (Johnson and Martin 1987; Bettis and Littke 1987) more detailed patterns of Holocene archaeological site formation relative to terrace soil development can be expected. In these cases, Holocene archaeological site formation is less straightforward than along the Trinity River, where all terrace sites are subsequent sites.

Along the South Platte River in Colorado, shallowly buried Paleoindian sites include Clovis and Agate Basin components on the Kersey terrace (Holliday 1987a). Since the Kersey floodplain was still aggrading during Clovis occupations of the Klein site, it is an antecedent terrace site. Downcutting (and formation of the Kersey terrace) apparently preceded Agate Basin occupations. Thus the Frazier Agate Basin site (Malde 1988), also located on the Kersey terrace, is a subsequent terrace site.

In the midcontinent, a number of studies of Holocene alluvial sequences provide examples that are instructive for analysis of alluvial soils and archaeology (McDowell 1983; Brackenridge 1981, 1984; May and Holen 1985; Johnson and Martin 1987; Mandel, this volume). In the Soap Creek watershed, southern Iowa, analysis of Holocene alluvium and soils resulted in a geologic framework for archaeological site prediction (Bettis and Littke 1987; Bettis, this volume). The results of their soils and geomorphic analysis also have implications for site formation processes and resultant archaeological records. The Gunder Member of the DeForest Formation is the fill for a 1–4 meter terrace. This alluvium accumulated between ca. 10,500–3000 B.P. Moderately well developed Mollisols or Alfisols, usually having argillic horizons, occur at the surface of the terrace. Below the argillic horizons are thick (ca. 2–3 meters) C horizons. Since buried soils are not present, it seems probable that any Paleoindian or Early–Middle Archaic archaeological occupation surfaces may have been buried rapidly, with minimal soils-related modification effects. However, Late Archaic materials buried in the upper part of the terrace fill would have undergone at least 3000 years of modification effects accompanying formation of the terrace surface soil.

CONCLUSIONS

This essay has addressed alluvial pedology as a potentially important contribution to geoarchaeological research. Soil formation in alluvial environments is influenced by a variety of physical and biotic factors that are relevant to different kinds of archaeological inquiry: sedimentary environments, biotic environments, paleolandforms, chronometric variables and processes of soil formation that directly alter archaeological records. The diversity of alluvial soils makes them suitable for investigation of relatively short-scale (hundreds to thousands of years) changes in environments and landforms. These scales are appropriate for investigation of changes in prehistoric cultures.

As part of geoarchaeological research, alluvial pedology should be implemented early in research projects when there is time for soil-geomorphologists to interact with archaeologists in planning research strategies. Prior mapping of soils and prior information concerning soils geomorphology in the project area will enable better prediction and evaluation of sites during survey and testing phases of research. During excavations, it is imperative that the pedologist and the archaeologist confer on strategies for reconstructing site formation processes. This should include selection of stratigraphic columns where detailed soils description and sampling are physically close to excavated archaeological material. This will enable analysis of vertical changes in artifact distributions and organic materials with the aid of data on soil formation, including physical and geochemical aspects of soil development.

Pedology is an integral component of Quaternary alluvial geology. Some of the related contributions to archaeology have been described in this paper, yet the review has been hampered by a surprisingly small number of detailed studies of alluvial pedology, let alone geoarchaeological applications. Continued interaction among pedologists and archaeologists during research in alluvial valleys should benefit both disciplines directly and also contribute to geoarchaeology, an emerging and maturing bridge between archaeology and the earth sciences.

ACKNOWLEDGMENTS

I thank Vance Holliday, Rolfe Mandel, and an anonymous reviewer for their valuable comments on an early draft of this chapter. Research reported here in the Trinity River Basin was supported by the U.S. Corps of Engineers, Fort Worth District.

REFERENCES

Albanese, J.
  1986   The Geology and Soils at the Colby Site. In *The Colby Mammoth Site*, by G. C. Frison and L. C. Todd, pages 143–163. University of New Mexico Press, Albuquerque.

Allen, J. R. L.
  1965   A Review of the Origin and Character of Recent Alluvial Sediments. *Sedimentology* 5:89–191.

Anderson, D. G., and J. Schuldenrein
  1983   Early Archaic Settlement on the Southeastern Atlantic Slope: A View from the Rucker's Bottom Site, Elbert County, Georgia. *North American Archaeologist* 4(3):177–210.

Artz, J. A.
  1985   A Soil-Geomorphic Approach to Locating Buried Late Archaic Sites in Northeast Oklahoma. *American Archaeology* 5(2):142–150.

Artz, J. A., and K. C. Reid
  1984   Part II: Geoarchaeological Investigations in Cotton Creek Valley. In *Hunter of the Forest Edge: Culture, Time and Process in the Little Caney Basin*, by K. C. Reid and J. A. Artz, pages 97–186. Contributions in Archaeology 14, University of Tulsa Laboratory of Archaeology, Tulsa.

Baker, V. R., R. C. Kochel, R. C. Patton, and G. Pickup
  1983   Paleohydrologic Analysis of Holocene Flood Slackwater Sediments. In *Modern and Ancient Fluvial Systems*, edited by J. D. Collinson and J. Lewin, pages 229–239. Special Publication No. 6, International Association of Sedimentologists. Blackwell, Oxford.

Baumgardner, R. W., Jr., and S. C. Caran
  1986   Stop 15: Measured Sections, Hensen Farm, near Quitaque, Texas. In *Geomorphology and Quaternary Stratigraphy of the Rolling Plains, Texas Panhandle*, edited by T. C. Gustavson, pages 67–72. Guidebook 22, Bureau of Economic Geology, The University of Texas at Austin, Austin.

Bettis, E. A. III, and J. P. Littke
  1987   *Holocene Alluvial Stratigraphy and Landscape Development in Soap Creek Water-*

shed, Appanoose, Davis and Wapello Counties, Iowa. Open File Report 87–2, Iowa Department of Natural Resources, Iowa City.

Birkeland, P. W.
1984   *Soils and Geomorphology.* Oxford University Press, New York.

Boison, P. J., and P. C. Patton
1985   Sediment Storage and Terrace Formation in Coyote Gulch Basin, South-central Utah. *Geology* 13: 31–34.

Brackenridge, G. R.
1981   Late Quaternary Floodplain Sedimentation along the Pomme de Terre River, Southern Missouri. *Quaternary Research* 15:62–76.
1984   Alluvial Stratigraphy and Radiocarbon Dating along the Duck River, Tennessee, Implications Regarding Floodplain Origin. *Geological Society of America Bulletin* 95: 9–25.

Brammer, H.
1971   Coatings in Seasonally Flooded Soils. *Geoderma* 6(5–6):10–16.

Bridge, J. S., and M. R. Leeder
1979   A Simulation Model of Alluvial Stratigraphy. *Sedimentology* 26:617–644.

Butzer, K.
1977   *Geomorphology of the Lower Illinois Valley, as a Spatial-Temporal Context for the Koster Archaic Site.* Reports of Investigations No. 34, Illinois State Museum, Springfield.
1982   *Archaeology as Human Ecology.* Cambridge University Press, Cambridge.

Corless, J. F., and R. V. Ruhe
1955   The Iowan Terrace and Terrace Soils of the Nishnabotna Valley in Western Iowa. *Proceedings of the Iowa Academy of Sciences* 62: 345–360.

Crook, W. W., Jr., and R. K. Harris
1957   Hearths and Artifacts of Early Man near Lewisville, Texas and Associated Faunal Materials. *Bulletin of the Texas Archeological Society* 28: 7–97.

Darwin, C.
1896   *The Formation of Vegetable Mould Through the Action of Worms.* D. Appleton and Company, New York.

Dijkerman, J. C., M. G. Cline, and G. W. Olson
1967   Properties and Genesis of Textural Subsoil Lamellae. *Soil Science* 104(1):7–16.

Eidt, R. C.
1985   Theoretical and Practical Considerations in the Analysis of Anthrosols. In *Archaeological Geology*, edited by G. Rapp, Jr., and J. A. Gifford, pages 155–183. Yale University Press, New Haven.

Evans, L. J.
1982   Dating Methods of Pleistocene Deposits and Their Problems: VII. Paleosols. *Geoscience Canada* 9(3):155–160.

Ferring, C. R.
1986a   Rates of Fluvial Sedimentation: Implications for Archaeological Variability. *Geoarchaeology* 1(3):259–274.
1986b   Late Quaternary Geology and Environments of the Upper Trinity Basin. In *An Assessment of the Cultural Resources in the Trinity Basin, Dallas, Tarrant, and Denton Counties, Texas,* edited by B. C. Yates and C. R. Ferring, pages 32–112, Institute of Applied Sciences, North Texas State University, Denton.
1986c   Late Holocene Cultural Ecology in the Southern Plains: Perspectives from Delaware Canyon, Oklahoma. *Plains Anthropologist* 31(114):55–82.
1987a   Archaeological Geology of the Upper Trinity River Basin. *Abstracts with Programs Geological Society of America* 19(7): 661.
1987b   Geoarchaeology of Site 41CO141, A Late Holocene Locality in the Upper Trinity River Basin, Cooke County, Texas. In *Test Excavations at 41CO141, Ray Roberts Reservoir, Cooke County Texas,* edited by D. J. Prikryl and B. C. Yates, pages 19–52. Contributions in Archaeology Number 4, Institute of Applied Sciences, North Texas State University, Denton.
in   Archaeological Geology of the Southern Plains. In *Archaeological Geology of*
press   *North America,* edited by J. Donahue and N. Lasca, Centennial Special Volume, Geological Society of America, Boulder.

Ferring, C. R., and S. A. Hall
1987   Domebo Canyon, In *Late Quaternary Stratigraphy, Neotectonics and Geoarchaeology of Southwestern Oklahoma,* edited by C. R. Ferring, pages 56–66. Friends of the Pleistocene South-Central Cell Field Trip Guidebook. North Texas State University, Denton.

Ferring, C. R., and D. E. Peter
1987   Geoarchaeology of the Dyer Site, A Prehistoric Occupation in the Western Ouachitas, Oklahoma. *Plains Anthropologist* 32(118):351–366.

Follmer, L. R.
1983   Sangamon and Wisconsinan Pedogenesis in the Midwestern United States. In *Late-Quaternary Environments of the United States,* edited by H. E. Wright, Jr., Vol. 1, *The Late Pleistocene,* edited by S. C. Porter, pages 138–144. University of Minnesota Press, Minneapolis.
1985   Surficial Geology and Soils of the Rhoads Archaeological Site Near Lincoln, Illinois. *American Archaeology* 5(2):150–160.

Foss, J. E.
1977   The Pedological Record at Several Paleoindian Sites in the Northeast. *Annals of the New York Academy of Sciences* 288:234–244.

Funk, R. E., and B. Wellman
1984   Evidence of Early Holocene Occupations in the Upper Susquehanna Valley, New York State. *Archaeology of Eastern North America* 12: 81–109.

Gardner, G. D., and J. Donahue
1985   The Little Platte Drainage, Missouri: A Model for Locating Temporal Surfaces in a Fluvial Environment. In *Archaeological Sediments in Context,* edited by J. K. Stein and W. R. Farrand, pages 69–89. Center for the Study of Early Man, Institute for Quaternary Studies, Orono.

Gerrard, A. J.
  1981   *Soils and Landforms*. George Allen and Unwin, London.

Gerrard, A. J. (editor)
  1987   *Alluvial Soils*. Van Nostrand Reinhold Company, New York.

Gile, L. H., J. W. Hawley, and R. B. Grossman
  1981   *Soils and Geomorphology in the Basin and Range Area of Southern New Mexico—Guidebook to the Desert Project*. Memoir 39, New Mexico Bureau of Mines and Mineral Resources, Socorro.

Gooding, A. M.
  1971   Postglacial Alluvial History in the Upper Whitewater Basin, Southeastern Indiana, and Possible Regional Relationships. *American Journal of Science* 271:389–401.

Gray, H. H.
  1984   Archaeological Sedimentology of Overbank Silt Deposits on the Floodplain of the Ohio River near Louisville, Kentucky. *Journal of Archaeological Science* 11: 421–432.

Guccione, M. J., R. H. Lafferty III, and L. S. Cummings
  1988   Environmental Constraints of Human Settlement in an Evolving Holocene Alluvial System, the Lower Mississippi Valley. *Geoarchaeology* 3(1): 65–84.

Gustavson, T. C. (editor)
  1986   *Geomorphology and Quaternary Stratigraphy of the Rolling Plains, Texas Panhandle*. Guidebook 22, Bureau of Economic Geology, The University of Texas at Austin, Austin.

Haas, H., V. Holliday, and R. Stuckenrath
  1986   Dating of Holocene Stratigraphy with Soluble and Insoluble Organic Fractions at the Lubbock Lake Archaeological Site, Texas: an Ideal Case Study. *Radiocarbon* 28(2A): 473–485.

Hall, S. A.
  1977   Geology and Palynology of Archaeological Sites and Associated Sediments. In *The Prehistory of Little Caney River, 1976 Field Season*, edited by D. O. Henry, pages 13–41. Contributions in Archaeology 1, Laboratory of Archaeology, University of Tulsa, Tulsa.
  1987   Carnegie Canyon. In *Late Quaternary Stratigraphy, Neotectonics and Geoarchaeology of Southwestern Oklahoma*, edited by C. R. Ferring, pages 67–79. Friends of the Pleistocene South Central Cell Field Trip Guidebook, Institute of Applied Sciences, North Texas State University, Denton.
  1988   Environment and Archaeology of the Central Osage Plains. *Plains Anthropologist* 22(120): 203–218.

Hall, S. A., and C. Lintz
  1984   Buried Trees, Water Table Fluctuations and 3000 Years of Changing Climate in West-Central Oklahoma. *Quaternary Research* 22:129–133.

Haynes, C. V., Jr.
  1968   Geochronology of Late Quaternary Alluvium. In *Means of Correlation of Quaternary Successions*, edited by R. B. Morrison and H. E. Wright, pages 591–631. Proceedings of the VII INQUA Congress, Volume 8. University of Utah Press, Salt Lake City.
  1970   Geochronology of Man-Mammoth Sites and Their Bearing on the Origin of the Llano Complex. In *Pleistocene and Recent Environments of the Central Great Plains*, edited by W. Dort, Jr., and J. K. Jones, Jr., pages 77–92. University Press of Kansas, Lawrence.
  1981   Geochronology and Paleoenvironments of the Murray Springs Clovis Site, Arizona. *National Geographic Society Research Reports* 14: 243–251.

Hayward, M., and I. Fenwick
  1983   Soils and Hydrologic Change. In *Background to Paleohydrology*, edited by K. J. Gregory, pages 167–187. John Wiley and Sons, New York.

Holliday, V. T.
  1987a Geoarchaeology and Late Quaternary Geomorphology of the Middle South Platte River, Northeastern Colorado. *Geoarchaeology* 2(4): 317–319.
  1987b A Reexamination of Late-Pleistocene Boreal Forest Reconstructions for the Southern High Plains. *Quaternary Research* 28: 238–244.

Irwin-Williams, C., H. Irwin, G. Agogino, and C. V. Haynes
  1973   Hell Gap: Paleo-Indian Occupation on the High Plains. *Plains Anthropologist* 18(59): 40–53.

Jenny, H.
  1941   *Factors of Soil Formation*. McGraw-Hill Book Company, Inc., New York.
  1962   Model of a Rising Nitrogen Profile in Nile Valley Alluvium, and its Agronomic and Pedogenic Implications. *Soil Science Society of America Proceedings* 26: 588–591.

Johnson, D. L.
  1989   Subsurface Stone Lines, Stone Zones, Artifact-Manuport Layers, and Biomantles Produced by Bioturbation via Pocket Gophers (*Thomomys bottae*). *American Antiquity* 54(2):370–389.

Johnson, W. C., and C. W. Martin
  1987   Holocene Alluvial-Stratigraphic Studies from Kansas and Adjoining States of the East-Central Plains. In *Quaternary Environments of Kansas*, edited by W. C. Johnson, pages 109–122. Guidebook Series 5, Kansas Geological Survey, Lawrence.

Knox, J. C.
  1976   Concept of the Graded Stream. In *Theories of Landform Development*, edited by W. N. Melhorn and R. C. Flemal, pages 169–198. Publications in Geomorphology, State University of New York, Binghamton.
  1983   Responses of River Systems to Holocene Climates. In *Late Quaternary Environments of the United States*, Vol. 2, *The Holocene*, edited by H. E. Wright, Jr., pages 26–41. University of Minnesota Press, Minneapolis.

Kraus, M. J., and T. M. Bown
1988 Pedofacies Analysis: A New Approach to Reconstructing Ancient Fluvial Sequences. In *Paleosols and Weathering Through Geologic Time: Principles and Applications*, Special Paper 216, Geological Society of America, edited by J. Reinhardt and W. R. Sigleo, pages 143–152. Geological Society of America, Boulder.

Leeder, M. R.
1973 Pedogenic Carbonates and Flood Sediment Accumulation Rates: a Quantitative Model for Alluvial Arid-Zone Lithofacies. *Geology Magazine* 112(3):257–270.

Leopold, L. B., and J. P. Miller
1954 *A Post-Glacial Chronology for Some Alluvial Valleys in Wyoming*. U.S. Geological Survey Water Supply Paper No. 1261. U.S. Geological Survey, Washington.

Lewin, J.
1978 Floodplain Geomorphology. *Progress in Physical Geography* 2:408–437.

Machette, M. N.
1985 Calcic Soils of the Southwestern United States. In *Soils and Quaternary Geology of the Southwestern United States*, Special Paper 203, Geological Society of America, edited by D. L. Weide, pages 1–22. Geological Society of America, Boulder.

Malde, H. E.
1988 Geology of the Frazier Site, Kersey, Colorado. In *Guidebook to the Archaeological Geology of the Colorado Piedmont and High Plains of Southeastern Wyoming*, edited by V. T. Holliday, pages 85–90. Department of Geography, University of Wisconsin, Madison.

May, D. W., and S. R. Holen
1985 A Chronology of Holocene Erosion and Sedimentation in the South Loup Valley, Nebraska. *Geographical Perspectives* 56:8–12.

McClelland, J. E., E. M. White, and F. F. Riecken
1950 Causes of Differences in Soil Series of Missouri River Bottomlands in Monona County. *Iowa Academy of Sciences Proceedings* 57: 253–258.

McDowell, P. F.
1983 Evidence of Stream Response to Holocene Climatic Change in a Small Wisconsin Watershed. *Quaternary Research* 19:100–116.

McFadden, L. D.
1988 Climatic Influences on Rates and Processes of Soil Development in Quaternary Deposits of Southern California. In *Paleosols and Weathering Through Geologic Time: Principles and Applications*, Special Paper 216, Geological Society of America, edited by J. Reinhardt and W. R. Sigleo, pages 153–177. Geological Society of America, Boulder.

McFadden, L. D., and D. M. Hendricks
    1985   Changes in the Content and Composition of Pedogenic Iron Oxyhydroxides
            in a Chronosequence of Soils in Southern California. *Quaternary Research* 23:
            189–204.

McFadden, L. D., and J. C. Tinsley
    1985   Rate and Depth of Pedogenic-Carbonate Accumulation in Soils: Formulation
            and Testing of a Compartment Model. In *Soils and Quaternary Geology of the
            Southwestern United States*, Special Paper 203, Geological Society of America,
            edited by D. L. Weide, pages 23–41. Geological Society of America, Boulder.

Miller, B. J., G. C. Lewis, J. J. Alford, and W. J. Day
    1984   *Loesses in Louisiana and at Vicksburg, Mississippi.* Guidebook for the Friends of
            the Pleistocene Field Trip. Louisiana Agricultural Center, Louisiana State Uni-
            versity, Baton Rouge.

— Morrison, R. B.
    1978   Quaternary Soil Stratigraphy—Concepts, Methods and Problems. In *Quater-
            nary Soils*, edited by W. C. Mahaney, pages 77–108. Geological Abstracts,
            Norwich, England.

Parsons, R. B., and R. C. Herriman
    1970   Haploxerolls and Argixerolls Developed in Recent Alluvium, Southern
            Willamette Valley, Oregon. *Soil Science* 109(299):302–309.

Pheasant, D. R.
    1982   Soils Analyses from Delaware Canyon. In *Late Holocene Prehistory of Delaware
            Canyon, Oklahoma*, edited by C. R. Ferring, pages 64–94. Contributions in
            Archaeology Number 1, Institute of Applied Sciences, North Texas State
            University, Denton.

Ponti, D. J.
    1985   The Quaternary Alluvial Sequence of the Antelope Valley, California. In *Soils
            and Quaternary Geology of the Southwestern United States*, Special Paper 203,
            Geological Society of America, edited by D. L. Weide, pages 79–96. Geologi-
            cal Society of America, Boulder.

Putnam, L. A., C. R. Cail, R. A. Cochran, W. J. Guckian, L. C. Lovelace, and
B. J. Wagner
    1979   *Soil Survey of Cooke County, Texas.* U.S. Department of Agriculture, Soil
            Conservation Service, Washington.

Reider, R. G.
    1980   Late Pleistocene and Holocene Soils of the Carter/Kerr-McGee Archaeological
            Site, Powder River Basin, Wyoming. *Catena* 7:301–315.
    1982   Soil Development and Paleoenvironments. In *The Agate Basin Site*, by G. C.
            Frison and D. J. Stanford, pages 331–344. Academic Press, Inc., New York.

Reider, R. G., M. A. Hayter, and G. M. Zeimens
    1987   Soil, Archaeological, Biotic and Climatic Relationships for the Late Holocene
            of the Wyoming Basin: The Case of the Garrett Allen (Elk Mountain) Site
            (48CR301). *Geoarchaeology* 2(4): 301–316.

Rockwell, T. K., D. L. Johnson, E. A. Keller, and G. R. Dembroff
  1985   A Late Pleistocene-Holocene Soil Chronosequence in the Ventura Basin,
         Southern California, USA. In *Geomorphology and Soils*, edited by K. S.
         Richards, R. R. Arnett, and S. Ellis, pages 309–327. George Allen and Un-
         win, London.

Ruhe, R. V.
  1970   Soils, Paleosols and Environment. In *Pleistocene and Recent Environments of the
         Central Great Plains*, edited by W. Dort, Jr., and J. K. Jones, Jr., pages 37–52.
         University Press of Kansas, Lawrence.
  1983   Aspects of Holocene Pedology in the United States. In *Late Quaternary En-
         vironments of the United States*, Vol. 2, *The Holocene*, edited by H. E. Wright,
         Jr., pages 12–25. University of Minnesota Press, Minneapolis.

Ruhe, R. V., and C. G Olson
  1980   Soil Welding. *Soil Science* 130(3): 132–139.

Schiffer, M. B.
  1983   Toward the Identification of Formation Processes. *American Antiquity* 48: 675–
         706.
  1987   *Formation Processes of the Archaeological Record*. University of New Mexico
         Press, Albuquerque.

Sellards, E. H.
  1923   Geologic and Soils Studies on the Alluvial Lands of the Red River Valley.
         University of Texas Bulletin 2327:27–87. Soil Survey Staff.
  1974   *Soil Taxonomy*. Agriculture Handbook No. 436. Soil Conservation Service,
         U.S. Department of Agriculture, Washington.

Stein, J. K.
  1983   Earthworm Activity: A Source of Potential Disturbance of Archaeological
         Sediments. *American Antiquity* 48: 277–289.

Stuiver, M., and P. J. Reimer
  1986   A Computer Program for Radiocarbon Age Calibration. *Radiocarbon* 28:
         1022–1030.

Villa, P.
  1982   Conjoinable Pieces and Site Formation Processes. *American Antiquity* 47(2):
         276–290.

Vreeken, W. J.
  1984   Relative Dating of Soils and Paleosols. In *Quaternary Dating Methods*, edited
         by W. C. Mahaney, pages 269–281. Developments in Paleontology and Strat-
         igraphy, 7. Elsevier, New York.

Walker, P. H., and R. J. Coventry
  1976   Soil Profile Development in Some Alluvial Deposits of Eastern New South
         Wales. *Australian Journal of Soil Research* 14:305–317.

Walker, P. H., and P. Green
  1976   Soil Trends in Two Valley Fill Sequences. *Australian Journal of Soils Research* 14:291–303.

Walker, R. G., and D. J. Cant
  1984   Sandy Fluvial Systems. In *Facies Models*, 2d ed., edited by R. G. Walker, pages 71–89. Geoscience Canada, Reprint Series 1. Geological Association of Canada Publications, Toronto.

Waters, M. R.
  1986   *The Geoarchaeology of Whitewater Draw, Arizona.* Anthropological Papers of the University of Arizona, No. 45. University of Arizona Press, Tucson.
  1988   The Impact of Fluvial Processes and Landscape Evolution on Archaeological Sites and Settlement Patterns Along the San Xavier Reach of the Santa Cruz River, Arizona. *Geoarchaeology* 3(3): 205–219.

Webb, W. S.
  1939   *An Archaeological Survey of Wheeler Basin on the Tennessee River in Northern Alabama.* Bulletin 122, Bureau of Ethnology. Smithsonian Institution, Washington.

White, E. M.
  1966   Subsoil Structure Genesis: Theoretical Consideration. *Soil Science* 101: 135–141.

Wood, W. R., and D. L. Johnson
  1978   A Survey of Disturbance Processes in Archaeological Site Formation. In *Advances in Archaeological Method and Theory*, edited by M. Schiffer, pages 315–381. Academic Press, New York.

2

ROLFE D. MANDEL

Soils and Holocene
Landscape Evolution in
Central and Southwestern
Kansas: Implications for
Archaeological Research

The history of landscape evolution preserved in Late Quaternary alluvium of the Great Plains offers great potential for predicting archaeological site distribution. However, until recently, archaeologists working in river valleys of the Plains have relied primarily on traditional
methods, such as surface reconnaissance and shallow shovel testing, to
locate prehistoric sites. With these methods, the detection of deeply buried sites is largely opportunistic, relying on chance exposures of buried
cultural materials in gullies or stream cutbanks. Also, the distribution
and ages of landform/sediment assemblages, such as floodplains, terraces, and alluvial fans, are not determined in most archaeological surveys. The absence of this information is a major limitation since these are
the geomorphic settings where buried archaeological sites are likely to
occur. Several researchers (e.g., Bettis and Thompson 1981; Artz 1985;
Gladfelter 1985; Mandel 1987a) have pointed out that inadequate sampling of the landscape, and failure to consider differential preservation of
Holocene alluvial deposits in fluvial systems, have led to erroneous conclusions about site distributions and therefore, about prehistoric cultures.

This chapter reports on two studies of Holocene landscape evolution within the central Great Plains: one in the Pawnee River Basin of

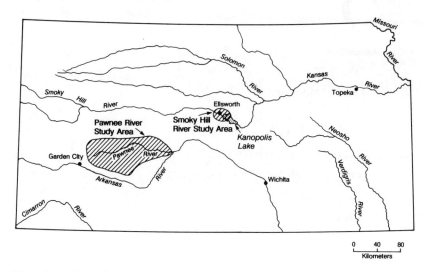

Figure 2-1. Map of Kansas showing location of study areas.

southwestern Kansas and the other in the Lower Smoky Hill River Basin
of central Kansas (Figure 2-1). Intensive and extensive absolute dating
was combined with basinwide alluvial stratigraphic investigations so as
to determine whether deposits of certain ages are differentially preserved
in the drainage networks. The investigations also focused on buried
Holocene soils as indicators of stable landscapes in alluvial settings. Information gleaned from these studies was used to predict where buried
archaeological sites dating to each cultural period are likely to be found in
the basins.

GENERAL SETTING

The Smoky Hill and Pawnee rivers are located in the central portion of
Fenneman's (1931) Great Plains physiographic province. The Smoky Hill
River Basin is a 11,621,688 ha watershed draining to the Kansas River.
The basin extends from the High Plains of western Kansas eastward to
the Flint Hills of central Kansas. Most of the Lower Smoky Hill River
system, which is the focus of the present study (Figure 2-1), is within the
Smoky Hills physiographic region. This region consists of a broad belt
of hills formed by the dissection of Cretaceous and Permian sedimentary
rocks (Merriam 1963). The interfluves are mantled with deposits of
Peoria loess that are 1–2 m thick in most locations (Frye and Leonard

1952). The Lower Smoky Hill River and its major tributaries have cut some rather deep, narrow canyons, with local relief ranging between about 30 and 80 m.

The Pawnee River Basin is a long, fairly wide, west-to-east trending drainage system in southwestern Kansas (Figure 2-1). The total area of this basin is approximately 639,354 ha and it is part of the Arkansas River drainage network. The Pawnee River originates in the High Plains and flows eastward through the extreme southwestern portion of the Smoky Hills before it enters the Arkansas River Lowlands. In the head-water area of the Pawnee River, the topography of the High Plains is monotonously flat, with local relief ranging between about 5 and 15 m. The High Plains are mantled by deposits of Peoria and Loveland loess that have a combined thickness of 3–5 m (Frye and Leonard 1952). In many areas, the loess overlies thick deposits of Pleistocene and Pliocene alluvium. The loess mantle thins eastward, and generally is less than 3 m thick in the Smoky Hills. The Pawnee River Valley deepens and widens as it crosses the Smoky Hills, with local relief ranging between about 30 and 40 m. The valley is flanked by pediments that are thinly veneered with gravel and silty pedisediment (Frye and Leonard 1952: 203). As the Pawnee River enters the Arkansas River Lowlands the landscape becomes an undulating plain with little relief.

The climate of the central Great Plains is continental; summers are hot and winters are cold. The Smoky Hill and Pawnee rivers are situated on a steep precipitation gradient from moist-subhumid central Kansas to semiarid southwestern Kansas. Mean annual precipitation decreases westward, ranging from 66 cm at Ellsworth (Bayne et al. 1971) to 48 cm at Garden City (Harner et al. 1965).

Natural vegetation in the Smoky Hill River Valley and the eastern two-thirds of the Pawnee River Basin is classified as mixed prairie (Kuchler 1974). This grassland is dominated by bluestems (*Andropogon* sp.) and gramas (*Bouteloua* sp.). Within the extreme western portion of the Pawnee River Basin, mixed prairie is replaced by short-grass prairie largely consisting of buffalo grass (*Buchloe dactyloides*) and gramas.

METHODS

The methodology for this study included several steps. First, the drainage basins selected for study were subdivided into small valleys (1st-through 3rd-order streams) and large valleys (greater than 3rd-order streams) using Strahler's (1964) stream classification system. Second, the general distribution of landforms, including floodplains, terraces, and alluvial fans, were mapped from U.S. Geological Survey 1:24,000-scale topographic maps as well as from 1:2,400-scale maps supplied by the USDA-Soil Conservation Service. In addition, 1:5,000-scale air photos were used to identify landforms in the stream valleys. Research localities were then selected in a number of small and large valleys within each drainage basin. Selection of research sites was based on access to property and/or presence of cutbank exposures revealing thick sections of Holocene valley fill.

Field work in the study area was undertaken with an approach similar to that employed by Thompson and Bettis (1980) in their study of Smokey Hollow Watershed of western Iowa. A Giddings hydraulic soil probe was used to obtain intact cores along cross-valley and longitudinal transects. Close-interval coring was supplemented with widely spaced backhoe trenching in order to examine microstratigraphy and stratigraphic relationships among valley deposits. Stratigraphic sequences also were examined in stream cutbanks and in gravel pits. Detailed descriptions of all cores and selected artificial exposures were made in the field using standard USDA procedures and terminology (Soil Survey Staff 1987). Stages of soil-carbonate morphology were noted using Birkeland's (1984: Table A-4) classification system.

A bipartite stratigraphic nomenclature was used in the present study. Stratigraphic designations are informal, and include units and soils. Allostratigraphic units are mappable stratified bodies of sedimentary rock or sediments whose boundaries are laterally traceable disconformities (North American Commission on Stratigraphic Nomenclature 1983). The upper boundaries of surface soils or laterally traceable buried soils were used as boundaries of allostratigraphic units. Many of the thin, weakly developed buried soils observed in some sections were not observed in others, i.e., they were not laterally traceable; hence, these soils were not used as allostratigraphic boundaries. Roman numerals were used to designate allostratigraphic units, beginning with I at the top. The individual units are site specific and do not always represent the same deposits at different localities. In addition, soils were numbered consecutively at each section, beginning with 1 (modern soil) at the top of a section. Altogether, the detailed subsurface investigations were used to determine the character, depth, and extent of deposits and buried paleosols, and to establish stratigraphic relationships among the deposits and buried paleosols.

Radiocarbon ages were determined on charcoal, wood, and bone recovered from cores and/or exposures at research localities. In addition, soil samples from organic-rich A and truncated B horizons of buried paleosols were collected for C-14 dating of humates. Radiocarbon ages determined on humates are mean residence times for all organic carbon in the soil samples (Campbell et al. 1967). Although mean residence time does not provide the absolute age of a buried soil, it does give a minimum age for the period of soil development, and it provides a limiting age on the overlying material (Birkeland 1984: 150). Radiocarbon assays were used to correlate alluvial fills and buried paleosols, and to establish a chronology of geomorphic events in stream valleys within the study areas.

GEOMORPHOLOGY, SOILS, AND STRATIGRAPHY

Lower Smoky Hill River Basin

The Lower Smoky Hill River Basin was investigated in the area of Kanopolis Lake near the town of Ellsworth, Kansas (Figure 2-1). Subsurface investigations were conducted in valleys of the Smoky Hill River and several major tributaries, including Ash, Thompson, and Alum creeks (Figure 2-2).

The valley floor of the Smoky Hill River is 1–2 km wide within the study area. Valley margins are noticeably asymmetric; south-facing slopes are longer, gentler, and composed of more stepped surface than are north-facing slopes.

Two terraces were identified on the valley floor of the Smoky Hill River (Figure 2-3). The highest of these terraces (T-2) has a gently sloping surface 4–5 m above the modern floodplain (T-0). Remnants of the T-2 terrace generally are unpaired and are scattered along the valley margin. The T-2 surface is graded to the level of the lowest terrace (T-1). T-1 is the best preserved and most continuous terrace in the Smoky Hill River Valley. This low terrace is characterized by broad, paired surfaces that stand 3–4 m above the adjacent floodplain.

Alluvial fans are common along margins of the valley floor of the Smoky Hill River. Large, low-angle fans occur where 2nd- and 3rd-order streams join the main valley, and small, low-angle fans developed where 1st-order upland drainages deliver sediment directly to the valley floor. In both cases, the fans merge with T-1 terraces.

The general topographic and stratigraphic relations of Quaternary

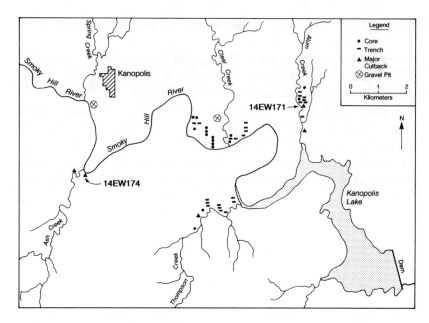

Figure 2-2. Map of the study area within the Lower Smoky Hill River Basin showing loci of cores, backhoe trenches, cutbank exposures, and buried archaeological sites.

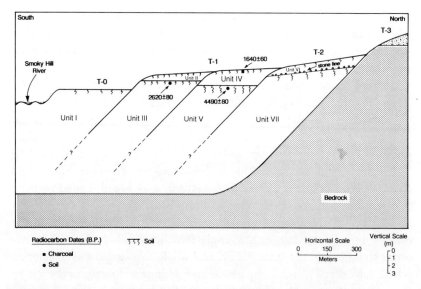

Figure 2-3. Diagrammatic cross section of the valley fill on the north side of the Smoky Hill River 5 km upstream from Kanopolis Lake.

deposits within the Lower Smoky Hill River Valley are shown in Figure 2-3. Two distinct stratigraphic units were identified below the T-2 surface: (1) a 17 m thick lower unit (Unit VII) composed of bedded sand and gravel grading upward to sandy loam, and (2) a 1–2 m thick upper unit (Unit VI) of poorly sorted pebbly sand and sandy loam. An erosional surface, marked by a stone line, separates the two units (Figure 2-3). The thick Bt horizon of a truncated paleosol developed in Unit VII is present immediately below the erosion surface (Table 2-1: Profile 1). This truncated paleosol is mantled by colluvium (Unit VI) that has been transported across the sloping tread of the T-2 terrace. A Typic Haplustoll with A–C horizonation is developed at the top of Unit VI.

Deposits associated with the T–2 terrace failed to produce materials that could provide numerical or relative ages. According to Bayne and others (1971), all fill in the valley bottom of the Smoky Hill River is Wisconsinan or Holocene in age; however, absolute age control is absent in their report. Although several archaeological sites were documented on the T-2 surface, they did not contain 14C-datable materials or culturally diagnostic artifacts.

Alluvial deposits beneath the T-1 terrace in the Smoky Hill River Valley are contained in at least four fills (Figure 2-3). The oldest T-1 fill, Unit V, consists of coarse-grained lateral accretion deposits at its base that grade upward to loamy and silty vertical accretion deposits. A fluvial erosion surface was traced across the top of Unit V in a series of cores and trenches. The Bk horizon of a truncated paleosol developed in Unit V was observed immediately below the erosion surface (Table 2-1: Profile 2). Humates from the upper 20 cm of the Bkb horizon yielded a radiocarbon age of 4490 ± 80 years B.P. Hence, stream erosion removed the upper horizons of this paleosol sometime after ca. 4500 B.P., and the erosion surface was subsequently mantled by Unit IV. Fine sandy loam at the base of Unit IV grades upward to loam. The surface soil developed in the upper part of Unit IV is a Cumulic Haplustoll with a thick, dark-colored A horizon above a C horizon (Table 2-1: Profile 2). Several Plains Woodland sites were documented on the surface of Unit IV. Charcoal from two of these sites, 14EW155 and 14EW172, yielded radiocarbon ages of 1640 ± 60 and 800 ± 90 years B.P., respectively.

Backhoe trenches revealed that Unit III is inset against units IV and V (Figure 2-3). A paleosol with A–C horizonation is developed in loamy alluvium at the top of Unit III (Table 2-1: Profile 3). Humates from the upper 20 cm of the 2Akb horizon yielded a radiocarbon age of 2620 ± 80 years B.P. Hence, Unit III was buried by Unit II sometime after ca. 2600

TABLE 2-1

Description of Soil Profiles 1–9 in the Lower Smoky Hill River Basin

PROFILE 1

Location: Smoky Hill River Valley; SE 1/4, SE 1/4 Sec. 4, R. 7 W., T. 15 S.
Landform: T-2 Terrace; Exposure: Core 5; Elevation: 455 m; Slope: 2%; Vegetation: Native grasses

Depth (cm)	Soil Horizon	Unit	Color (moist-dry)	Texture[a] (USDA)	Structure[b]	Consistence[c]	Reaction (10% HCL)	Carbonate Morphology	Lower Boundary
0–20	Ap	VI	10YR 3/3–10YR 4/3	SL	1 f gr	v. friable	none	none	clear
20–49	A	VI	10YR 3/2–10YR 4/3	SL	1 f gr	v. friable	none	none	gradual
49–58	AC	VI	10YR 3/3–10YR 4/3	S	1 f gr	sl hrd, fri	none	none	gradual
58–97	C	VI	10YR 4/4–10YR 5/4	GS	single grain	loose	none	none	abrupt
97–121	2Btb1	VII	7.5YR 4/4–7.5YR 5/4	SCL	2 m sbk	sl hrd, fri	none	none	gradual
121–142	2Btb2	VII	7.5YR 4/4–7.5YR 5/6	SCL	2 m sbk	firm	none	none	gradual
142–157	2BCb	VII	10YR 4/4–10YR 5/4	SL	1 f sbk	firm	none	none	gradual
157–190	2C1	VII	10YR 4/4–10YR 5/4	LS	massive	friable	none	none	gradual
190–381	2C2	VII	10YR 4/4–10YR 5/6	GS	single grain	loose	none	none	—

PROFILE 2

Location: Smoky Hill River Valley; NW 1/4, NE 1/4, Sec. 10, R. 7 W., T. 16 S.
Landform: T-1 terrace; Exposure: Trench 4; Elevation: 453 m; Slope: 1%; Vegetation: Crops

Depth (cm)	Soil Horizon	Unit	Color (moist-dry)	Texture[a] (USDA)	Structure[b]	Consistence[c]	Reaction (10% HCL)	Carbonate Morphology	Lower Boundary
0–25	Ap	IV	10YR 2/2–10YR 4/2	L	1 f gr	friable	strong	none	clear
25–37	A	IV	10YR 3/3–10YR 4/3	L	1 f gr	friable	strong	none	gradual
37–58	ACk	IV	10YR 3/3–10YR 5/3	SL	1 f gr	friable	violent	Stage I	gradual
58–200	Ck	IV	10YR 4/3–10YR 6/3	SL	massive	friable	violent	Stage I	abrupt
200–248	2Bkb	V	10YR 4/3–10YR 5/3	SiCL	2 m sbk	friable	violent	Stage I+	gradual
248–260	2BCkb	V	10YR 4/3–10YR 5/3	SiL	2 m sbk	friable	violent	Stage I+	—

PROFILE 3

Location: Smoky Hill River Valley; NW 1/4, NW 1/4, Sec. 10, R. 7 W., T. 16 S.

Landform: T-1 terrace; Exposure: Trench 5; Elevation: 453 m; Slope: 1%; Vegetation: Crops

0–20	Ap	II	10YR 2/2–10YR 4/2	SiL	1 f gr	friable	strong	none	clear
25–35	A	II	10YR 3/3–10YR 4/3	L	1 f gr	friable	strong	none	clear
37–56	ACk	II	10YR 4/3–10YR 5/3	L	1 f gr	friable	strong	Stage I	gradual
56–130	Ck	II	10YR 4/4–10YR 6/4	L	massive	friable	violent	Stage I	abrupt
130–190	2Akb	III	10YR 3/3–10YR 4/3	SiL	1 f gr	friable	violent	Stage I	gradual
190–220	2ACkb	III	10YR 4/3–10YR 5/3	SiL	1 f gr	friable	violent	Stage I	gradual
220–250	2C	III	10YR 4/4–10YR 5/4	L	massive	friable	violent	none	gradual

PROFILE 4

Location: Smoky Hill River Valley; SW 1/4, NW 1/4, Sec. 10, R. 7 W., T. 16 S.

Landform: T-0 floodplain; Exposure: Core 4; Elevation: 450 m; Slope: < 1%; Vegetation: Crops

0–20	Ap	I	10YR 3/1–10YR 4/1	SiCL	1 f gr	friable	weak	none	abrupt
20–36	A	I	10YR 3/1–10YR 4/1	SiCL	2 m gr	friable	weak	none	gradual
36–117	AC	I	10YR 3/2–10YR 6/4	SiL	2 f gr	sl hrd, fri	strong	none	gradual
117–221	C1	I	10YR 5/4–10YR 6/4	L	massive	sl hrd, fri	strong	none	gradual
221–348	C2	I	10YR 5/4–10YR 6/4	SL	massive	sl hrd, fri	strong	none	gradual
348–453	C3	I	10YR 5/4–10YR 6/4	LS	single grain	loose	violent	none	gradual
453–584	C4	I	10YR 4/3–10YR 5/3	S	single grain	loose	violent	none	—

(continued)

TABLE 2-1 (Continued)

PROFILE 5
Location: Smoky Hill River Valley; SW 1/4, NE 1/4, Sec. 14. R. 8 W., T. 16 S.
Landform: Low-angle alluvial fan; Exposure: Cutbank; Elevation: 457.2 m; Slope: 2–3%; Vegetation: Native grasses

Depth (cm)	Soil Horizon	Unit	Color (moist-dry)	Texture[a] (USDA)	Structure[b]	Consistence[c]	Reaction (10% HCL)	Carbonate Morphology	Lower Boundary
0–16	Ap	I	10YR 3/3–10YR 4/3	SiL	1 f gr	friable	none	none	clear
16–30	A	I	10YR 3/3–10YR 5/3	SiL	1 f gr	friable	none	none	gradual
30–36	AB	I	10YR 3/3–10YR 4/3	SiL	2 m gr	friable	none	none	gradual
36–105	Bw1	I	10YR 4/4–10YR 5/4	SiCL	2 f sbk	sl hrd, fri	none	none	clear
105–145	2Ab(Bw2)*	II	10YR 4/3–10YR 4/4	SiCL	2 f sbk	sl hrd, fri	none	none	gradual
145–151	2C	II	10YR 4/4–10YR 5/4	SiL	massive	hrd, firm	none	none	clear
151–178	2Ck	II	10YR 5/4–10YR 6/4	SiL	massive	hrd, firm	weak	Stage I	clear
178–198	3Ab	III	10YR 3/3–10YR 5/3	SiL	2 m gr	hrd, fri	weak	none	abrupt
198–231	4Btb	IV	10YR 3/3–10YR 4/3	SiCL	2 m sbk	sl hrd, fri	none	none	gradual
231–285	4Btkb	IV	10YR 3/3–10YR 5/3	SiCL	2 m abk	sl hrd, fri	strong	Stage 1+	clear
285–308	4C1	IV	10YR 5/4–10YR 6/4	SiL	massive	soft	violent	none	abrupt
308–316	4C2	IV	10YR 4/3–10YR 5/3	C	massive	very firm	violent	none	clear
316–327	4Ck	IV	10YR 3/3–10YR 4/3	SiCL	w f sbk	firm	violent	Stage II	abrupt
327–420	5Akb	V	10YR 3/3–10YR 4/3	SiCL	2 f gr	friable	weak	Stage I	gradual

PROFILE 6

Location: Smoky Hill River Valley; SW 1/4, NE 1/4, Sec. 4, R. 7 W., T. 16 S.

Landform: High-angle alluvial fan; Exposure: Trench 1; Elevation: 455.6 m; Slope: 4%; Vegetation: Native grasses

Depth	Horizon	Unit	Color	Texture	Structure	Consistence	Effervescence	Stage	Boundary
0–35	A	I	10YR 3/1–10YR 4/1	SiL	1 f gr	friable	weak	none	gradual
35–50	AC	I	10YR 3/1–10YR 4/2	SiL	1 f gr	friable	strong	none	clear
50–53	C1	I	10YR 3/1–10YR 4/2	GL	massive	friable	strong	none	abrupt
53–57	C2	I	10YR 3/1–10YR 4/1	SiCL	massive	firm	strong	none	abrupt
57–63	Ck	I	10YR 3/3–10YR 4/3	SL	massive	sl hrd, fri	violent	Stage I+	abrupt
63–97	2Ab	II	10YR 3/1–10YR 3/2	SiL	1 f gr	friable	weak	none	gradual
97–117	2C1	II	10YR 4/4–10YR 5/6	SL	massive	soft	none	none	abrupt
117–122	2C2	II	10YR 4/4–10YR 5/6	GS	sing	loose	none	none	abrupt
122–217	2C3	II	10YR 4/4–10YR 5/6	SL	massive	friable	none	none	abrupt
217–230	3Akb	III	10YR 3/2–10YR 4/2	SiL	2 m gr	friable	strong	Stage I+	gradual
230–251	3ABkb	III	10YR 3/3–10YR 4/3	SiCL	2 c gr	friable	strong	Stage I+	gradual
251–293	3Bwb	III	10YR 4/4–10YR 5/4	SiCL	1 f sbk	friable	strong	none	clear
293–353	3C	III	10YR 4/3–10YR 5/3	SL	massive	soft	strong	none	—

PROFILE 7

Location: Alum Creek Valley; SE 1/4, SW 1/4, Sec. 31, R. 6 W., T. 15 S.

Landform: T-2 terrace; Exposure: Trench 22; Elevation: 455.6 m; Slope: 1%; Vegetation: Native grasses

Depth	Horizon	Unit	Color	Texture	Structure	Consistence	Effervescence	Stage	Boundary
0–18	Ap	I	10YR 3/1–10YR 4/2	L	1 f gr	friable	none	none	clear
18–35	A	I	10YR 3/1–10YR 4/2	L	1 m gr	friable	none	none	gradual
35–45	AB	I	10YR 3/3–10YR 4/3	L	1 m gr	friable	none	none	gradual
45–84	Bt1	I	10YR 4/4–10YR 5/4	SiCL	2 f sbk	hrd, firm	none	none	gradual
84–116	Bt2	I	10YR 4/4–10YR 5/4	SiCL	2 f sbk	hrd, firm	none	none	gradual
116–138	BCk	I	10YR 4/4–10YR 5/4	SL	1 f sbk	hrd, firm	strong	Stage I+	gradual
138–178	C	I	10YR 4/4–10YR 5/4	SL	massive	hrd, firm	none	none	—

51

TABLE 2-1 (*Continued*)

PROFILE 8
Location: Alum Creek Valley; NW 1/4, NW 1/4, Sec. 6, R. 6 W., T. 15 S.
Landform: T-1 terrace; Exposure: Cutbank (Site 14EW171); Elevation: 451 m; Slope: 1%; Vegetation: Native grasses

Depth (cm)	Soil Horizon	Unit	Color (moist-dry)	Texture[a] (USDA)	Structure[b]	Consistence[c]	Reaction (10% HCL)	Carbonate Morphology	Lower Boundary
0–25	A	I	10YR 3/3–10YR 4/2	SL	1 f gr	friable	none	none	clear
25–43	AC	I	10YR 3/3–10YR 4/3	SL	1 f gr	friable	none	none	abrupt
43–97	2Ab	II	10YR 3/1–10YR 4/2	L	1 f gr	friable	none	none	gradual
97–104	2ABb	II	10YR 3/2–10YR 4/2	L	1 m sbk	friable	none	none	gradual
104–168	2Bwb	II	10YR 4/3–10YR 5/3	SiL	2 f sbk	sl hrd, fri	none	none	gradual
168–185	2BCb	II	10YR 4/3–10YR 5/3	SiL	2 f sbk	sl hrd, fri	none	none	gradual
185–279	2C1	II	10YR 4/3–10YR 5/3	L	massive	sl hrd, fri	none	none	gradual
279–317	2C2	II	10YR 4/3–10YR 5/3	SCL	massive	hrd, firm	none	none	gradual
317–421	2Cg	II	2.5YN 3/1–2.5YN 4/1	SiC	massive	hrd, firm	none	none	abrupt
421+	R	—	—	—	—	—	—	—	—

PROFILE 9

Location: Thompson Creek Valley; NW 1/4, SE 1/4, Sec. 21, R. 7 W., T. 16 S.

Landform: T-1 terrace; Exposure: Cutbank; Elevation: 452 m; Slope: 1%; Vegetation: Riparian woodland

0–30	A	I	10YR 3/2–10YR 4/2	SiL	1 f gr	friable	none	none	gradual
30–46	AC	I	10YR 3/3–10YR 4/3	SiL	1 f gr	friable	none	none	gradual
46–215	C1	I	10YR 4/3–10YR 5/4	SiL	massive	friable	none	none	clear
215–336	C2	II	10YR 4/3–10YR 5/3	SL	massive	sft, fri	none	none	abrupt
336–425	2Ab	II	10YR 3/2–10YR 3/3	SiL	1 f gr	friable	none	none	gradual
425–450	2ACb	II	10YR 3/3–10YR 4/3	SiL	1 f gr	friable	none	none	—

aG = gravelly, S = sand, Si = silt, L = loam, C = clay.

b1 = weak, 2 = moderate, 3 = strong; f = fine, m = medium, c = coarse; gr = granular, abk = angular blocky, sbk = subangular blocky structure; mass = massive, sing = single grain; strat = stratified.

csl = slightly, hrd = hard, fri = friable, sft = soft.

*Welded soil

B.P. The top of Unit II aggraded to about the same elevation as the surface of Unit IV (Figure 2-3), and a Cumulic Haplustoll with a thin A-C profiles developed in the upper part of Unit II (Table 2-1: Profile 3).

Two deep cores were taken on the modern floodplain (T-0) of the Smoky Hill River. The T-0 fill consists of bedded sand and gravel that grades upward into stratified loamy and fine-silty deposits. These deposits collectively make up Unit I (Figure 2-3). No buried paleosols were detected in Unit I , and the modern surface soil is a Fluventic Haplustolls with a thin A-C profile (Table 2-1: Profile 4). A survey of the floodplain surface recorded no prehistoric sites. Historic materials, such as nails and barbed wire, were recovered at depths of 3–4 m below the T-0 surface at sand-pit operations in the study area. Hence, the T-0 surface appears to be less than 200 years old, and deposits of historic alluvium compose at least the upper 3–4 m of the T-0 fill.

Several large, low-angle alluvial fans were investigated along the southern margin of the valley floor of the Smoky Hill River. At site 14EW174 (Eagle's Roost), a large fan emerges from a 2nd-order stream that extends into the uplands. The Smoky Hill River has migrated into the fan, creating a steep cutbank that exposes a transverse section through its midsection (Figure 2-4). Alluvium stored in the fan generally is silty and loamy, and there are multiple fining-upward sequences. Paleosols are developed at the top of most of these sequences (Figure 2-5), indicating that sedimentation on the fan was interrupted by periods of stability. Some of the paleosols have been partially or deeply truncated. For example, the A horizon of Soil 4 has been stripped off, leaving only the resistant Btk horizon as evidence of soil formation (Table 2-1:Profile 5). Erosion of Soil 3 is indicated by concentrations of calcium carbonate concretions and pebbles (stone lines) at the top of this buried paleosol. The modern soil on the fan surface is a Pachic Haplustoll with an A-Bw profile.

Temporal data indicate that the large, low-angle fans developed during the middle Holocene. At site 14EW174, radiocarbon ages of 5110 ± 70 and 5750 ± 60 years B.P. were determined on humates from the upper 20 cm of soils 4 and 5, respectively (Figure 2-5). Fan sedimentation ceased sometime after ca. 5100 B.P. when the stream feeding the fan incised, and the fan-head trench developed.

Backhoe trenches were excavated across several of the small, high-angle alluvial fans that have developed along margins of the valley bottom. These fans occur at the mouths of short gullies that extend up the steeply sloping valley walls of 4th-order and larger streams. Trenches

Figure 2-4.   View of vertical section exposed at the Eagle's Roost alluvial fan (site 14EW174). Radiocarbon ages were determined on humates from the upper 20 cm of soils 4 and 5.

excavated across distal portions of small fans revealed that fan deposits interfinger and grade into valley fill underlying T-1 terraces. The fan deposits generally consist of fine sandy loam grading upward to silt loam, and a few angular cobbles and pebbles (colluvium) were observed in the loamy matrix. Paleosols are developed at the top of some fining-upward sequences. These buried soils are Mollisols with A-C or A-Bw horizonation (Table 2-1: Profile 6). The presence of weakly developed soils suggests episodic aggradation of fans, with only short intervals of nondeposition. Modern surface soils developed into alluvium and col-luvium at the top of the fans are Typic Ustipsamments with thin A-C profiles. The occurrence of these weakly developed soils suggests that modern fan surfaces have been stable for relatively short periods of time.

As many as two terraces are present in valley bottoms of Ash, Thompson, and Alum creeks. The surface of the highest terrace (T-2) is 6–7 m above the modern floodplain. This terrace only occurs as scattered remnants along the lower reaches (4th-order) of these streams, and is absent in middle and upper reaches. A low, broad, terrace (T-1) domi-

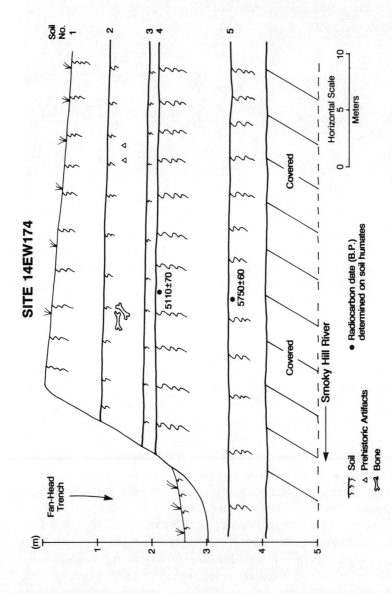

Figure 2-5. Diagram of vertical section exposed at the Eagle's Roost alluvial fan.

nates valley floors of major tributaries. T-1 is a paired terrace, and is separated from the modern floodplain (T-0) by a short, 3-m-high scarp. Floodplains generally are less than 30 m wide and are 1–3 m above channel bottoms.

Valley fill beneath remnants of the T-2 terrace along lower Alum and Thompson creeks was examined in backhoe trenches and cores. Subsurface observations revealed a Typic Argiustoll with a thick A-Bt profile developed at the top of the T-2 fill (Table 2-1: Profile 7).

The age of the T-2 fill is unknown. However, it must be older than ca. 3700 years B.P. based on a radiocarbon age from the T-1 fill in Thompson Creek Valley. The presence of a thick, oxidized Bt horizon developed within the upper 2 m of T-2 fill suggests that the underlying alluvium is at least middle Holocene in age.

Alluvium beneath T-1 terraces in the valleys of Ash, Thompson, and Alum creeks is contained in two distinct sediment groups: (1) a 1–2 m thick lower increment consisting of bedded sand and gravel overlying bedrock, and (2) a 3–5 m thick upper increment of fine sandy loam, loam, and silt loam. The T-1 fill is laterally inset against bedrock in the upper and middle reaches of these tributaries (2nd- and 3rd-order streams), and it abuts T-2 fill in portions of lower reaches (4th-order streams).

At least one buried paleosol was observed at every exposure of T-1 fill in small valleys. Most of these paleosols are developed in the upper portion of the T-1 fill, and many are Cumulic or Pachic Haplustolls (A-C and A-Bw profiles) buried beneath a 0.5–3.5 m thick mantle of Historic alluvium (Table 2-1: Profiles 8 and 9).

Radiocarbon assays suggest that the bulk of the fill in small valleys is late Holocene in age. For example, wood recovered from the base of the T-1 fill at site 14EW171 in Alum Creek Valley (Figure 2-2) yielded a radiocarbon age of 2090 ± 60 years B.P. Also, humates from buried paleosols near the base of T-1 fill in Ash and Thompson creek valleys yielded radiocarbon ages of 4170 ± 60 and 3680 ± 80 years B.P., respectively. No early- or middle-Holocene terraces, deposits, or soils were documented in valleys of 3rd-order or smaller streams.

A comparison of stratigraphic records from large and small valleys in the Lower Smoky Hill River Basin (Figure 2-6) reveals that late-Holocene alluvial deposits and buried soils occur in both large and small valleys. However, middle-Holocene deposits and buried soils appear to be restricted to large valleys and alluvial fans.

Comparison of surface-soil morphology in valley bottoms

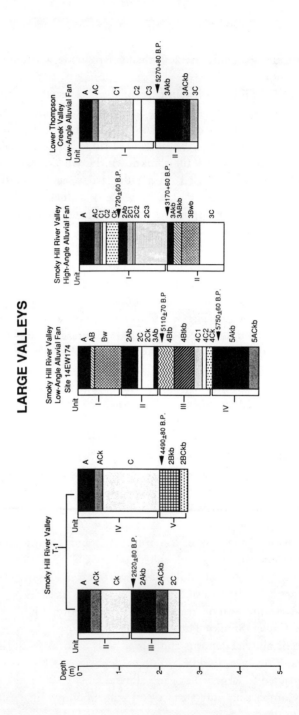

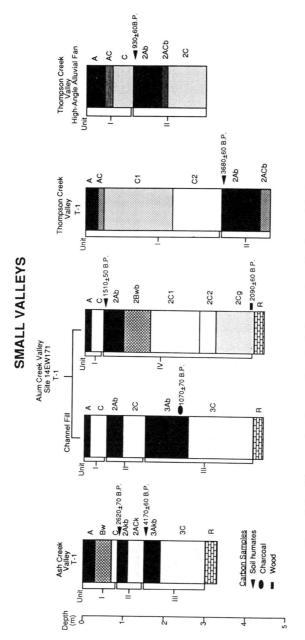

Figure 2-6. Diagram showing stratigraphy in large and small valleys of the Lower Smokey Hill River Basin.

PAWNEE RIVER DRAINAGE BASIN

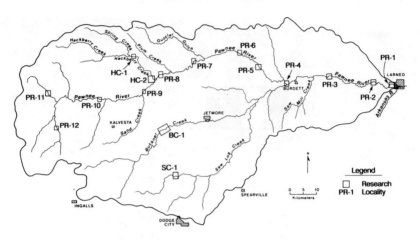

Figure 2-7. Map of the Pawnee River Basin showing localities where detailed soil stratigraphic investigations were conducted.

throughout the Lower Smoky Hill River drainage network also reveals a pattern. With the exception of soils developed at the top of T-2 fill in major tributary valleys, *all* surface soils have A-C or A-Bw horizonation. Hence, surfaces of most landforms in valley bottoms appear to be relatively young. Radiocarbon assays support this observation; ages determined on charcoal and humates from buried paleosols indicate that overlying deposits, and hence modern surface soils, often are less than about 3000 years old.

Pawnee River Valley

The Pawnee River was investigated from its confluence with the Arkansas River at Larned, Kansas, west to its source area near Kalvesta, Kansas (Figure 2-7). The valleys of Buckner, Saw Log, and Hackberry creeks also were studied. Detailed subsurface investigations, including coring and examination of trench silos and stream cutbanks, were conducted at 16 localities within the Pawnee River Basin (Figure 2-7).

The valley floor within the lower and middle reaches of the Pawnee River is 6.5–1.5 km wide, and it becomes progressively narrower in the upper reaches of this river. As many as three terraces occur in portions of the Pawnee Valley. The highest terrace (T-3) has a broad, gently sloping surface that is 7–8 m above the modern floodplain. This terrace is paired and is nearly continuous along the course of the Pawnee River. Deep coring revealed a 1- to 2-m-thick deposit of Peoria loess on the T-3 surface. A Typic Argiustoll with an A-Btk-Bk profile has developed in the upper part of the loess (Table 2-2: Profile 1). The loess overlies a truncated Bt horizon developed into alluvium. Valley fill beneath the truncated paleosol consists of 2–3 m of loamy overbank deposits above sandy and gravelly lateral accretion deposits.

An intermediate terrace (T-2) occupies a portion of the valley floor in the middle reach of the Pawnee River, but is absent in the upper and lower reaches. This terrace usually is unpaired, and it has a broad, flat surface 5–6 m above the floodplain. One natural exposure of T-2 deposits was examined in the project area along the left bank of the Pawnee River in Locality PR-8 (Figure 2-7). Here, a 6-m-thick unit of massive, brown and pale brown, silty sediment extends from the T-2 surface to the base of the exposure. A Pachic Haplustoll with A-Bw-Bk horizonation is developed at the top of the fill (Table 2-2: Profile 2). No buried paleosols were detected in the exposure, and the age of the fill is unknown.

The lowest terrace (T-1) has a broad, flat surface that dominates the valley bottom along the entire length of the Pawnee River. This terrace is on both sides of the river, and it is separated from the modern floodplain by a 3–5 m high scarp. Valley fill underlying the T-1 terrace is up to 40 m thick in the middle and lower reaches of the Pawnee River. Deposits at the base of the fill largely consist of bedded sands and gravels. These lateral accretion deposits are mantled by fine-textured alluvium composing vertical accretion deposits. Surface soils on the T-1 terrace are Haplustolls with A-C or A-Bw horizonation.

Buried paleosols are common in the upper 5–7 m of the T-1 fill. Most of the buried late-Holocene paleosols have A-C or thin A-Bk profiles. However, early- and middle-Holocene soils usually are well-developed and have thick Bt or Bk horizons. Also, some of the early- and middle-Holocene soils have been truncated by erosion, and in some cases, only their B horizons remain. For example, at Locality PR-4 (Figure 2-8), stream erosion removed the surface horizons of an early-Holocene soil (humates: 7900 ± 160 years B.P.), leaving a Btk horizon at the top of Unit III (Table 2-2: Profile 3) .

Radiocarbon ages determined on humates from buried paleosols in

TABLE 2-2
DESCRIPTION OF SOIL PROFILES 1–8 IN THE PAWNEE RIVER BASIN

PROFILE 1

Location: Pawnee River Valley; Locality PR-2; SW 1/4, SE 1/4, Sec. 29, R. 17 W., T. 21 S.

Landform: T–3 terrace; Exposure: Core; Elevation: 621.8 m; Slope: 1%; Vegetation: Crops

Depth (cm)	Soil Horizon	Unit	Color (moist-dry)	Texture[a] (USDA)	Structure[b]	Consistence[c]	Reaction (10% HCL)	Carbonate Morphology	Lower Boundary
0–20	Ap	I	10YR 3/2–10YR 5/3	SiL	1 f gr	sl hrd, fri	none	none	abrupt
20–42	A	I	10YR 3/2–10YR 5/2	SiL	2 m gr	sl hrd, fri	none	none	gradual
42–71	ABk	I	10YR 3/2–10YR 5/2	SiL	2 f sbk	hrd, firm	strong	Stage II	gradual
71–109	Btk	I	10YR 3/3–10YR 5/3	SiCL	2 m sbk	hrd, firm	weak	Stage I	gradual
109–190	Bk	I	10YR 3/3–10YR 5/3	SiCL	2 m sbk	hrd, firm	none	none	gradual
190–215	BC	I	10YR 5/3–10YR 6/3	SiL	1 f sbk	hrd, firm	none	none	gradual
215–292	C	I	10YR 5/3–10YR 5/3	SiL	mass	sl hrd, fri	none	none	abrupt
292–355	2Btb1	II	7.5YR 4/6–7.5YR 6/6	SiCL	2 m sbk	v hrd, firm	none	none	gradual
355–457	2Btb2	II	10YR 5/6–10YR 6/6	SiCL	2 f sbk	hrd, firm	none	none	gradual
457–469	2BCb	II	10YR 4/4–10YR 6/4	L	1 f sbk	hrd, firm	none	none	gradual
469–490	2C1	II	10YR 4/4–10YR 6/4	SL	mass	sl hrd, fri	none	none	gradual
490–571	2C2	II	10YR 4/4–10YR 6/4	LS	mass	mass, sft	none	none	clear
571–722	2C3	II	10YR 4/4–10YR 5/4	SiL	massive	sl hrd, fri	none	none	clear
722–853	3Bkb	III	10YR 4/4–10YR 5/4	SiCL	2 m sbk	hrd, firm	strong	Stage II	—

PROFILE 2

Location: Pawnee River Valley; Locality PR-8; SW 1/4, SW 1/4, Sec. 17, R. 25 W., T. 21 S.

Landform: T-2 terrace; Exposure: Cutbank; Elevation: 709.5 m; Slope: <1%; Vegetation: Crops

Depth	Horizon		Color	Texture	Structure	Consistence	Effervescence	Carbonate	Boundary
0–20	Ap	I	10YR 3/2–10YR 4/2	SiL	1 f gr	sl hrd, fri	none	none	clear
20–34	A	I	10YR 2/2–10YR 4/2	SiL	2 m gr	sl hrd, fri	none	none	gradual
34–48	AB	I	10YR 3/2–10YR 4/2	SiCL	1 f sbk	hrd, firm	none	none	gradual
48–62	Bw	I	10YR 3/3–10YR 5/3	SiCL	2 m sbk	hrd, firm	weak	none	gradual
62–94	Bk	I	10YR 4/3–10YR 5/3	SiCL	2 m sbk	hrd, firm	strong	Stage II	gradual
94–155	BCk	I	10YR 5/3–10YR 6/3	SiCL	1 m sbk	hrd, firm	strong	Stage I+	gradual
155–205	Ck1	I	10YR 5/3–10YR 6/3	SiL	massive	hrd, fri	strong	Stage I+	gradual
205–415	Ck2	I	10YR 5/4–10YR 6/4	SiL	massive	sl hrd, fri	strong	Stage I	gradual
415–610	Ck3	I	10YR 6/4–10YR 6/3	SiL	massive	sl hrd, fri	strong	Stage I	—

PROFILE 3

Location: Pawnee River Valley; Locality PR-4; SW 1/4, NW 1/4, Sec. 31, R. 20 W., T. 21 S.

Landform: T-1 terrace; Exposure: Cutbank; Elevation: 643.1 m; Slope: <1%; Vegetation: Native grasses

Depth	Horizon		Color	Texture	Structure	Consistence	Effervescence	Carbonate	Boundary
0–27	Ap	I	10YR 3/2–10YR 4/2	SiL	1 f gr	sl hrd, fri	weak	none	clear
27–38	A	I	10YR 3/2–10YR 5/2	SiL	1 f gr	sl hrd, fri	strong	Stage I	gradual
38–48	AC	I	10YR 4/2–10YR 5/3	SiL	1 f gr	sl hrd, fri	strong	Stage I	gradual
48–105	C	I	10YR 4/2–10YR 5/3	SL, SiL, SiCL	mass, strat	sl hrd, fri	strong	none	abrupt
105–145	2Ab	II	10YR 3/1–10YR 4/1	SiL	1 f gr	sl hrd, fri	none	none	gradual
145–175	2ACkb	II	10YR 4/3–10YR 5/3	SiL	1 f gr	sl hrd, fri	violent	Stage I	gradual
175–273	2Ck	II	10YR 5/3–10YR 6/3	SiL	1 f gr	hrd, fri	violent	Stage I	gradual
273–441	2C	II	10YR 6/3–10YR 7/3	SiL, SL	mass, strat	soft, fri	violent	none	abrupt
441–482	3Bkb	III	10YR 4/4–10YR 5/4	SiCL	2 f&m sbk	hrd, fri	strong	Stage II	diffuse
482–528	3Btkb	III	10YR 3/3–10YR 5/2	SiCL	2 m sbk	hrd, firm	weak	Stage II	gradual
528–564	3BCkb	III	10YR 4/3–10YR 5/3	SiCL	2 f sbk	hrd, fri	weak	Stage I	abrupt
564–604	4Btkb	IV	10YR 4/4–10YR 5/4	SiCL	2 f sbk	hrd, frm	strong	Stage I+	gradual
604–820	4BCkb	IV	10YR 4/4–10YR 5/4	SiCL	1 f sbk	hrd, fri	strong	Stage I+	—

(continued)

TABLE 2-2 (*Continued*)

PROFILE 4

Location: Pawnee River Valley; Locality PR–3; NW 1/4, NW 1/4, Sec. 36, R. 19 W., T. 21 S.

Landform: T-1 terrace; Exposure: Trench Silo and core; Elevation: 630.9 m; Slope: <1%; Vegetation: Native grasses

Depth (cm)	Soil Horizon	Unit	Color (moist-dry)	Texture[a] (USDA)	Structure[b]	Consistence[c]	Reaction (10% HCL)	Carbonate Morphology	Lower Boundary
0–10	Ap	I	10YR 3/1–10YR 4/2	SiL	1 f gr	sl hrd, fri	none	none	clear
10–24	A	I	10YR 3/2–10YR 5/2	SiL	1 f gr	sl hrd, fri	none	none	gradual
24–45	AC	I	10YR 4/2–10YR 5/2	SiL	1 vf gr	sl hrd, fri	none	weak	abrupt
45–75	2Akb	II	10YR 3/2–10YR 4/2	SiCL	1 f&m gr	sl hrd, fri	weak	Stage I	gradual
75–105	2ABBkb	II	10YR 3/2–10YR 4/2	SiCL	1 f sbk	hrd, fri	strong	Stage I+	gradual
105–142	2Bkb1	II	10YR 3/3–10YR 5/3	SiC	2 m sbk	hrd, firm	strong	Stage I+	gradual
142–183	2Bkb2	II	10YR 4/3–10YR 5/3	SiC	2 m sbk	v hrd, firm	strong	Stage II	gradual
183–216	2BCkb	II	10YR 4/3–10YR 5/3	L	1 f sbk	hrd, fri	strong	Stage II	gradual
216–251	2Ck	II	10YR 4/3–10YR 5/3	L	mass, strat	sft, fri	strong	Stage I	gradual
251–296	2C	II	10YR 5/2–10YR 5/3	SL, L, SiL, SiCL, SiC	mass, strat	sft, fri	moderate	none	clear
296–338	3Btb1	III	7.5YR 5/4–7.5YR 6/6	SiC	2 f sbk	hrd, firm	none	none	clear
338–405	3Btb2	III	10YR 4/4–10YR 5/4	SiCL	2 f sbk	hrd, firm	none	Stage I	—

PROFILE 5

Location: Pawnee River Valley; Locality HC-5; NW 1/4, NW 1/4, Sec. 7, R. 21 W., T. 21 S.
Landform: T-0 floodplain; Exposure: Cutbank; Elevation: 649.2 m; Slope: <1%; Vegetation: Riparian forest

0–25	A	I	10YR 3/2–10YR 5/2	SiL	1 f gr	sl hrd, fri	moderate	none	gradual
25–55	AC	I	10YR 4/2–10YR 6/2	SiL	1 gr	sl hrd, fri	strong	none	gradual
55–105	C	I	10YR 4/2–10YR 6/2	SiL	mass, strat	sft, fri	strong	none	abrupt
105–140	2Ab	II	10YR 3/2–10YR 6/2	SiL	1 f gr	sl hrd, fri	moderate	none	gradual
140–165	2ACb	II	10YR 4/2–10YR 5/2	SiL	1 vf gr	sl hrd, fri	strong	none	gradual
165–260	2C	II	10YR 5/3–10YR 6/3	L, SiL, SiCL	mass, strat	sft, fri	strong	none	—

PROFILE 6

Location: Hackberry Creek Valley; Locality HC-2; SE 1/4, SE 1/4, Sec. 13, R. 26 W., T. 21 S.
Landform: T-2 terrace; Exposure: Cutbank; Elevation: 719.3 m; Slope: <1%; Vegetation: Crops

0–12	Ap	I	10YR 3/2–10YR 4/2	SiL	1 f gr	sl hrd, fri	none	none	clear
12–43	A	I	10YR 3/2–10YR 3/3	SiL	1 m gr	sl hrd, fri	none	none	gradual
43–65	Bw	I	10YR 4/3–10YR 5/3	SiCL	2 c sbk	sl hrd, fri	none	none	gradual
65–103	Bk	I	10YR 4/3–10YR 6/3	SiCL	2 c sbk	sl hrd, fri	strong	Stage I+	gradual
103–155	Ck	I	10YR 5/3–10YR 6/3	SiL	mass	hrd, fri	strong	Stage I	abrupt
155–176	2Akb	I	10YR 3/2–10YR 4/2	SiCL	2 m&f gr	hrd, fri	strong	Stage I+	gradual
176–207	2ACkb	I	10YR 4/2–10YR 5/2	SiL	2 f gr	hrd, fri	strong	Stage I	abrupt
207–233	3Akb	I	10YR 3/2–10YR 4/2	SiL	1 f gr	hrd, fri	strong	Stage I	gradual
233–245	3ACkb	I	10YR 3/3–10YR 4/3	SiL	1 f gr	hrd, fri	strong	Stage I	abrupt
245–271	4Akb	II	10YR 3/2–10YR 4/2	Sil	1 m&f gr	hrd, fri	strong	Stage I	gradual
271–323	4ACkb	II	10YR 3/3–10YR 5/3	SiL	1 f gr	hrd, fri	strong	Stage I	abrupt
323–335	5Akb	II	10YR 3/3–10YR 4/3	SiL	1 f gr	hrd, fri	strong	Stage I+	gradual
335–349	5ACkb	II	10YR 3/3–10YR 5/3	SiL	1 f gr	hrd, fri	strong	Stage I+	abrupt
349–365	6Akb	II	10YR 3/3–10YR 4/3	SiL	1 f gr	hrd, fri	strong	Stage I+	gradual
365–417	6C	II	10YR 3/3–10YR 5/3	L, SL	mass, strat	sft, fri	strong	none	abrupt

(continued)

TABLE 2-2 (Continued)

Depth (cm)	Soil Horizon	Unit	Color (moist-dry)	Texture[a] (USDA)	Structure[b]	Consistence[c]	Reaction (10% HCL)	Carbonate Morphology	Lower Boundary
417–432	7Akb	II	10YR 3/3–10YR 4/3	SiL	1 f gr	hrd, fri	strong	Stage I	gradual
432–451	7ACkb	II	10YR 3/3–10YR 5/3	L	1 f gr	hrd, fri	strong	Stage I	abrupt
451–491	8Akb	III	10YR 3/3–10YR 4/3	SiL	1 f gr	hrd, fri	strong	Stage II	gradual
491–536	8Bkb	III	10YR 3/3–10YR 4/3	SiCL	1 f sbk	hrd, fri	strong	Stage II	gradual
536–595	8BCkb	III	10YR 3/3–10YR 5/3	SiL	1 f gr	hrd, fri	strong	Stage II	gradual
595–654	8Ck	III	10YR 4/3–10YR 5/3	L	1 f gr	hrd, fri	strong	Stage II	abrupt
654–705	9Akb	IV	10YR 3/3–10YR 4/3	SiL	1 f gr	hrd, fri	strong	Stage I	gradual
705–724	9ACkb	IV	10YR 4/3–10YR 5/3	L	1 f gr	hrd, fri	strong	Stage I	gradual
724–805	9Ck	IV	10YR 4/3–10YR 5/3	L, SL	mass, strat	soft, fri	weak	Stage I	irregular

PROFILE 7

Location: Buckner Creek Valley; Locality BC-1; SW 1/4, NE 1/4, Sec. 16, R. 25 W., T. 23 S.
Landform: T-1 terrace; Exposure: Cutbank; Elevation: 731 m; Slope: <1%; Vegetation: Native grasses

Depth (cm)	Soil Horizon	Unit	Color (moist-dry)	Texture[a] (USDA)	Structure[b]	Consistence[c]	Reaction (10% HCL)	Carbonate Morphology	Lower Boundary
0–18	Ap	I	10YR 3/2–10YR 4/3	SiL	1 m gr	sl hrd, fri	none	none	gradual
18–38	A	I	10YR 3/2–10YR 5/2	SiL	2 m gr	sl hrd, fri	moderate	none	gradual
38–46	AB	I	10YR 4/3–10YR 5/2	SiL	2 m gr	sl hrd, fri	moderate	none	clear
46–61	Bk1(2Ab)*	I	10YR 3/2–10YR 3/3	SiL	2 mc>f gr	hrd, fri	strong	Stage I	clear
61–86	Bk2	I	10YR 4/3–10YR 5/2	SiL	2 mc>f gr	hrd, fri	strong	Stage I+	gradual
86–119	BCk	I	10YR 4/3–10YR 5/2	SiL	1 fi & m gr	hrd, fri	strong	Stage I+	abrupt
119–147	3Akb	I	10YR 4/2–10YR 5/2	SiL	1 m gr	hrd, fri	strong	Stage I+	gradual
147–176	3ACkb	I	10YR 4/2–10YR 5/2	SiL	1 f gr	hrd, fri	strong	Stage I+	abrupt
176–210	4Ab	II	10YR 3/1–10YR 4/1	SiL	2 m gr	hrd, fri	none	none	gradual

210–241	4Akb	II	10YR 3/2–10YR 3/2	SiL	2 m gr	hrd, fri	strong	none	gradual
241–271	4ACkb	II	10YR 4/2–10YR 5/3	SiL	1 fi & m gr	hrd, fri	strong	Stage I	gradual
271–317	4Ck	II	10YR 5/3–10YR 6/3	SiL	massive	hrd, fri	violent	Stage II	abrupt
317–345	5Akb	II	10YR 3/3–10YR 5/2	SiL	1 f gr	hrd, fri	strong	Stage II	gradual
345–394	5Ck	II	10YR 5/3–10YR 5/2	SiL	massive	hrd, fri	strong	Stage 1+	abrupt
394–432	6Akb1	III	10YR 3/2–10YR 4/2	SiL	2 m gr	hrd, fri	strong	none	gradual
432–471	6Akb2	III	10YR 4/2–10YR 5/2	SiL	2 m gr	hrd, fri	strong	Stage I	gradual
471–523	6Bkb	III	10YR 4/3–10YR 5/2	SiL	1 f sbk	hrd, fri	violent	Stage II	gradual
523–658	6BCkb	III	10YR 4/3–10YR 6/3	SiL	massive	hrd, fri	violent	Stage II	gradual
658–712	6Ck	III	10YR 4/3–10YR 5/3	GS/SL	mass, strat	hrd, fri	strong	Stage I	irregular
712+	R	—	—	—	—	—	—	—	—

PROFILE 8

Location: Hackberry Creek Valley; Locality HC-1; NE 1/4, SE 1/4, Sec. 29, R. 26 W., T. 20 S.

Landform: T-1 terrace; Exposure: Cutbank; Elevation: 746.7 m; Slope: <1%; Vegetation: Crops

0–15	Ap	I	10YR 4/3–10YR 5/2	SiL	1 m gr	sl hrd, fri	moderate	none	gradual
15–48	A	I	10YR 3/2–10YR 5/2	SiL	2 m gr	sl hrd, fri	moderate	none	gradual
48–55	AB	I	10YR 4/3–10YR 5/2	SiL	2 m gr	sl hrd, fri	moderate	none	gradual
55–67	Bk1(2Ab)*	I	10YR 3/2–10YR 4/2	SiL	2 m c>f gr	hrd, fri	strong	Stage I	gradual
67–85	Bk2	I	10YR 3/3–10YR 4/3	SiL	2 mc>mgr	hrd, fri	strong	Stage I	gradual
85–107	BC	I	10YR 4/3–10YR 6/3	SiL	2 mc>mgr	hrd, fri	strong	none	abrupt
107–151	3Ab	II	10YR 3/2–10YR 4/2	SiL	2 m gr	hrd, fri	strong	none	gradual
151–168	3ACb	II	10YR 5/2–10YR 6/3	SiL	2 m gr	hrd, fri	strong	none	gradual
168–200	3Ck1	II	10YR 5/3–10YR 6/3	SiL	massive	v hrd, fri	violent	Stage 1+	gradual
200–415	3Ck2	II	10YR 5/3–10YR 7/3	SiL	massive	v hrd, fri	violent	Stage 1+	abrupt
415–455	4Akb1	IV	10YR 3/2–10YR 5/2	SiL	2 m gr	hrd, fri	strong	Stage I	gradual

(continued)

67

TABLE 2-2 (*Continued*)

Depth (cm)	Soil Horizon	Unit	Color (moist-dry)	Texture[a] (USDA)	Structure[b]	Consistence[c]	Reaction (10% HCL)	Carbonate Morphology	Lower Boundary
455–510	4Akb2	IV	10YR 4/3–10YR 5/3	SiL	2 m gr	hrd, fri	strong	Stage I	gradual
510–532	4Bkb	IV	10YR 4/3–10YR 6/3	SiL	1 f sbk	hrd, fri	violent	Stage II+	gradual
532–545	4BCkb	IV	10YR 4/3–10YR 7/3	SiL	1 f sbk	v hrd, fri	violent	Stage II+	gradual
545–628	4Ck	IV	10YR 4/3–10YR 7/3	L	massive	v hrd, fri	violent	Stage I+	abrupt
628–645	4C	IV	10YR 4/3–10YR 5/3	LS	mass, strat	loose	strong	none	abrupt
645–662	4Ck1	IV	10YR 4/3–10YR 5/3	SL	massive	hrd, fri	violent	Stage I+	abrupt
662–670	4Ck2	IV	10YR 4/3–10YR 6/3	GSL	sing	loose	violent	Stage I	abrupt
670–713	4Ck3	IV	10YR 5/3–10YR 6/3	SL	massive	hrd, fri	violent	Stage I	abrupt
713–734	4Ck4	IV	10YR 5/2–10YR 6/2	GLS	sing	loose	violent	Stage I	irregular
734+	R	—	—					—	—

PROFILE 9

Location: Buckner Creek Valley; Locality BC-1; NW 1/4, NW 1/4, Sec. 20, R. 25 W., T. 23 S.

Landform: T-0 floodplain; Exposure: Cutbank; Elevation: 727.5 m; Slope: <1%; Vegetation: native grasses

Depth (cm)	Soil Horizon	Unit	Color (moist-dry)	Texture[a] (USDA)	Structure[b]	Consistence[c]	Reaction (10% HCL)	Carbonate Morphology	Lower Boundary
0–30	A	I	10YR 3/2–10YR 4/2	SiL	1 f gr	sl hrd	weak	none	gradual
30–42	AC	I	10YR 4/2–10YR 5/2	SiL	1 f gr	sl hrd, fri	strong	none	clear
42–59	C1	I	10YR 6/2–10YR 6/3	SiL	mass, strat	sl hrd, fri	strong	Stage I	abrupt
59–230	C2	I	10YR 4/2–10YR 5/2	SiL	massive	hrd, fri	strong	Stage I	abrupt
230–361	C3	I	10YR 4/2–10YR 5/2	GL	mass, strat	sl hrd, fri	strong	Stage I	irregular
361+	R	—	—					—	—

[a]G = gravelly, S = sand, Si = silt, L = loam, C = clay.

[b]1 = weak, 2 = moderate, 3 = strong; vf = very fine, f = fine, m = medium, c = coarse; gr = granular, abk = angular blocky, sbk = subangular blocky structure; mass = massive, sing = single grain, strat = stratified, > = parting to.

[c]sl = slightly, hrd = hard, v hrd = very hard, fri = friable, sft = soft.

*Welded soil.

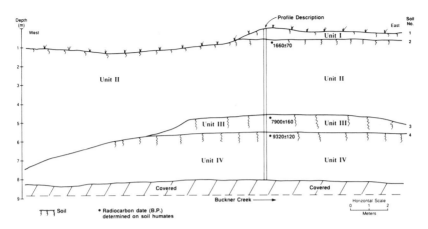

Figure 2-8. Diagram of vertical section at the confluence of Buckner Creek and the Pawnee River in Locality PR-4. Valley fill in the section underlies the T-1 terrace.

T-1 fill indicate that alluviation during the early, middle, and late Holocene was punctuated by floodplain stability and concomitant soil formation. However, since no 14C-datable materials, such as charcoal or wood, were found within T-1 fill, numerical ages of alluvial deposits could not be determined. Instead, relative ages of deposits were inferred from the paleosol record where more than one buried soil was dated within a section. Despite this limitation, the identification of early-, middle-, and late-Holocene paleosols within T-1 fill of the Pawnee River has important implications for archaeological research, which will be discussed later.

Deposits of Historic alluvium up to 2 m thick cover much of the T-1 terrace in the middle and lower reaches of the Pawnee River Valley. These deposits consist of stratified silts and clays, and they often contain Historic artifacts. Surface soils developed at the top of Historic fill are Fluventic Haplustolls with thin A-C profiles (Table 2-2: Profile 4). The mantle of Historic alluvium generally becomes thinner with increasing distance from the modern channel of the Pawnee River, and often is absent near margins of the valley floor. This factor accounts for soil variability observed along some cross-valley transects. For example, in area PR-3 (Figure 2-7), a very young surface soil with a thin A-C profile is developed into deposits of Historic alluvium that form natural levees on the T-1 terrace. The Historic alluvium mantles a late-Holocene soil with an A-Bk profile developed into T-1 fill. This buried late-Holocene soil is the surface soil where the mantle of Historic alluvium is absent.

The modern floodplain of the Pawnee River (T-0) is about 20–50 m wide, and its surface is 2–3 m above the bottom of the channel. The T-0 fill is largely composed of sandy lateral accretion deposits capped by silty and clayey overbank deposits. Archaeological and soils evidence suggests that T-0 surfaces are Late Prehistoric to Historic in age. At site 14HO5 in Locality PR-9 (Figure 2-7), Middle Ceramic pot sherds were found in a cultural horizon 1 m below the T-0 surface. Hence, deposits above the cultural horizon are no greater than 1,000 years old, and may be less than 500 years old. Buried paleosols and modern surface soils observed in T-0 fill are characterized by A-C horizonation (Table 2-2: Profile 5). The surface soils are Typic Ustifluvents or Fluventic Haplustolls with thin A-C profiles; they have not developed long enough to have B horizons. The morphology of these soils suggests that T-0 surfaces are very young.

All of the tributaries of the Pawnee River are 4th-order or smaller streams. The valley floors of 2nd- and 3rd-order streams are comprised of two landforms: a narrow floodplain (T-0) and a low, broad terrace (T-1). The T-1/T-0 terrace sequence also characterizes most reaches of 4th-order streams, but a second terrace (T-2) is present near their confluences with the Pawnee River.

The T-2 terrace is unpaired, and its surface is 6–7 m above the modern floodplain. A detailed subsurface investigation of the T-2 fill was conducted at Locality HC-2 along Lower Hackberry Creek (Figure 2-7). This creek has migrated laterally across its floor, cutting into the T-2 fill and creating an 8-m-high cutbank at site 14HO316 (Figure 2-9). Coring revealed that bedrock is less than 1 m below the base of the cutbank. Eight buried paleosols were identified below the T-2 surface (Figure 2-10). With the exception of soils 4, 8, and 9, all of the paleosols are characterized by thin Ak-ACk profiles (Table 2-2: Profile 6). Soils 4 and 9 have thick, dark-colored Ak horizons above Ck horizons, and soil 8 has an A-Bk profile. Humates from the upper 20 cm of soils 4, 8, and 9 yielded radiocarbon ages of 4970 ± 100, 7170 ± 120, and 9820 ± 110 years B.P., respectively (Figure 2-10). Based on these ages, a large proportion of the alluvium beneath T-2 accumulated during the early and middle Holocene. Unit I at the top of the section aggraded sometime after ca. 4970 years B.P. but before ca. 2700 years B.P. The upper bounding date is inferred from a radiocarbon age of 2680 ± 80 years B.P. determined on charcoal near the base of the T-1 fill at a nearby archaeological site (14HO308) in Hackberry Creek Valley. Stream entrench-

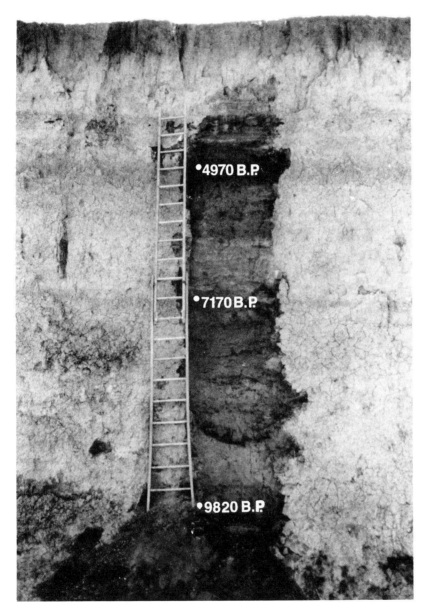

Figure 2-9.   View of vertical section at site 14HO316 on the north bank of Hackberry Creek in Research Locality HC-2. Valley fill in the section underlies the T-2 terrace. The ladder is 6 m long.

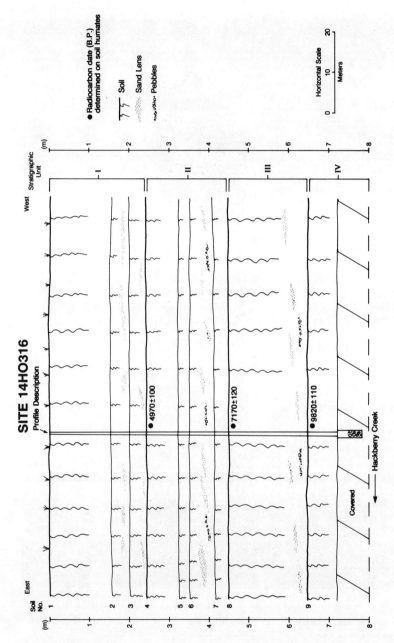

Figure 2-10. Diagram of vertical section seen in Figure 2-9.

ment also occurred sometime between ca. 4970 and 2680 years B.P., isolating the T–2 surface from flooding. A Pachic Haplustoll with A–Bw–Bk horizonation has developed into the upper part of Unit I (Table 2-2: Profile 6).

The T–1 terrace usually is on both sides of small streams in the Pawnee River Basin, and is separated from the modern floodplain by a 3–4 m high scarp. Deposits underlying this low terrace were examined at over 100 cutbank exposures, and detailed investigations were conducted at localities HC-1, BC-1, and SC-1 (Figure 2-7). Bedded sand and gravel at the base of the T–1 fill grades upward into loamy and silty alluvium. As many as five buried paleosols were identified in the T–1 fill. Most of these paleosols are thin, discontinuous, weakly developed A horizons. However, two paleosols are relatively well developed and can be traced laterally throughout the low-order drainages. These soils were first recognized at site 14HO306 (Figures 2-11 and 2-12) in Buckner Creek Valley (Locality BC-1 in Figure 2-7). The oldest of the two buried soils, informally named the Hackberry Creek Paleosol (Mandel 1988), has a 50–100 cm thick cumulic A horizon above a Bk horizon (Table 2-2: Profiles 7 and 8). This paleosol usually is developed in loamy alluvium near the base of the T–1 fill. At some localities, such as site 14NS308 (Locality HC-1 in Figure 2-7), a deep channel is cut into the Hackberry Creek Paleosol and underlying fill (Figure 2-12). The channel is filled with cross-bedded sands.

Four radiocarbon ages were determined on charcoal from multi-component Late Archaic sites in the Hackberry Creek Paleosol. The oldest age of 2820 ± 260 years B.P. is from a hearth in the lower 10 cm of this paleosol at site 14HO306 (Figure 2-11). Charcoal from a hearth in the upper 10 cm of the Hackberry Creek Paleosol at site 14NS308 (Figure 2-12) yielded a radiocarbon age of 2450 ± 90 years B.P., which is the youngest of the four dates. In addition, three radiocarbon ages were determined on humates from the Hackberry Creek Paleosol. At site 14NS308, humates from the upper and lower 30 cm of the paleosol yielded ages of 1950 ± 50 years B.P. and 2170 ± 50 years B.P., respectively. Humates from the upper 30 cm of the Hackberry Creek Paleosol at site 14FD311 in Saw Log Creek Valley (Locality SC-1 in Figure 2-7) yielded a radiocarbon age of 2260 ± 80 years B.P. These radiocarbon ages suggest that formation of the Hackberry Creek Paleosol began around 2800 years B.P. and continued until at least 2000 years B.P.

A younger buried soil, informally named the Buckner Creek Paleosol (Mandel 1988), has a thick, dark-colored A–C profile (Figure 2-13;

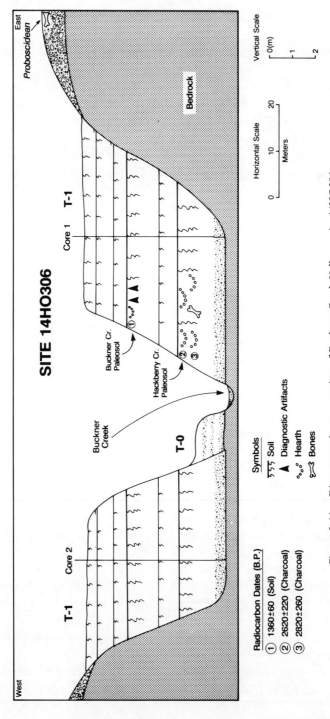

Figure 2-11. Diagrammatic cross section of Buckner Creek Valley at site 14HO306 showing soil stratigraphy, radiocarbon dates, and cultural horizons.

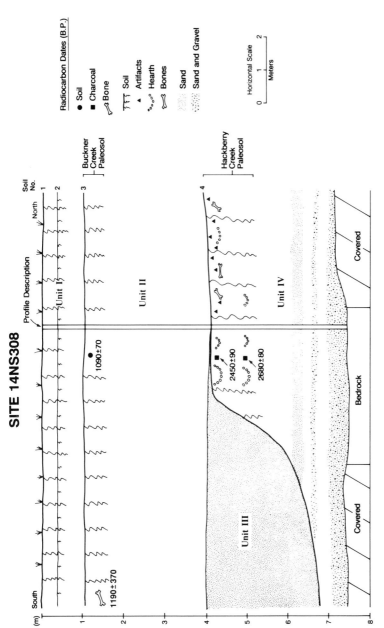

Figure 2-12. Diagram of the vertical section at site 14NS308 on the west bank of Hackberry Creek in Research Locality HC-1. Valley fill in the section underlies the T-1 terrace.

Figure 2-13.   View of vertical section at site 14HO306 on the east bank of Buckner Creek in Research Locality BC-1. The alluvial deposits underlie the T-1 terrace. Note hearth in the Buckner Creek Paleosol, which also contains Plains Woodland archaeological materials. The Hackberry Creek Paleosol near the lower portion of the section contains a stratified Late Archaic site.

Table 2-2: Profiles 7 and 8). This paleosol is developed in silty alluvium near the top of the T-1 fill (Figures 2-11 and 2-12). At site 14HO306, several hearths, many bone fragments, and several lithic artifacts were identified in the Buckner Creek Paleosol (Figure 2-11). The artifact assemblage included a projectile point characteristic of the Keith variant of the Plains Woodland period. Radiocarbon assays from the High Plains place the Keith variant from ca. 1600 to 1200 years B.P. (Grange 1980: 126). A radiocarbon age of 1360 ± 60 B.P. determined on humates from the upper 25 cm of the Buckner Creek Paleosol at 14HO306 falls within this period. At site 14NS308 (Figure 2-12), apatite and collagen from bison bones recovered 40 cm below the surface of the Buckner Creek Paleosol yielded radiocarbon ages of 1310 ± 130 and 1190 ± 370 years B.P., respectively. Humates from the upper 20 cm of this paleosol at 14NS308 yielded a radiocarbon age of 1090 ± 70 years B.P. Altogether, the archaeological evidence and radiocarbon assays suggest that the Buckner Creek Paleosol developed from about 1350 to at least 1000 years B.P.

The Buckner Creek Paleosol is mantled by 1–2 m of silty alluvium composing the upper portion of the T-1 fill. Surface soils developed at the top of the T-1 fill are Typic Haplustolls with thin A-Bk profiles (Table 2-2: Profile 7 and 8).

Floodplain (T-0) deposits abut the T-1 fill in small valleys (Figure 2-11). Deep cores and cutbank exposures revealed 1–2 m of fine-textured alluvium above alternating beds of sandy loam, sand, and gravel. Deposits underlying T-0 are distinct from those beneath T-1 in that the former are coarser, much more stratified, and rarely contain buried paleosols. The absolute age of T-0 fill, however, has not been firmly established. Only one radiocarbon age has been determined on materials from T-0 deposits: 1010 ± 410 years B.P. on apatite from bison bones recovered 1 m below the T-0 surface. No prehistoric archaeological sites were discovered on or below the T-0 surface, and historic artifacts are common in the upper 1 m of the fill. The presence of Haplustolls with thin A-C profiles developed at the top of the T-0 fill suggests that floodplain surfaces are very young (Table 2-2: Profile 9).

A comparison of stratigraphic records from large and small valleys in the Pawnee River Basin (Figure 2-14) reveals a pattern similar to the one observed in the Lower Smoky Hill River Basin. Specifically, late-Holocene alluvial deposits and buried paleosols are present in both large and small valleys. However, middle- and early-Holocene deposits and buried paleosols were documented only in the main valley of the Pawnee River, and in the lower reaches of major tributaries near their confluence with the Pawnee.

The morphology of surface soils in valley bottoms of the Pawnee River Basin is fairly consistent. With the exception of soils developed into the Peoria loess on the T-3 terrace, all surface soils are Haplustolls characterized by A-C, A-Bw, or weakly-developed A-Bk profiles. The presence of weakly developed soils suggests that surfaces of landforms in valley bottoms are relatively young. Radiocarbon ages determined on charcoal and humates from buried paleosols in large and small valleys indicate that overlying deposits, and hence modern surface soils, often are less than 2000 years old.

HOLOCENE VALLEY HISTORY

Radiocarbon ages, combined with age estimates based on temporally diagnostic archaeological materials, were used to outline the chronology

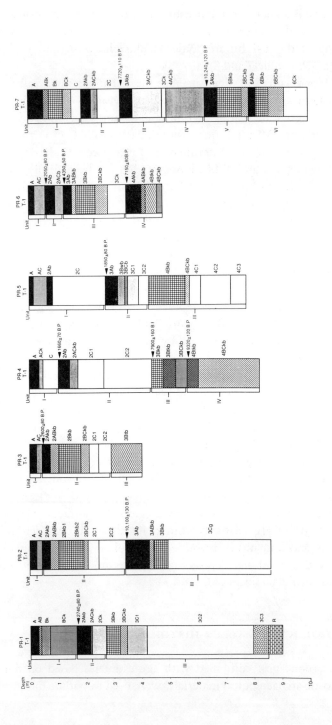

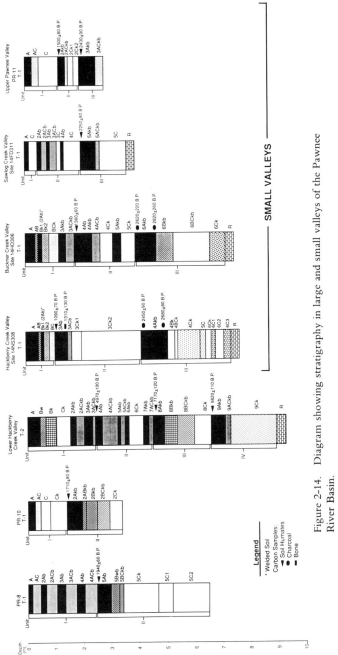

Figure 2-14. Diagram showing stratigraphy in large and small valleys of the Pawnee River Basin.

of Holocene landscape evolution in the Pawnee and Lower Smoky Hill river basins. The ages on which this chronology is based roughly span the Holocene (Table 2-3).

During the early Holocene (ca. 10,500–7000 B.P.), alluviation in large valleys of the Pawnee River Basin was punctuated by floodplain stability and soil formation. Buried paleosols dating to this period were documented in T-1 fill of the Pawnee River, and in T-2 fill of Lower Hackberry Creek near its confluence with the Pawnee.

The type of fluvial activity that characterized the Lower Smoky Hill River during the early Holocene is not known. However, radiocarbon ages from other large valleys in the Kansas River drainage network indicate episodic floodplain stability, marked by soil development, interrupting alluviation at times between ca. 10,500 and 8000 years B.P. (Johnson and Martin 1987).

During the middle Holocene, between about 7000 and 4500 B.P., 2nd- and 3rd-order streams in the Pawnee and Lower Smoky Hill river basins were characterized by net transport of alluvium, with little or no long-term storage. It is likely that small streams were migrating laterally and actively downcutting and lengthening during this period. Some sediment transported out of these parts of the lower Smoky Hill River Basin was stored in large, low-angle alluvial fans that prograded into large valleys. Although there is no evidence for alluvial-fan development in the Pawnee River Basin, alluvium accumulated as valley fill in the middle reach of the Pawnee River and in lower reaches of its major tributaries during the middle Holocene. This fill is stored beneath T-1 terraces of the Pawnee River, and is beneath T-2 terraces of 4th-order streams near their confluence with the Pawnee. Although mid-Holocene deposits may be preserved in the vast quantity of valley fill stored beneath T-1 terraces of the lower Pawnee and Smoky Hill rivers, its presence has not yet been documented.

Sedimentation on alluvial fans in the Smoky Hill River Valley and on mid-Holocene floodplains of major tributaries in the Pawnee River Basin was episodic with intervening periods of stability and soil formation. The episodic nature of fan and floodplain development indicates that transport of sediment out of the small basins draining to the fans and lower reaches of major tributaries was cyclic during the middle Holocene.

A major shift in the locus of sediment storage took place during the late Holocene in both study areas. Following the mid-Holocene episode of downcutting and lateral erosion, 2nd- and 3rd-order streams, for-

TABLE 2-3

Radiocarbon Ages from the Study Areas

Stream Valley	Landform	Material Dated	Depth Below Surface (m)	C-14 Years B.P.	Lab. No.
SMOKY HILL RIVER BASIN					
Large Valleys					
Smoky Hill	T-1	Soil	2.00–2.20	4490 ± 80	TX-5827
Smoky Hill	T-1	Soil	1.30–1.60	2620 ± 80	TX-5826
Smoky Hill	T-1	Charcoal	0.01–0.20	1640 ± 60	TX-5812
Smoky Hill	T-1	Charcoal	0.52–0.54	800 ± 90	TX-5813
Smoky Hill	LAF[a]	Soil	3.27–3.47	5750 ± 60	TX-5817
Smoky Hill	LAF	Soil	1.98–2.30	5110 ± 70	TX-5816
Smoky Hill	HAF[b]	Soil	2.17–2.30	3170 ± 60	TX-5822
Smoky Hill	HAF	Soil	0.63–0.83	720 ± 60	TX-5821
Thompson Cr.	LAF	Soil	1.83–2.05	5270 ± 80	TX-5823
Thompson Cr.	HAF	Soil	1.15–1.35	930 ± 60	TX-5824
Small Valleys					
Thompson Cr.	T-1	Soil	3.36–3.56	3680 ± 60	TX-5825
Alum Cr.	T-1	Wood	4.00–4.05	2090 ± 60	TX-5815
Alum Cr.	T-1	Soil	0.47–0.60	1510 ± 50	TX-5820
Alum Cr.	T-1	Charcoal	2.32–2.38	1070 ± 70	TX-5811
Ash Cr.	T-1	Soil	2.52–2.72	4170 ± 60	TX-5819
Ash Cr.	T-1	Soil	0.79–1.00	2620 ± 70	TX-5818
PAWNEE RIVER BASIN					
Large Valleys					
Pawnee R.	T-1	Soil	6.20–6.40	10,240 ± 120	TX-6391
Pawnee R.	T-1	Soil	3.45–3.70	10,100 ± 130	TX-6374
Pawnee R.	T-1	Soil	5.63–5.83	9320 ± 120	TX-6396
Pawnee R.	T-1	Soil	5.28–5.48	7900 ± 160	TX-6392
Pawnee R.	T-1	Soil	3.30–3.35	7720 ± 110	TX-6476
Pawnee R.	T-1	Soil	3.50–3.70	7150 ± 110	TX-6398
Pawnee R.	T-1	Soil	1.25–1.55	4350 ± 50	TX-6389
Pawnee R.	T-1	Soil	1.42–1.62	2740 ± 80	TX-6375
Pawnee R.	T-1	Soil	0.45–0.65	2600 ± 80	TX-6394
Pawnee R.	T-1	Soil	0.60–0.95	2050 ± 80	TX-6390
Pawnee R.	T-1	Soil	1.80–2.00	1940 ± 60	TX-6393
Pawnee R.	T-1	Soil	2.75–2.95	1850 ± 80	TX-6397
Pawnee R.	T-1	Soil	1.20–1.40	1710 ± 80	TX-6475
Pawnee R.	T-1	Soil	1.05–1.45	1660 ± 70	TX-6395
Hackberry Cr.	T-2	Soil	6.50–6.70	9820 ± 110	TX-6480
Hackberry Cr.	T-2	Soil	4.51–4.71	7170 ± 120	TX-4732
Hackberry Cr.	T-2	Soil	2.45–2.65	4970 ± 100	TX-5731
Small Valleys					
Pawnee Cr.	T-1	Soil	1.95–2.15	2430 ± 90	TX-6474
Pawnee Cr.	T-1	Soil	1.20–1.35	1500 ± 80	TX-6473

(continued)

TABLE 2-3 (*Continued*)

Stream Valley	Landform	Material Dated	Depth Below Surface (m)	C-14 Years B.P.	Lab. No.
Hackberry Cr.	T-1	Charcoal	5.05–5.15	2680 ± 80	TX-5640
Hackberry Cr.	T-1	Charcoal	4.20–4.30	2450 ± 90	TX-5641
Hackberry Cr.	T-1	Charcoal	4.10–4.15	2340 ± 400	TX-5639
Hackberry Cr.	T-1	Soil	2.90–3.30	2170 ± 50	TX-5649
Hackberry Cr.	T-1	Soil	2.10–2.50	1950 ± 50	TX-5645
Hackberry Cr.	T-1	Bone[c]	1.55–1.60	1310 ± 130	TX-5643
Hackberry Cr.	T-1	Bone[d]	1.55–1.60	1190 ± 370	TX-5643
Hackberry Cr.	T-1	Soil	1.07–1.37	1090 ± 70	TX-5646
Buckner Cr.	T-1	Charcoal	4.64–4.69	2820 ± 260	TX-5730
Buckner Cr.	T-1	Charcoal	3.94–4.04	2620 ± 220	TX-5729
Buckner Cr.	T-1	Charcoal	5.28–5.33	1610 ± 100	TX-5642
Buckner Cr.	T-1	Soil	4.98–5.28	1430 ± 50	TX-5644
Buckner Cr.	T-1	Soil	1.76–2.00	1360 ± 60	TX-5642
Buckner Cr.	T-0	Bone[d]	1.00–1.05	1010 ± 410	TX-5651
Sawlog Cr.	T-1	Soil	2.00–2.30	2260 ± 80	TX-5647

[a] Low-angle alluvial fan.
[b] High-angle alluvial fan.
[c] Apatite.
[d] Collagen.

merly zones of net transport, became zones of sediment storage. Although valley bottoms of small streams experienced cut-and-fill episodes during the late Holocene, net storage of alluvium occurred as evidenced by preservation of large volumes of late-Holocene valley fill beneath T-1 terraces.

Sediment storage on low-angle alluvial fans within the main valley of the Smoky Hill River ceased sometime after ca. 5100 years B.P. The development of fan-head trenches during the late Holocene allowed sediment from higher in the drainage network to bypass the fans and reach the floodplain of the Smoky Hill River.

In large valleys, late-Holocene entrenchment and lateral channel migration reworked some deposits stored during the early and middle Holocene. The entrenchment left the late-Holocene floodplains as T-1 terraces. Alluvium derived primarily from reworking of older deposits is stored beneath modern floodplains of large valleys.

The drainage networks of the Pawnee and Smoky Hill rivers appear to have been overwhelmed with sediment during the Historic period. It is likely that various human activities, such as land clearance and cultivation, increased sediment delivery to all drainage elements. The bulk of the Historic alluvium has accumulated on modern floodplains (T-0) and composes flood drapes that mantle T-1 terraces in large valleys.

REGIONAL CORRELATIONS OF HOLOCENE ALLUVIAL SEQUENCES

When the Holocene alluvial records of the Pawnee and Lower Smoky Hill river basins are compared with each other and with those of other stream systems in the Midwest, there is not an episode-to-episode correlation between any of the records. However, a general pattern is evident in the timing of fluvial events across the region as a whole. This pattern is similar to the one described by Knox (1983) for the Midwest and western Great Plains. Many of the alluvial chronologies used for comparison in the present study, as was the case in Knox's (1983) investigation, are tied to Holocene paleosol records from stream valleys. Buried paleosols in valley fills are readily dated by radiocarbon analysis, and they have long been recognized as indicators of episodic change in stream systems (Johnson and Martin 1987; Ferring, this volume). Caution must be exercised, however, when comparing radiocarbon ages determined on different materials, such as humates, charcoal, and bone, from different soils.

The timing of Holocene landscape stability and concomitant soil development in the Pawnee and Lower Smoky Hill river basins was separated into two principle categories: episodes in large valleys vs. small valleys (Figure 2-15). In the case of large valleys, the paleosol records were further subdivided by landform type: soil development in valley fills vs. fan deposits. This categorization reveals that while some episodes of landscape stability were basinwide, others were not. The paleosol records for these two drainage systems were then compared with records for other drainage systems in the Central Plains (Figure 2-15).

Within the main valley of the Pawnee River, soil formation was underway by at least 10,300 to 10,100 years B.P. based on mean residence time for humates from the upper 20 cm of buried paleosols. This period occurs during the Pleistocene-Holocene transition in the Midwest: a time of major atmospheric circulation shifts that resulted in dramatic hydrologic changes. Deposits and associated soils of such antiquity have been documented at few localities within the Central Plains (Figure 2-15).

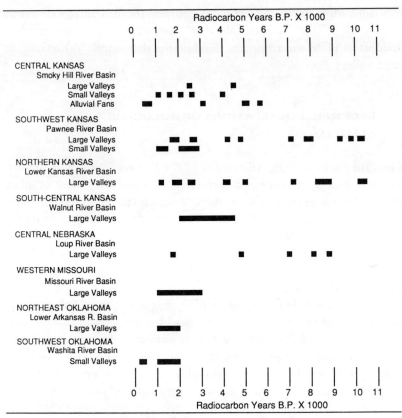

Figure 2-15. Diagram Showing periods of Holocene floodplain stability and soil formation in the Central Plains. Records are based on radiocarbon assays from the regions.

Mean residence time for humates from buried paleosols in large valleys of the Pawnee River suggests that the period 10,000 to 7000 years B.P. was punctuated by episodes of floodplain stability and soil development. A similar pattern of early-Holocene soil development is indicated by radiocarbon assays from the Loup and Lower Kansas river valleys (Figure 2-15).

Holocene valley fills in the Pawnee and Lower Smoky Hill river systems are void of any indications of soil development between 7000 and 5000 years B.P. (Table 2-2). However, mean residence time for humates from buried paleosols indicate soil formation on large, low-angle alluvial fans in the Smoky Hill River Valley at least by ca. 5100–5300 and 5750 years B.P., partially filling the gap in the middle-Holocene paleosol record. Several studies suggest that the middle Holocene was a time of stream-system instability, or at least low potential for strong soil development in the Central Plains (Johnson and Martin 1987). For example, at the Coffey site in the Big Blue River Valley of northeastern Kansas, Schmits (1980) recorded aggradation at ca. 6300 B.P. May (1986a) noted that alluvial fill at the Horn site on the South Loup River shows no evidence of soil development, in the form of buried paleosols, from ca. 7000 to 4780 years B.P. Elsewhere in the South Loup River Valley, Ahlbrandt and others (1983) reported ten radiocarbon ages from organic-rich zones in sandy alluvial fill. None of these dates, however, are within the period 7000 to 5000 years B.P., suggesting an absence of floodplain stability and/or sufficient biomass for organic enrichment.

Radiocarbon assays suggest that soil formation was underway by at least 5000 years B.P. on floodplains of large valleys in the Pawnee River Basin. Corroborative evidence for this episode of landscape stability once again comes from the Kansas and Loup river systems (Figure 2-15).

The timing of late-Holocene floodplain stability and soil formation in the Pawnee and Lower Smoky Hill river basins shows some variation according to the size of the streams. Radiocarbon assays indicate two discrete periods of paleosol development in large valleys: one at 2750 to 2600 years B.P., and another at 2000 to 1600 B.P. (Figure 2-15). The older of these two episodes is correlative with the soil-forming period radiocarbon dated ca. 2800 to 2000 B.P. in small valleys. However, the most recent episode of paleosol development in large valleys, 2000 to 1600 years B.P., overlaps only the beginning of the soil-forming period dated 1600 to 1000 years B.P. in small valleys. Hence, late-Holocene deposition appears to have been time transgressive throughout the entire extent of the drainage basins.

Very good indication for fluvial stability and soil formation during the late Holocene is found elsewhere in the Midwest, including the Great Plains (Figure 2-15). Late-Holocene paleosols have been documented in valley fills throughout much of the Central Plains (Johnson and Martin 1987; Bettis and Mandel 1989; Ferring, this volume).

There are exceptions to the synchronous pattern of fluvial stability and soil development in Midwestern stream valleys during the

Holocene. For example, an episode of soil development radiocarbon-dated ca. 600 to 400 years B.P. (Delaware Creek Paleosol) in small stream valleys within southwestern Oklahoma (Ferring 1986) has not been documented in the Central Plains. Similarly, a major episode of soil development dated ca. 6500 to 6000 years B.P. within the Des Moines River Valley (Bettis and Hoyer 1986) has not been recorded in central or southwestern Kansas.

Despite some variations in timing of erosion, sedimentation, and landscape stability, regional synchroneity is indisputable. For example, upland erosion and wholesale removal of sediment from small valleys occurred during the early and middle Holocene (ca. 8000–4000 years B.P.) across much of the Midwest. Sediment transported out of small valleys accumulated on alluvial fans and floodplains in large valleys. This episode of upland erosion and fan development has been documented in the lower Illinois River Valley (Butzer 1977; Hajic 1981; Wiant et al. 1983), the Des Moines River Valley (Bettis and Benn 1984; Bettis and Hoyer 1986), and in large valleys of the lower Missouri River system (Ahler 1973; Hoyer 1980; Thompson and Bettis 1980). Sedimentation on fans was accompanied by aggradation in many large valleys, including the Wisconsin River Valley in southern Wisconsin (Knox 1972), the Des Moines River Valley in central Iowa (Bettis and Hoyer 1986), the Pomme de Terre River Valley in west-central Missouri (Ahler 1973; Haynes 1976; Brakenridge 1981), the South Loup River Valley in central Nebraska (May 1986a), and the lower Kansas River Valley in northeastern Kansas (Johnson and Martin 1987).

The alluvial chronologies of midwestern stream systems, combined with paleoenvironmental data from the region, suggest that wholesale removal of sediment from small valleys during the early and middle Holocene was a result of major bioclimatic change. Specifically, during the early Holocene the waning of the Laurentide ice sheet favored strong zonal westerly circulation over the Great Plains (Bryson and Hare 1974). Such zonal flow restricted the northward penetration of moist, tropical air masses into the Plains, thereby triggering the warm, dry Altithermal climate that prevailed in the Midwest from about 8000 to 5000 years B.P. (Antevs 1955; Deevey and Flint 1957; Bryson et al. 1970; Webb and Bryson 1972). The Altithermal caused prairies to expand far eastward into Iowa and Illinois (Brush 1967; Wright 1968, 1971; Durkee 1971; Van Zant 1979). As tall- and mixed-grass prairies in the Central Plains were replaced by sparser short-grass prairie, hillslopes would have been prone to erosion. It also is likely that frequent fires during this dry period removed ground cover and thereby accelerated erosion on hill-slopes. In addition, the northward retreat of the Laurentide ice sheet during the early Holocene and the sharp north–south temperature gradient at its southern margin probably triggered a change from frequent widespread but gentle rains associated with airmass fronts to less frequent precipitation but more intense and erosive thunderstorms in the Midwest (Knox 1983: 34). The net effect of of these climatic and vegetative changes would have been high erosion rates and large sediment yields in small streams during early- through mid-Holocene time (Bettis and Mandel 1989). As Chorley and others (1984: 53–54) pointed out, sediment delivery ratios are greater for small drainage basins than for larger ones under normal conditions. They attribute this inverse relationship to the following properties of small basins in relation to larger ones:

1. They commonly have steeper valley-side and stream-channel gradients, encouraging more rapid rates of erosion.
2. Lack of broad floodplains gives less opportunity for sediment storage within the basin after weathering and removal from slopes.
3. Small basins may be totally blanketed by high-intensity storm events, giving high maximum erosion rates per unit area.

Hence, infrequent but intense thunderstorms during the Altithermal, combined with sparse vegetative cover on hillslopes, would have favored (1) widespread erosion in small watersheds, and (2) transport of sediment out of small valleys and into larger ones. As the sediment supplied to the large valleys exceeded the conveyance capacity of streams, there would be net increases in alluvial storage, with only a small portion of eroded sediment leaving the basin (Phillips 1987). It is likely that alluviation and storage of sediment would occur both on fans and floodplains in high-order stream valleys.

The change of atmospheric circulation from frequent zonal dominance during the early and middle Holocene to mixed zonal and meridional dominance during the late Holocene influenced the regional distribution of vegetative communities and thus the activity of fluvial systems (Knox 1983:31). The increased frequency of meridional atmospheric circulation after ca. 4000 years B.P. is significant because it allowed warm, moist, tropical air masses from the Gulf of Mexico to penetrate deep into the central Great Plains. Mean annual precipitation and large floods probably increased significantly because of frequent frontal activity in the collision zone between polar and tropical air masses (Knox 1983:39). As mean annual precipitation increased during the late Holocene, forests expanded across floodplains and hillslopes in the Midwest (Wright 1971).

Vegetation density increased in upland areas of the Central Plains as short-grass prairies were replaced by mixed and tall-grass prairies. Denser vegetative cover would have promoted greater soil porosity and infiltration capacity. Altogether, the late-Holocene vegetational change probably reduced erosion rates on hillslopes, which in turn, would have reduced mean annual sediment concentrations in small streams. When stream loads were highest, during large floods, the forested floodplains would have served as sediment traps and promoted alluvial storage in small valleys. Thus, vegetative cover on floodplains would account for the preservation of large volumes of late-Holocene alluvium in low-order drainage elements. It also would explain storage of alluvium in small, high-angle fans where gullies deliver sediment from uplands to the valley floors. As conveyance capacities of high-order streams were no longer satisfied by sediment imposed from tributaries, entrenchment and lateral channel migration into floodplain deposits of large valleys enhanced sediment loads in this part of the fluvial system (Bettis and Mandel 1989).

There is no question that major bioclimatic changes have affected Holocene landscape evolution in stream valleys of the Midwest, including the Great Plains. The development of alluvial fans during the early and middle Holocene is a case in point. However, when basinwide Holocene alluvial chronologies are examined, it is apparent that each erosional and depositional event did not occur in response to one simultaneous external change, such as climate. Also, the number, magnitude, and duration of erosional and depositional events not only varied from valley to valley in the Midwest, but also varied in different parts of the same basin. Thus, fluvial events were not in phase everywhere, suggesting that some episodes of erosion, deposition, and landscape stability did not occur in response to a single external control (Bettis and Mandel 1989).

GEOLOGIC PRESERVATION POTENTIALS FOR CULTURAL RESOURCES

The preceding discussion noted that alluvial deposits of certain ages are differentially but systematically preserved in various drainage elements of both the Pawnee and Lower Smoky Hill river basins. This phenomenon has important implications for predicting the locations of prehistoric cultural resources, and for explaining apparent gaps in the archaeological record.

Geomorphic, chronostratigraphic, and soil-stratigraphic data were used to predict where buried sites for each cultural period are likely to occur in the river basins (Table 2-4). The potential for buried sites is based on the presence or absence of Holocene deposits and buried paleosols within the different drainage elements of the basins (after Bettis and Benn 1984: 22).

The presence/absence of buried paleosols, especially A horizons, is an important factor in the evaluation of geologic site-preservation potential. Buried paleosols indicate periods of landscape stability during formation of landform/sediment assemblages—an important aspect of the evolution of the Holocene landscapes inhabited by prehistoric people (Holliday 1989, this volume; Ferring, this volume). Hoyer (1980: 61) commented: "Buried A1 horizons represent previous land surfaces which were exposed for sufficient periods of time to develop recognizable soil profile characteristics. Thus, they represent stable land surfaces. If one assumes that the probability of human use of a particular landscape position was equal for each year, it follows that the surfaces which remain exposed for the longest time would represent those with the highest probability of containing cultural resources. As the paleosols represent these surfaces, evidence for occupation would most likely be associated with them." Hoyer was quick to point out that an archaeological site, even a rich one, also may be found in sediment that has not been modified by soil development. Hence, the presence/absence of buried paleosols cannot be used as the sole criterion for evaluating geologic site-preservation potential.

The geologic potential for buried prehistoric sites older than Plains Village in T-0 deposits of large and small valleys within both study areas is considered low to nonexistent. Archaeological evidence suggests that the bulk of the fill beneath modern floodplains in the region is very late Holocene to Recent in age, and no paleosols were found at depths of more than 2 m below the T-0 surface. Also, preservation of sedimentary features throughout most of the T-0 fill indicates rapid deposition. Altogether, these lines of evidence suggest that buried prehistoric sites probably are rare in T-0 deposits, and sites that occur are likely to be Plains Village occupations. There is high potential, however, for Historic sites and artifacts below the surfaces of modern floodplains.

Based on radiocarbon assays and the paleosol record, there is high

TABLE 2-4

Preservation Potentials for Buried Archaeological Sites in the Study Areas

Cultural Periods	Lower Smoky Hill River Basin Landforms							Pawnee River Basin Landforms					
	Large Valleys					Small Valleys		Large Valleys				Small Valleys	
	T-0	T-1	T-2	HAF~	LAF~	T-0	T-1	T-0	T-1	T-2*	T-3	T-0	T-1
Paleoindian	−	?	?	−	?	−	−	−	+++	+++	++	−	−
Early Archaic	−	?	?	−	?	−	−	−	+++	+++	+	−	−
Middle Archaic	−	+++	?	+	+++	−	−	−	+++	+++	+	−	−
Late Archaic	+	+++	?	+++	+++	−	+++	+	+++	++	−	−	+++
Plains Woodland	+	+++	?	+++	++	+	+++	+	+++	+	−	+	+++
Plains Village	++	+++	?	+++	+	++	+++	++	+++	−	−	++	++
Historic	+++	+++	?	+++	−	+++	+++	+++	+++	−	−	+++	+

Note: +, low potential; ++, moderate potential; +++, high potential; −, impossible; ?, unknown; ~ HAF = High-angle alluvial fan; ~ LAF = Low-angle alluvial fan.

*Applies only to T-2 terraces in valleys of 4th-order streams.

potential for deeply buried sites dating from the Late Archaic through the Historic period in T-1 fill of the Smoky Hill River. The oldest and youngest radiocarbon ages determined on humates from buried paleosols in the T-1 fill are ca. 4500 years B.P. and 2600 years B.P., respectively. The age of deposits underlying the oldest paleosol is not known; hence, the potential for early sites in T-1 fill of the Smoky Hill River could not be determined.

There is high potential for buried archaeological sites dating to all cultural periods in T-1 fill of the Pawnee River Valley. Paleoindian and Early Archaic sites are likely to be found on or within early-Holocene soils documented 3.5–9.0 m below the T-1 surface. Also, Middle Archaic sites may occur at the top of these buried soils. Late Archaic and younger sites are likely to be associated with buried late-Holocene soils documented at many localities within the Pawnee Valley. Most of these late-Holocene soils are beneath Historic alluvium that mantles large areas of the T-1 terrace.

Alluvial deposits and paleosols beneath T-1 terraces in small valleys of both study areas are likely to contain Late Archaic and Plains Woodland sites, but there will be no Middle Archaic or older sites associated with these terraces. Only late-Holocene deposits are stored in T-1 fill of 2nd- and 3rd-order streams, precluding an early archaeological record. Deposits of post-settlement alluvium probably conceal most if not all of the archaeological sites on T-1 terraces of small streams in the Lower Smoky Hill River Basin. Deep entrenchment of small streams in the Pawnee River Basin, however, isolated T-1 surfaces from Historic floods and concomitant sedimentation. Thus, Historic and very late Prehistoric sites will be present on these surfaces in the Pawnee Basin. This has been confirmed by a recent archaeological survey in small valleys of the Pawnee River Basin (Timberlake 1988).

The geologic potential for buried archaeological sites in valley fill underlying T-2 terraces of the Pawnee and Lower Smoky Hill rivers is unknown because the age of the fill has not been determined. However, T-2 fill in the lower reaches of 4th-order tributaries to the Pawnee River contains early- and mid-Holocene deposits and paleosols; hence, it may contain sites dating from the Paleoindian through the Late Archaic period. Although a T-2 terrace also is present in lower reaches of 4th-order tributaries that join the Smoky Hill River, the absence of temporal data from its fill precludes an assessment of the geologic potential for buried sites.

Alluvial deposits underlying the T-3 terrace of the Pawnee River are too old to contain archaeological sites. Paleoindian sites may, however, be buried in Peoria loess that mantles the T–3 fill. Prehistoric sites of all cultural periods are likely to be found on the T–3 surface, except where shallow burial has resulted from pedoturbation and colluviation

Alluvial fans in the lower Smoky Hill River Basin offer great potential for buried prehistoric sites, though the archaeological record will vary depending on the type of fan. Large, low-angle fans that developed where 2nd-order streams join large valleys are composed of mid- and late-Holocene deposits with multiple buried paleosols. These fans are likely to contain Middle Archaic, Late Archaic, and Plains Woodland sites. Small, high-angle fans at the mouths of ephemeral gullies, however, are composed only of late-Holocene deposits with buried paleosols. Hence, the small fans may contain sites dating to the Late Archaic and more recent cultural periods.

If the time–space distribution of alluvial deposits in the study areas holds true for other drainage basins of the Great Plains, as suggested earlier, it may explain the paucity of Archaic and Paleoindian sites in the region. Within large valleys, most of the archaeological record may be deeply buried in early- through late-Holocene terrace and fan deposits. Within small valleys, erosion during the early and middle Holocene probably removed most of the early sites, and aggradation during the late Holocene and Historic period favored deep burial of Late Archaic and younger sites. Also, surfaces of landforms that dominate valley bottoms throughout the drainage systems are geologically quite young, often post-dating 2000 B.P. Hence, apparent gaps in the archaeological record may be a result of (1) deep burial of sites, (2) removal of deposits that contain sites, and (3) young surfaces dominating valley landscapes.

CONCLUSIONS

The foregoing discussion described the nature of valley landscapes in the Pawnee and Lower Smoky Hill river basins, and focused on the stratigraphy and chronology of alluvial deposits composing landform/sediment assemblages in different drainage elements of the basins. Radiocarbon data indicate that entrenchment and alluviation, as well as periods of net transport and storage of sediment were diachronous through the individual basins, but were roughly synchronous in similar-sized parts of the different basins. The results of these phenomena are differential preservation of Holocene deposits in different parts of individual drainage basins, and broadly similar alluvial stratigraphic records across the region as a whole. More specifically, early, middle, and late-Holocene deposits are stored in valley fill of large streams (> 3rd-order), but only late-Holocene deposits are present in valley bottoms of small streams. Within the Lower Smoky Hill River Basin, the early- and middle-Holocene depositional record that is missing in small valleys is present in large, low-angle alluvial fans that formed where 2nd- and 3rd-order streams join larger valleys. Similarly, early- and middle-Holocene deposits are stored beneath terrace remnants in the lower reaches of small tributaries near their confluence with the Pawnee River.

The similarity in alluvial stratigraphic records is attributed to broadly similar activity of streams in basins throughout the Midwest during the Holocene. Major climatic changes appear to be the underlying cause behind synchronous patterns of fluvial activity that are detected in the stratigraphic records of streams within the region. However, extrinsic and intrinsic factors in the fluvial system interact to produce periods of stability and instability that may be detected in the stratigraphic record of one stream but not in that of another within the same basin.

The basinwide geomorphic and stratigraphic evidence provides an explanation for the paucity of recorded Early and Middle Archaic sites in the Central Plains. A number of authors (e.g., Malouf 1958; Syms 1969; Benedict 1978) suggested that a cultural hiatus occurred in the Plains during the early- to mid-Holocene Altithermal as a result of increased aridity. According to Benedict (1978), inhabitants were forced to leave the core of the Central Plains between ca. 8000 and 4000 B.P. because of extremely adverse environmental conditions and displacement of native game animals. However, Reeves (1973) argued that the lack of evidence for human occupation in the Plains during the Altithermal is a result of sampling, geological variables, and nonrecognition of artifact types. The results of the present study suggest that geologic processes have affected the archaeological record by either removing or burying sites that date to the Altithermal. For example, all or most early- and middle-Holocene deposits have been removed from small valleys by erosion. Thus, Middle Archaic and older sites associated with these deposits also would have been removed. Sediment transported out of small valleys during the early and middle Holocene was stored in alluvial fans and/or terrace fills within large valleys. Buried paleosols in the fans and valley fills have great potential for containing Archaic and Paleoindian sites, but there is limited exposure of deeply buried soils. Also, it is important to note that some of the early- and middle-Holocene paleosols have been truncated by erosion; hence, archaeological sites may have been stripped off former stable surfaces. Nevertheless, it is likely that early sites will be discovered in terrace fills and alluvial fans within large valleys as deep testing, i.e., trenching and coring, become an integral part of future archaeological surveys.

In addition to providing an explanation for gaps in the archaeological record, the basinwide, three-dimensional landscape analysis allows the archaeologists to concentrate survey and testing efforts in potentially productive localities (Bettis and Hoyer 1986: 67; Bettis, this volume; Ferring, this volume). For example, a search for Middle Archaic and older sites in the Pawnee River Basin should focus on T-1 fill of 5th-order and larger streams. This search would be unnecessary in 3rd-order and smaller valleys since the alluvial deposits are too young to contain early sites. However, a search for Late Archaic and Plains Woodland sites should concentrate on the Hackberry Creek and Buckner Creek paleosols in small valleys. These buried soils are useful stratigraphic markers in late-Holocene valley fill beneath T-1 terraces, and can be used to identify stratigraphic positioning of Late Archaic and Plains Woodland sites.

The history of Holocene landscape evolution stored in valley fills of the Central Plains is complex and fragmentary; not all erosional or depositional events are preserved at one location or, necessarily, among several locations. Therefore, the interpretation of soil-stratigraphic records is almost always inferential and highly dependent upon the spatial scale, the level of observation, and the time depth of the record (Gladfelter 1985). This problem may be overcome, however, by adopting a basinwide stratigraphic approach that includes three-dimensional analysis of landform/sediment assemblages. When this approach is taken, regional models of soil and Holocene landscape evolution can be developed to evaluate the existing archaeological record and to provide sound information which can be used to search for as yet undiscovered parts of that record.

ACKNOWLEDGMENTS

Parts of the research were supported by grants from the U.S. Soil Conservation Service and the U.S Army Corps of Engineers, Kansas City District. Special thanks are due to Robert Timerlake and Michael Fosha, who provided valuable field assistance. Thanks also to Laura Poracsky, who prepared many of the diagrams. The essay benefited greatly from critical reviews by Vance T. Holliday, E. Arthur Bettis III, and Joseph Schuldenrein.

REFERENCES

Ahlbrandt, T. S., J. B. Swinehart, and D. G. Maroney
  1983   The Dynamic Holocene Dune Fields of the Great Plains and Rocky Mountain Basins, U.S.A. In *Eolian Sediments and Processes*, edited by M. E. Brookfield and T. S. Ahlbrandt, pp. 379–406. Elsview, Amsterdam.

Ahler, S. A.
  1973   Post-Pleistocene Depositional Processes at Rodgers Shelter. *Plains Anthropologist* 18:1–26.

Antevs, E.
  1955   Geologic-Climatic Dating in the West. *American Antiquity* 20: 317–335.

Artz, J. A.
  1983   The Soils and Geomorphology of the East Branch Walnut Valley: Contexts of Human Adaptation in the Kansas Flint Hills. Unpublished M.A. Thesis, Department of Anthropology, University of Kansas, Lawrence.
  1985   A Soil-Geomorphic Approach in Locating Buried Late-Archaic Sites in Northeastern Oklahoma. *American Archaeology* 5: 142–150.

Bayne, C. K., P. C. Franks, and W. Ives, Jr.
  1971   *Geology and Groundwater Resources of Ellsworth County, Central Kansas.* Kansas Geological Survey, Bulletin 201, Lawrence.

Benedict, J. B.
  1978   Getting Away from It All: A Study of Man, Mountains, and the Two-Drought Altithermal. *Southwestern Lore* 45: 1–12.

Bettis, E. A. III, and D. W. Benn
  1984   An Archaeological and Geomorphological Survey in the Central Des Moines River Valley, Iowa. *Plains Anthropologist* 29: 211–227.

Bettis, E. A. III, and B. E. Hoyer
  1986   *Late Wisconsinan and Holocene Landscape Evolution in the Saylorville Lake Area, Central Des Moines Valley, Iowa.* Iowa Geological Survey, Open File Report 86–1, University of Iowa, Iowa City.

Bettis, E. A. III, and R. D. Mandel
  1989   Holocene Landscape Evolution in Midwestern Stream Systems, USA. Ms. on file at the Iowa Department of Natural Resources Geologic Survey Bureau, Iowa City.

Bettis, E. A. III, and D. M. Thompson
  1981   Holocene Landscape Evolution in Western Iowa—Concepts, Methods, and

Implications for Archaeology. In *Current Directions in Midwestern Archaeology: Selected Papers from the Mankato Conference*, edited by S. F. Anfinson, pp. 1–14. Occasional Papers in Minnesota Archaeology 9, Minnesota Archaeological Society, St. Paul.

Birkeland, P. W
1984 *Soils and Geomorphology*. Oxford University Press, New York.

Bowman, M. W.
1985 A Disparity in the Rate of Lateral Channel Cutting Between Two Reaches of the Kansas River. Unpublished M.A. Thesis, Department of Geography, University of Kansas, Lawrence.

Brakenridge, G. R.
1981 Late Quaternary Floodplain Sedimentation along the Pomme de Terre River, Southern Missouri. *Quaternary Research* 15: 62–76.

Brice, J. C.
1964 *Channel Patterns and Terraces of the Loup River in Nebraska*. U.S. Geological Survey Professional Paper 422-D.

Brush, G. S.
1967 Pollen Analysis of Late-Glacial and Postglacial Sediments in Iowa. In *Quaternary Paleoecology*, edited by E. J. Cushing and H. E. Wright, Jr., pp. 99–115. Yale University Press, New Haven, Connecticut.

Bryson, R. A., D. A. Baerreis, and W. M. Wendland
1970 The Character of Late-Glacial and Post-Glacial Climatic Changes. In *Pleistocene and Recent Environments of the Central Great Plains,* edited by W. Dort, Jr. and J. K. Jones, Jr., pp. 53–76. University of Kansas Special Publication No. 3, University Press of Kansas, Lawrence.

Bryson, R. A., and F. K. Hare
1974 *Climates of North America*. Elsevier, New York.

Butzer, K. W.
1977 *Geomorphology of the Lower Illinois Valley as Spatial-Temporal Context for the Koster Archaic Site*. Illinois State Museum Reports of Investigations No. 34.

Campbell, C. A., E. A. Paul, D. A. Rennie, and K. J. McCallum
1967 Factors Affecting the Accuracy of the Carbon-Dating Method in Soil Humus Studies. *Soil Science* 104: 81–85.

Chorley, R. C. , S. A. Schumm, and D. E. Sugden
1984 *Geomorphology*. John Wiley & Sons, New York.

Deevey, E. S., and R. F. Flint
1957 Postglacial Hypsithermal Interval. *Science* 125: 182–184.

Durkee, L. H.
1971 A Pollen Profile from Woden Bog in North-Central Iowa. *Ecology* 52: 837–844.

Fenneman, N. M.
1931   *Physiography of the Western United States.* McGraw-Hill, New York.

Ferring, C. R.
1986   Late Holocene Cultural Ecology in the Southern Plains: Perspective from Delaware Canyon. *Plains Anthropologist Memoir* 21, Vol. 31–114 (2): 55–82.

Frye, J. C., and A. B. Leonard
1952   *Pleistocene Geology of Kansas.* Kansas Geological Survey, Bulletin 99, Lawrence.

Gladfelter, B. G.
1985   On the Interpretation of Archaeological Sites in Alluvial Settings. In *Archaeological Sediments in Context*, edited by J. K. Stein and W. R. Farrand, pp. 41–
52. Center for the Study of Early Man, Institute for Quaternary Studies, Peo-
pling of the Americas Edited Volume Series 1, University of Maine, Orono.

Grange, R. T., Jr.
1980   *Archaeological Investigations in the Red Willow Reservoir.* Nebraska State Historical Society Publications in Anthropology No. 9, Lincoln.

Hajic, E. R.
1981   Geology and Paleopedology of the Koster Archaeological Site, Greene County, Illinois. Unpublished M.A. thesis, Department of Geology, University of
Iowa, Iowa City.

Hall, S. A.
1977a   Holocene Geology and Paleoenvironmental History of the Hominy Creek
Valley. In *Prehistory and Paleoenvironment of Hominy Creek Valley*, edited by
D. O. Henry, pp. 12–42. University of Tulsa, Laboratory of Archaeology,
Contributions in Archaeology 2.
1977b   Geological and Paleoenvironmental Studies. In *Prehistory and Paleoenvironment
of Birch Creek Valley*, edited by D. O. Henry, pp. 11–31. University of Tulsa,
Laboratory of Archaeology, Contributions in Archaeology 3.
1977c   Geology and Palynology of Archaeological Sites and Associated Sediments. In
Prehistory of the Little Caney River: 1976 Season, edited by D. O. Henry, pp.
13–41. University of Tulsa, Laboratory of Archaeology, Contributions in Archaeology 2.
1982   Geology of the Delaware Canyon. In *The Late Holocene Prehistory of the Delaware Canyon, Oklahoma*, edited by C. R. Ferring, pp. 47–63. Institute of Applied Sciences, Contributions in Archaeology No. 1, North Texas State
University, Denton.

Harner, R. F., R. C. Augell, M. A. Lobmeyer, and D. R. Jantz
1965   *Soil Survey of Finney County, Kansas.* U.S. Department of Agriculture, Soil
Conservation Service, Washington, D.C.

Haynes, C. V.
1976   Late Quaternary Geology of the Lower Pomme de Terre Valley. In *Prehistoric Man and His Environments: A Case Study in the Ozark Highlands*, edited by
W. R. Wood and R. B. McMillan, pp. 47–61. Academic Press, New York.

Holliday, V. T.
1989   Paleopedology in Archeology. *Paleopedolgy, Catena Supplement* 16: 187–206.

Hoyer, B. E.
1980   The Geology of the Cherokee Sewer Site. In *The Cherokee Excavations: Holocene Ecology and Human Adaptations in Northwestern Iowa*, edited by D. C. Anderson and H. A. Semken, pp. 21–66. Academic Press, New York.

Johnson, W. C., and C. W. Martin
1987   Holocene Alluvial-Stratigraphic Studies from Kansas and Adjoining States of the East-Central Plains. In *Quaternary Environments of Kansas*, edited by W. C. Johnson, pp. 109–122. Kansas Geological Survey, Guidebook Series 5, Lawrence.

Knox, J. C.
1972   Valley Alluviation in Southwestern Wisconsin. *Annals of the Association of American Geographers* 62: 401–410.
1983   Responses of River Systems to Holocene Climates. In *Late Quaternary Environments of the United States*, vol. 2, *The Holocene*, edited by H. E. Wright, Jr., pp. 26–41. University of Minnesota Press, Minneapolis.

Kuchler, A. W.
1974   A New Vegetation Map of Kansas. *Ecology* 55: 586–604.

Lintz, C., and S. A. Hall
1983   *The Geomorphology and Archaeology of Carnegie Canyon, Fort Cobb Laterals watershed, Caddo County, Oklahoma.* Oklahoma Conservation Commission, Archaeological Research Report No. 10, Oklahoma City.

Malouf, C.
1958   Indian Tribes of Montana. In *Montana Almanac*, pp. 106–128. Montana State University Press, Missoula.

Mandel, R. D.
1985   Geomorphology of the Little Blue Drainage Basin. In *Prehistory of the Little Blue River Valley, Western Missouri*, edited by L. J. Schmits, pp. 35–46. ESA Cultural Resources Management Report No. 29, submitted to the U. S. Army Corps of Engineers, Kansas City District.
1987a   Late-Quaternary Environments of the Great Plains: Implications for Cultural Resource Management. In *Kansas Prehistoric Archaeological Preservation Plan*, edited by K. L. Brown and A. H. Simmons, pp. IV-1—IV-28. University of Kansas Museum of Anthropology, report submitted to the Kansas State Historical Society, Topeka, Kansas.
1987b   Geomorphology of the Wakarusa River Valley, Northeastern Kansas. In *Archaeological Investigations in the Clinton Lake Project Area, Northeastern Kansas: National Register Evaluation of 27 Prehistoric Sites*, edited by B. Logan, pp. 20–34. Report submitted to the U.S. Army Corps of Engineers, Kansas City District.
1988   Geomorphology of the Pawnee River Valley, Southwest Kansas. In *Phase II Archaeological and Geomorphological Survey of the Proposed Pawnee River Watershed Covering Subwatersheds 3 through 7, Ness, Ford, Lane, Hodgeman, and Finney*

Counties, Southwest Kansas, edited by R. D. Timberlake, pp. 79–134. Kansas State Historical Society, report submitted to the U.S. Department of Agriculture, Soil Conservation Service, Salina, Kansas.

Mandel, R. D., C. J. Sorenson, and L. J. Schmits
  1986   Geology and Geomorphology of the Lower Perche-Hinkson Drainage, Central Missouri. In *Prehistory of the Lower Perche-Hinkson Drainage, Central Missouri*, edited by L. J. Schmits, pp. 45–66. Environmental Systems Analysis, Inc., Cultural Resources Management Report No. 16.

May, D. W.
  1986a   *Holocene Alluviation, Soil Genesis, and Erosion in the South Loup Valley, Nebraska*. Unpublished Ph.D. dissertation, Department of Geography, University of Wisconsin, Madison.
  1986b   Geomorphology. In *Along the Pawnee Trail: Cultural Resource Survey and Testing at Wilson Lake, Kansas*, edited by D. Blakeslee, R. Blasing, and H. Garcia, pp. 72–86. Report submitted to the U.S. Army Corps of Engineers, Kansas City District.

Merriam, D. F.
  1963   *The Geologic History of Kansas*. Kansas Geological Survey, Bulletin 162, Lawrence.

North American Commission on Stratigraphic Nomenclature
  1983   North American Stratigraphic Code. *The American Association of Petroleum Geologists Bulletin* 67: 841–875.

Phillips, J. D.
  1987   Sediment Budget Stability in the Tar River Basin, North Carolina. *American Journal of Science* 287: 780–794.

Reeves, B.
  1973   The Concept of an Altithermal Cultural Hiatus in Northern Plains Prehistory. *American Anthropologist* 75: 1221–1253.

Schmits, L. J.
  1980   Holocene Fluvial History and Depositional Environments at the Coffey Site, Kansas. In *Archaic Prehistory on the Prairie Plains Border*, edited by A. E. Johnson, pp. 79–105. University of Kansas Publications in Anthropology 12, Lawrence.

Soil Survey Staff
  1987   *Keys to Soil Taxonomy*. SMSS Technical Monograph 6, Agency for International Development, U. S. Depertment of Agriculture, Soil Management Support Services, Cornell University, Ithaca, New York.

Strahler, A. N.
  1964   Quantitative Geomorphology of Drainage Basin and Channel Networks. In *Handbook of Applied Hydrology*, edited by V. T. Chow, pp. 39–76. McGraw-Hill, New York.

Syms, L.
1969   The McKean Complex as a Horizon Marker in Manitoba and on the Northern Great Plains. Unpublished M.A. Thesis, Department of Anthropology, University of Manitoba, Winnipeg.

Thompson, D. M., and E. A. Bettis
1980   Archaeology and Holocene Landscape Evolution in the Missouri Drainage of Iowa. *Journal of the Iowa Archeological Society* 27: 1–60.

Timberlake, R. D.
1988   *Phase II Archaeological and Geomorphological Survey of the Proposed Pawnee River Watershed, Covering Subwatersheds 3 through 7, Ness, Ford, Lane and Finney Counties, Southwestern Kansas.* Kansas State Historical Society, report submitted to the U.S. Department of Agriculture, Soil Conservation Service, Salina, Kansas.

Van Zant, K. L.
1979   Late-Glacial and Postglacial Pollen and Plant Micro-Fossils from Lake West Okoboji, Northwestern Iowa. *Quaternary Research* 12: 358–380.

Webb, T., and R. A. Bryson
1972   Late- and Post-Glacial Climatic Change in the Northern Midwest, USA: Quantitative Estimates Derived from Fossil Pollen Spectra by Multivariate Analysis. *Quaternary Research* 2: 70–115.

Wiant, M. D, E. R. Hajic, and T. R. Styles
1983   Napoleon Hallow and Koster Site Stratigraphy: Implications for Holocene Landscape Evolution and Studies of Archaic Period Settlement Patterns in the Lower Illinois River Valley. In *Archaic Hunters and Gatherers in the American Midwest*, edited by J. L. Phillips and J. A. Brown, pp. 147–164. Academic Press, New York.

Wright, H. E., Jr.
1968   History of the Prairie Peninsula. In *The Quaternary of Illinois*, edited by R. E. Bergstrom, pp. 78–88. Special Report 14, College of Agriculture, University of Illinois, Champaign-Urbana.
1971   Late Quaternary Vegetation History of North America. In *Late Cenozoic Glacial Ages*, edited by K. K. Turekian, pp. 425–462. Yale University Press, New Haven, Connecticut.

3

VANCE T. HOLLIDAY

Soil Formation, Time, and Archaeology

Soils have long been recognized as important in the interpretation of archaeological sites and regions. The broadest systematic application of soils in archaeological research is probably in the area of soil chemistry as an indicator of habitations, habitation patterns, and agricultural activity (e.g., Eidt 1977, 1985; Hassan 1981; Sjoberg 1976; Solecki 1951). Soils in archaeological contexts have been used commonly and successfully as stratigraphic markers (e.g., Bettis and Thompson 1982; Goldberg 1986; Haynes 1968, 1975; Hoffecker 1987; Wiant et al. 1983). Such soils have also been used, with varying degrees of success, for paleoenvironmental reconstruction (e.g., Holliday 1985a; Paulissen and Vermeersch 1987; Ranov and Davis 1979; Reeves and Dormaar 1972; Reider 1980). Soils in archaeological contexts have received considerably less attention, however, as pedologic entities, i.e., as types of surface weathering phenomena with unique physical and chemical characteristics.

The presence of a soil or soils in a stratigraphic sequence at an archaeological site can be of even more direct and fundamental significance to the interpretation of the archaeological record than for correlation or paleoenvironmental interpretation. Such an understanding of the archaeological significance and interpretation of soils can be gained by using the principles of pedology (the area of soil science devoted to the study of soils in their natural setting; their morphology, genesis and classification). There are several general discussions of the applications of pedology (Holliday 1990; Lotspeich 1961; Olson 1981; Rutter 1978; Tamplin 1969). The purpose of this paper is to provide further discussion of soils as pedologic entities, focusing on their development over time and the significance of this characteristic of soils in archaeological situations.

The term "soil" has a variety of definitions and uses. A soil in the pedologic sense is the result of the complex interaction of a variety of physical, chemical, and biological processes acting on rock or sediment over time. The nature and degree of influence of these processes is controlled by various environmental factors. This concept of what a soil is, and the factors that influence soil formation can be expressed in the classic formula of Jenny (1941)

$$S \text{ or } s = f(cl, o, r, p, t, \dots)$$

where the state of a soil (S) or soil property (s) is considered to be the result of the factors of climate (cl), organisms (o), relief (r), parent material (p), time (t) and local or unspecified factors (. . .). A soil is a natural entity that is a type of weathering phenomena occurring at the immediate surface of the earth in sediment and rock, acting as a medium for plant growth, and the result of the effects of the sediment or rock parent material, climate, flora, fauna, and landscape position, all acting through time (Holliday 1990).

Jenny's equation as a whole has never been solved, but Jenny (1961, 1980) proposed solving the equation by studying variation in the state of a soil as a function of one factor, keeping the others constant or accounted for. The "state factor" approach to the study of soil genesis is not without criticism, summarized by Birkeland (1984:162–168). For example, it is difficult to find situations where vegetation varies independently of climate. Additionally, there are few areas that have not experienced significant climate changes over time. Moreover, quantitative solutions for the state factor equation can be difficult to find because many factors are difficult to quantify (e.g., biota). For the most part, however, the general validity of the state factor approach has been upheld, particularly in studies of age variability or topographic variability of soils (Birkeland 1984; Bockheim 1980; Yaalon 1975).

Although quantitative expressions of the state factor equation are rare, qualitative statements, called sequences (see Holliday and Goldberg, this volume), are common (Birkeland 1984; Jenny 1961, 1980). A chronosequence, therefore, is a group of soils whose properties vary primarily as a function of age variability. For example, many chronosequences are defined for the surfaces of a set of alluvial terraces whose ages vary but where the parent materials and landscape settings are the same and the climate and biota have changed little or the changes can be controlled for. In a chronosequence defined for a set of terraces, the soils on the higher terraces will have more strongly developed profiles than the soils on the lower terraces because the higher terraces are older and there has been more time for pedogenesis (e.g., Birkeland and Burke 1988; Dethier 1988; Machette 1975; Rockwell et al. 1985).

Isolation of the time factor in the soil formation equation allow soils to be used as dating tools in archaeological research. Soils that vary as a function of time can provide information concerning rates of formation of soils or specific pedologic features (e.g., horizons of carbonate or clay accumulation) (Birkeland 1984). These kinds of data derived from a chronosequence can be used to estimate the age of other soils in similar settings, including archaeological sites, and therefore date associated sediments and cultural debris. Bischoff et al. (1981), Foss (1977), and Holliday (1988) are several of the very few examples of this particular area of geoarchaeology.

Soils as pedologic entities have a broader potential application in archaeology, however, beyond their use as dating tools or in their more traditional role as stratigraphic or environmental indicators. Soils require some amount of time to form and soil development requires a relatively stable landscape, one that is neither aggrading nor eroding (Catt 1986:166–167; Gerrard 1981:7–8). The principal exceptions are bogs or marshes, characterized by organic matter accumulation and alteration, and very weakly developed soils that occur along floodplains or toe slopes, characterized simply by accumulation of organic matter (from both in situ growth and redeposition) and some bioturbation and depositional mixing. The presence of a soil, therefore, denotes the passage of some amount of time under conditions of relative landscape stability. Furthermore, a buried soil in a stratigraphic sequence denotes a hiatus between depositional events; a kind of unconformity. In such a sequence the sediment, which is the parent material for the soil, may have accumulated rapidly or slowly, but a significant period of nondeposition had to occur in order for the soil to form. Under some circumstances deposition can occur relatively instantaneously; possibly in a matter of days, years or decades. Soil formation, in contrast, almost always takes longer (ex-

103

cept as noted above); usually at least a century or several centuries and commonly millennia (e.g., Birkeland 1984). In alluvial or eolian depositional environments where sedimentation is episodic and buried soils are common, soil formation may take up a significant amount of the time represented in a stratigraphic sequence (e.g., Holliday 1985b; Kraus and Bown 1986; Pawluk 1978).

Archaeological materials associated with the surface of a soil could, therefore, represent accumulations of artifacts over a long time and from multiple occupations. This consideration of the archaeological significance of soils is complementary to the implications of the rates of fluvial sedimentation in archaeological contexts (Ferring 1986). "Rapid sedimentation promotes superposition of artifacts and features that resulted from serial occupation of sites. . . . Conversely, slow deposition during multiple episodes of occupation results in accumulation of archaeological debris as mixed assemblages . . . on paleosurfaces" (Ferring 1986:264). In the latter situation, the debris will most likely be associated with a soil because soil formation will generally occur when deposition is slow.

In dealing with soils in archaeological sites, consideration of the time factor and landscape stability are important in interpreting artifact associations and contexts, and cultural chronologies. These considerations are also important in the more standard geoarchaeological investigations of site stratigraphy, depositional and landscape history, and geochronology. These points can be illustrated using several case histories.

CASE HISTORIES

Three case histories serve to illustrate the archaeological significance of considering soils as pedologic entities, with the emphasis on the time factor and use of soils as markers of time passage: the Wilson–Leonard and Lubbock Lake sites, both in Texas (Figure 3-1), and the Cherokee Sewer site in Iowa. The three sites contain thick sedimentary sequences with several buried soils, good age control, and long records of human occupation.

Wilson–Leonard Site

The Wilson–Leonard site (41WM235) is located in central Texas, near the eroded northeastern edge of the Edwards Plateau, approximately 32

Figure 3-1.   Map of Texas with the location of the Lubbock Lake and Wilson–Leonard archaeological sites and the principal physiographic features mentioned in the text.

km (20 miles) north of Austin (Figure 3-1). The site is along Spanish Oak Creek, a low-order tributary of Brushy Creek, within the Brazos River system. The site contains a stratified record of late Paleoindian through late Prehistoric occupation, including a late Paleoindian (ca. 9500 B.P.) burial (Weir 1985; Young 1983). Geoarchaeological research was carried out at Wilson–Leonard in 1983 (Holliday 1989a) and is summarized below.

The archaeological material at Wilson–Leonard is contained within a sedimentary sequence, primarily alluvial, about 6.5 m thick, that constitutes the middle of three terraces of Spanish Oak Creek. The sediments accumulated episodically (Figure 3-2) and are divided into six stratigraphic units, numbered 1 through 6, oldest to youngest (Figure 3-2). Soils formed in several of the strata and each soil was named (Figure 3-2).

Strata 5 and 6 and associated soils are of primary concern here. Alluviation at the site began before 10,000 yr B.P. and by 9000 yr B.P. about 4.5 m of sediment had accumulated (strata 1–4). Stratum 5, averaging 50 cm thick, rests unconformably on stratum 4 and consists of silty overbank deposits. The Stiba soil is a moderately well-developed soil with an A-Bw or A-Bt profile formed in stratum 5. The A horizon is dark and particularly prominent and was a useful stratigraphic marker. Deposition of stratum 5 occurred about 9000 yr B.P. Pedogenesis then began and continued until about 7000 yr B.P. when stratum 5 and the associated Stiba soil were buried.

105

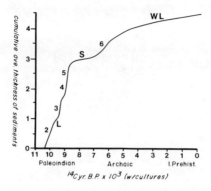

Figure 3-2. Plot of average sedimentation rates at the Wilson-Leonard site over the past 10,000 years. Numbers refer to stratigraphic units and letters refer to soils (L = Leanne soil, not discussed, S = Stiba soil, WL = Wilson-Leonard soil).

Stratum 6 is the surficial deposit at the site. The unit lies unconformably on stratum 5, is up to 1.5 m thick, and is also composed of silty overbank sediments. The Wilson-Leonard soil formed in stratum 6 and is moderately well developed with an A-Bw, A-Bwk, or A-Bt profile. The lower half of stratum 6 was deposited between about 7000 and 4000 yr B.P. and the upper half has slowly aggraded over the past 4000 years. Formation of the Wilson-Leonard soil probably began about 4000 yr B.P. and kept pace with the slow aggradation.

Archaeological material is common throughout the alluvium at Wilson-Leonard and is especially dense in upper stratum 5 (A horizon of the Stiba soil) and upper stratum 6 (A horizon of the Wilson-Leonard soil). The associations of various types of time-diagnostic artifacts recovered from the upper portions of strata 5 and 6 were initially confusing in the field until the pedological relationships were established. In upper stratum 5 projectile points of the Angostura and Gower types were found together, along with considerable occupation debris. These types appear to be chronologically distinct and span the late Paleoindian and Early Archaic periods (as defined in Central Texas by Prewitt 1981, 1983; see also Turner and Hester 1985). The surface represented by the Stiba soil was clearly stable for several thousand years spanning the late-Paleoindian to Early-Archaic transition, based on the pedologic information and available age control. Stone tools, lithic manufacturing debris, and refuse from successive occupations during this time were, therefore, deposited on the surface of by the A horizon of the Stiba Soil.

Similarly, archaeological material from the Late Archaic and Late Prehistoric periods (Prewitt 1981, 1983) were found concentrated in the A horizon of the Wilson-Leonard soil, which began forming by 4000 B.P. The surface associated with this soil (the surface of the terrace at the site) has been relatively stable for the past several thousand years and, therefore, archaeological materials from occupations spanning the Late Archaic through Late Prehistoric stages were concentrated in the relatively thin zone of the A horizon.

Lubbock Lake Site

The Lubbock Lake site (41LU1) is located on the Southern High Plains of northwestern Texas, in the city of Lubbock along Yellowhouse Draw, a now dry headwaters tributary of the Brazos River (Figure 3-1). Sediment has accumulated episodically in the draw since alluvial activity ended 11,000 years ago. Archaeological material is found throughout the deposits and includes almost 90 kill and butchering locales and camping features (Johnson 1987a; Johnson and Holliday 1989). Geoarchaeological investigations have been an integral component of the continuing archaeological research program at the site that began in 1972 (Johnson 1987a). The geoarchaeology of the site, summarized below, is described and discussed by Stafford (1981), Holliday (1985a, 1985b, 1985c) and Holliday and Allen (1987).

Yellowhouse Draw at Lubbock Lake has filled with alluvial, lacustrine, marsh, and eolian sediments, with a combined thickness of about 8 m. The sediments are divided into five principal strata, numbered 1 through 5, oldest to youngest (Figure 3-3). Soils formed in most of these strata and they are named (Figure 3-3). Yellowhouse Draw began filling sometime before 11,000 yr B.P., and by 8500 yr B.P., 3 to 4 m of alluvial sediment (stratum 1) and lacustrine and eolian sediment (stratum 2) had accumulated. The Firstview Soil formed in upper stratum 2 from about 8500 to about 6400 yr B.P. The soil is weakly developed and includes a lowland, valley axis facies with an A-Cg profile and a well-drained valley margin facies with an A-Bw profile.

Strata 3 and 4 combined are up to 4 m thick and both include eolian and marsh sediments. These deposits accumulated between about 6400 and 4500 yr B.P., with a period of nondeposition and formation of the Yellowhouse Soil separating the two and occurring sometime between about 6000 and 5000 yr B.P. The Lubbock Lake Soil developed in the

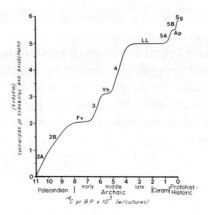

Figure 3-3. Plot of average sedimentation rates at Lubbock Lake over the past 11,000 years. Numbers refer to stratigraphic units and letters refer to soils (Fv = Firstview Soil, not discussed, Yh = Yellowhouse Soil, LL = Lubbock Lake Soil, Ap = Apache Soil, Sg = Singer Soil) (modified from Holliday 1985c:Figure 6).

eolian facies of stratum 4 and, where not buried, is the present surface soil at the site. Following deposition of stratum 4 minor sedimentation occurred along the valley axis of the draw and within the last thousand years localized deposits of eolian, slopewash, and marsh sediment (stratum 5) have accumulated.

The sedimentologic/pedologic situation at Lubbock Lake makes it virtually impossible to establish a cultural chronology for the latest Paleoindian to Early Archaic occupations or the Late Archaic to early Ceramic occupations. Although archaeological material is common in most deposits at Lubbock Lake (Johnson 1987a; Johnson and Holliday 1989), the site is best known for its Paleoindian occupations. The Paleoindian materials are well stratified within strata 1 and 2, the result of essentially continuous sedimentation from 11,000 to 8500 yr B.P. (Johnson 1987a). Nondeposition, marked by soil formation, occurred during several significant cultural periods: the late Paleoindian to Early Archaic transition occurred during formation of the Firstview Soil; and Late Archaic, Ceramic, Protohistoric and Historic occupations took place on the developing Lubbock Lake Soil. Cultural debris from these occupations is compressed into the relatively thin A horizons of the respective soils (Johnson and Holliday 1986). In some areas, however, late Ceramic through Historic material is well stratified within stratum 5 (Holliday 1987a; Johnson et al. 1977; Johnson 1987b).

The stratigraphic and pedologic record at Lubbock Lake is essentially representative of that in draws throughout much of the Southern High Plains (Holliday 1989b), including the Clovis site (Haynes 1975; Haynes and Agogino 1966; Hester 1972; Holliday 1985d), Plainview site (Holliday 1985d, 1986), Marks Beach site (Honea 1980; author's unpublished data), and Mustang Springs (Hill and Meltzer 1987; Meltzer and Collins 1987). There was little deposition during the Early and Late Archaic and, therefore, conditions were not suitable for preservation of remains from discrete occupations. As a result, the record of the Archaic occupation of the Southern High Plains is poorly known (Johnson and Holliday 1986).

The well-dated soil-stratigraphic sequence at Lubbock Lake also provides an opportunity to examine rates of Holocene soil formation (Holliday 1985c, 1988). These data compare favorably with pedologic information from other draw localities on the Southern High Plains (Holliday 1985d, 1985e). These results suggest, therefore, that the degree of development of various pedologic features such as argillic and calcic horizons can be used to correlate and date deposits at other draw localities in the region.

Cherokee Sewer Site

Cherokee Sewer is located in northwestern Iowa, along the eastern margin of the Great Plains (Anderson and Semken 1980). The site is in an alluvial fan formed along the valley wall of the Little Sioux River. The fan developed throughout the Holocene and within its alluvial deposits are two late Paleoindian bison kills and two Archaic bison kills.

Hoyer (1980) describes and discusses the soils and stratigraphy of the Cherokee Sewer site. The stratigraphic sequence is 12–15 m thick with 20 sedimentary units and 19 soils (Figure 3-4). Of the four cultural horizons identified within the deposits, three of the occupation zones were found in buried A horizons. Most of the sediments were deposited and most of the soils formed in the early to middle Holocene (10,000–4600 yr B.P.). There were no long periods of nondeposition during this time and, therefore, most of the buried soils are weakly developed (with A–C or A–Bw profiles). The strongest pedogenic expression is seen in the surface soil and in the three buried soils which formed over the past 4600 years, resulting in a "complex, polygenetic" soil (Hoyer 1980:34) with, very generally, an A–Bt profile. The cultural horizons were in the

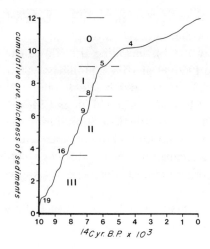

Figure 3-4. Plot of average sedimentation rates at the Cherokee site over the past 10,000 years (compiled from data presented by Hoyer 1980). Roman numerals refer to principal stratigraphic units ("Sedimentary Units" of Hoyer 1980) and Arabic numerals refer to soils.

early to middle Holocene sediments and soils, below the upper soil complex, and, therefore, the geologic/pedologic situation (i.e., nearly continuous sedimentation with only brief periods of stability) allowed for the preservation and recognition of the remains from several short-term occupations. A similar geoarchaeological situation is reported from alluvial fans and colluvial deposits in the lower Illinois River valley (Wiant et al. 1983).

CONCLUSIONS

The formation of a soil at an archaeological site can profoundly influence the nature of the archaeological record and interpretations of the cultural history of the locality. Long spans of time can be represented by the surface of a soil and long records of habitation can be compressed into zones only a few centimeters thick. The proper recognition and interpretation of soils in an archaeological context is essential for a more complete understanding of the geological and cultural record.

The number and degree of development of soils in a stratigraphic sequence can be a significant clue to the time-span and nature of the archaeological record in a stratified site. In sites such as Wilson–Leonard and Lubbock Lake, the presence of a few but well-developed soils is a good indicator of episodic sedimentation separated by long periods of nondeposition and landscape stability. Therefore, the debris from successive occupations are often concentrated in thin zones on the paleosurfaces and these thin zones represent long spans of time. In contrast, in archaeological sites with numerous, but weakly developed soils, sedimentation was more nearly continuous and the depositional hiatuses were probably shorter and, therefore, there is a greater likelihood that successive occupations will be stratified and preserved as discrete associations of habitation debris. Cherokee Sewer is an excellent example of such a situation.

Soil chronosequences are very useful for correlating and dating archaeological sites. Moreover, archaeological sites such as Lubbock Lake can often provide the age control necessary for establishing a chronosequence. Nonetheless, establishment and use of chronosequences must be done with considerable care and caution (Birkeland 1984). The rates and nature of pedogenesis can vary through time as climate and vegetation varies. Parent material variations, including seemingly minor changes in texture, can influence soil formation. Local variation in rates of sedimentation will also affect rates of pedogenesis.

A number of chronosequences are available in different regions of the United States, both with and without archaeological contexts, in addition to those cited earlier, but all clearly have potential for geoarchaeological applications. For example, Shlemon (1978) and McFadden et al. (1986) define chronosequences in the Mojave Desert of California and McFadden and Weldon (1987) establish rates of soil development in terraces in the Transverse Ranges of California. Karlstrom (1988) discusses a chronosequence associated with human occupation on Black Mesa, in northeast Arizona. A classic soil-geomorphic study from the Rio Grande Valley of south-central New Mexico is summarized by Gile et al. (1981). Holliday (1987b) discusses soil-geomorphic relations on terraces of the South Platte River in eastern Colorado, an area famous for its numerous Paleoindian sites, and in southeastern Wyoming, Reider et al. (1974) document a late-Quaternary chronosequence and incorporate their data into related archaeological investigations. Several Holocene chronosequences are also available from the eastern United States, including central Pennsylvania (Bilzi and Ciolkosz 1977) and the upper Susquehanna River basin of New York (Scully and Arnold 1981).

Although soil investigations of various kinds have a long history in archaeological research, clearly much more archaeological information can be gained from soils. In this paper one fundamental aspect of soils, time, and its relationship to studies of landscape evolution and human occupation is outlined as part of what is hoped will become a systematic approach to applying pedology to archaeological problems.

ACKNOWLEDGMENTS

I thank E. Arthur Bettis (Iowa Geological Survey), William R. Farrand (University of Michigan), Paul Goldberg (Hebrew University), Angela R. Linse (University of Washington), and Julie K. Stein (University of Washington) for their valuable and insightful comments on various versions of this essay.

REFERENCES

Anderson, Duane C., and Holmes A. Semken (editors)
    1980   *The Cherokee Excavations*. Academic Press, New York.

Bettis, E. A., and D. M. Thompson
    1982   *Interrelationships of Cultural and Fluvial Deposits in Northwest Iowa*. Association of Iowa Archaeologists Fieldtrip Guidebook, University of South Dakota Archaeology Laboratory, Vermillion.

Bilzi, A. F., and E. J. Ciolkosz
    1977   Time as a Factor in the Genesis of Four Soils Developed in Recent Alluvium in Pennsylvania. *Soil Science Society of America Journal* 41:122–127.

Birkeland, Peter W.
    1984   *Soils and Geomorphology*. Oxford University Press, New York.

Birkeland, Peter W., and R. M. Burke
    1988   Soil Catena Chronosequences on Eastern Sierra Nevada Moraines, California, U.S.A. *Arctic and Alpine Research* 20:473–484.

Bischoff, J. L., R. J. Shlemon, T. L. Ku, R. D. Simpson, R. J. Rosenbauer, and F. E. Budinger
    1981   Uranium-series and Soil-geomorphic Dating of the Calico Archaeological Site, California. *Geology* 9: 576–582.

Bockheim, James G.
    1980   Solution and Use of Chronofunctions in Studying Soil Development. *Geoderma* 24:71–85.

Catt, John A.
    1986   *Soils and Quaternary Geology: A Handbook for Field Scientists.* Oxford Science Publications, Monographs on Soil and Resources Survey 11, England.

Dethier, David P.
    1988   *The Soil Chronosequence along the Cowlitz River, Washington.* U.S. Geological Survey Bulletin 1590-F.

Eidt, Robert C.
    1977   Detection and Examination of Anthrosols by Phosphate Analysis. *Science* 197:1327–1333.
    1985   Theoretical and Practical Considerations in the Analysis of Anthrosols. In *Archaeological Geology*, edited by George Rapp, Jr. and John A. Gifford, pp. 155–190. Yale University Press, New Haven.

Ferring, C. Reid
    1986   Rate of Fluvial Sedimentation: Implications for Archaeological Variability. *Geoarchaeology* 1:259–274.

Foss, J. E.
    1977   The Pedological Record at Several Paleoindian Sites in the Northeast. In *Amerinds and their Paleoenvironments in Northeastern North America*, edited by W. S. Newman and B. Salwen, pp. 234–244. Annals of the New York Academy of Sciences, vol. 228.

Gerrard, A. J.
    1981   *Soils and Landforms.* Allen and Unwin, London.

Gile, L. H., J. W. Hawley, and R. B. Grossman
    1981   *Soils and Geomorphology in the Basin and Range Area of Southern New Mexico— Guidebook to the Desert Project.* New Mexico Bureau of Mines and Mineral Resources Memoir 39.

Goldberg, Paul
    1986   Late Quaternary Environmental History of the Southern Levant. *Geoarchaeology* 1:225–244.

Hassan, Fekri A.
    1981   Rapid Quantitative Determination of Phosphate in Archaeological Sediments. *Journal of Field Archaeology* 8:384–387.

Haynes, C. Vance, Jr.
    1968   Geochronology of Late-Quaternary Alluvium. In *Means of Correlation of Quaternary Successions*, edited by Roger B. Morrison and H. E. Wright, Jr., pp. 591–631. University of Utah Press, Salt Lake City.
    1975   Pleistocene and Recent Stratigraphy. In *Late Pleistocene Environments of the Southern High Plains*, edited by Fred Wendorf and James J. Hester, pp. 59–96. Ft. Burgwin Research Center, Publication 9. Southern Methodist University, Dallas.

Haynes, C. Vance, Jr., and George A. Agogino
 1966   Prehistoric Springs and Geochronology of the Clovis Site, New Mexico.
         American Antiquity 31:812–821.

Hester, James J.
 1972   *Blackwater Draw Locality No. 1.* Ft. Burgwin Research Center Publication 8.
         Southern Methodist University, Dallas.

Hill, Christopher L., and David J. Meltzer
 1987   Late Pleistocene to Middle Holocene Depositional Environments at Mustang
         Springs, Southern Llano Estacado. *Current Research in the Pleistocene* 4:127–
         130.

Hoffecker, John F.
 1987   Upper Pleistocene Loess Stratigraphy and Paleolithic Site Chronology on the
         Russian Plain. *Geoarchaeology* 2:259–284.

Holliday, Vance T.
 1985a   Early Holocene Soils at the Lubbock Lake Archeological Site, Texas. *Catena*
         12:61–78.
 1985b   Archeological Geology of the Lubbock Lake Site, Southern High Plains of
         Texas. *Geological Society of America Bulletin* 96:1483–1492.
 1985c   Morphology of Late Holocene Soils at the Lubbock Lake Archeological Site,
         Texas. *Soil Science Society of America Journal* 49:938–946.
 1985d   New Data on the Stratigraphy and Pedology of the Clovis and Plainview
         Sites, Southern High Plains. *Quaternary Research* 23:388–402.
 1985e   Holocene Soil-geomorphological Relationships in a Semi-arid Environment:
         The Southern High Plains of Texas. In *Soils and Quaternary Landscape Evolu-
         tion*, edited by John Boardman, pp. 321–353. John Wiley & Sons, Chichester,
         United Kingdom.
 1986   *Guidebook to the Archaeological Geology of Classic Paleoindian Sites on the South-
         ern High Plains, Texas and New Mexico.* Geological Society of America
         Guidebook, Department of Geography, Texas A&M University.
 1987a   Cultural Chronology. In *Lubbock Lake: Late Quaternary Studies on the Southern
         High Plains*, edited by Eileen Johnson, pp. 22–25. Texas A&M University
         Press, College Station.
 1987b   Geoarchaeology and Late Quaternary Geomorphology of the Middle South
         Platte River, Northeastern Colorado. *Geoarchaeology* 2:317–329.
 1988   Genesis of a Late-Holocene Soil Chronosequence at the Lubbock Lake Ar-
         chaeological Site, Texas. *Annals of the Association of American Geographers*
         78:594–610.
 1989a   *Geoarchaeological Investigations at the Wilson-Leonard Site.* Report submitted to
         the Archaeology Division, Texas Department of Highways and Public Trans-
         portation.
 1989b   Middle Holocene Drought on the Southern High Plains. *Quaternary Research*
         31:74–82.
 1990   Pedology in Archaeology. In *Archaeological Geology of North America*, edited
         by Norman Lasca and Jack Donahue, pp. 525–540. Geological Society of
         America, Centennial Special Volume 4.

Holliday, Vance T., and B. L. Allen
 1987   Geology and Soils. In *Lubbock Lake: Late Quaternary Studies on the Southern*

High Plains, edited by Eileen Johnson, pp. 14–21. Texas A&M University Press, College Station.

Honea, Kenneth
  1980   Marks Beach Stratified Paleoindian Site, Lamb County, Texas: Preliminary Report. *Bulletin of the Texas Archeological Society* 51:243–269.

Hoyer, Bernard E.
  1980   The Geology of the Cherokee Sewer Site. In *The Cherokee Excavations,* edited by Duane C. Anderson and Holmes A. Semken, pp. 21–66. Academic Press, New York.

Jenny, Hans
  1941   *Factors of Soil Formation.* McGraw-Hill, New York.
  1961   Derivation of State Factor Equations of Soils and Ecosystems. *Soil Science Society of America Proceedings* 25:385–388.
  1980   *The Soil Resource.* Springer-Verlag, New York.

Johnson, Eileen (editor)
  1987a   *Lubbock Lake: Late Quaternary Studies on the Southern High Plains.* Texas A&M University Press, College Station.
  1987b   Cultural Activities and Interactions. In *Lubbock Lake: Late Quaternary Studies on the Southern High Plains,* edited by Eileen Johnson, pp. 120–158. Texas A&M University Press, College Station.

Johnson, Eileen, and Vance T. Holliday
  1986   The Archaic Record at Lubbock Lake. *Plains Anthropologist Memoir* 21: 7–54.
  1989   Lubbock Lake: Late Quaternary Cultural and Environmental Change on the Southern High Plains, USA. *Journal of Quaternary Science* 4: 145–165.

Johnson, Eileen, Vance T. Holliday, Michael J. Kaczor, and Robert Stuckenrath
  1977   The Garza Occupation at the Lubbock Lake Site. *Bulletin of the Texas Archeological Society* 48:83–109.

Karlstrom, Eric T.
  1988   Rates of Soil Formation on Black Mesa, Northeast Arizona: A Chronosequence in Late Quaternary Alluvium. *Physical Geography* 9: 301–327.

Kraus, Mary, and Thomas M. Bown
  1986   Paleosols and Time Resolution in Alluvial Stratigraphy. In *Paleosols: Their Recognition and Interpretation,* edited by V. P. Wright, pp. 180–207. Princeton University Press, Princeton.

Lotspeich, F. B.
  1961   Soil Science in the Service of Archaeology. In *Paleoecology of the Llano Estacado,* edited by Fred Wendorf, pp. 137–139. Ft. Burgwin Research Center, Publication 1. The Museum of New Mexico Press, Santa Fe.

Machette, Michael N.
  1975   Geologic Map of the Lafayette Quadrangle, Adams, Boulder, and Jefferson Counties, Colorado. *U.S. Geological Survey Map* MF-656.

McFadden, Leslie D., and Ray J. Weldon
1987　Rates and Processes of Soil Development on Quaternary Terraces in Cajon Pass, California. *Geological Society of America Bulletin* 98:280–293.

McFadden, Leslie D., Stephen G. Wells, and John C. Dohrenwend
1986　Influences of Quaternary Climate Changes on Processes of Soil Development on Desert Loess Deposits of the Cima Volcanic Field, California. *Catena* 13:361–389.

Meltzer, David J., and Michael B. Collins
1987　Prehistoric Water Wells on the Southern High Plains: Clues to Altithermal Climate. *Journal of Field Archaeology* 14:9–28.

Olson, G. W.
1981　*Soils and the Environment: A Guide to Soil Surveys and Their Applications.* Chapman and Hall, New York.

Paulissen, E., and P. M. Vermeersch
1987　Earth, Man and Climate in the Egyptian Nile Valley during the Pleistocene. In *Prehistory of Arid North Africa: Essays in Honor of Fred Wendorf,* edited by A. E. Close, pp. 29–67. Southern Methodist University Press, Dallas.

Pawluk, S.
1978　The Pedogenic Profile in the Stratigraphic Section. In *Quaternary Soils,* edited by W. C. Mahaney, pp. 61–75. Geo Abstracts, Norwich, UK.

Prewitt, Elton R.
1981　Cultural Chronology in Central Texas. *Bulletin of the Texas Archeological Society* 52:65–89.
1983　From Circleville to Toyah: Comments on Central Texas Chronology. *Bulletin of the Texas Archeological Society* 54:201–238.

Ranov, V. A., and R. S. Davis
1979　Toward a New Outline of the Soviet Central Asian Paleolithic. *Current Anthropology* 20:249–270.

Reeves, Brian O. K., and John F. Dormaar
1972　A Partial Holocene Pedological and Archaeological Record for the Southern Alberta Rocky Mountains. *Arctic and Alpine Research* 4:325–336.

Reider, Richard G.
1980　Late Pleistocene and Holocene Soils of the Carter/Kerr-McGee Archeological Site, Powder River Basin, Wyoming. *Catena* 7:301–315.

Reider, Richard G., Nelson J. Kuniansky, David M. Stiller, and Peter J. Uhl
1974　Preliminary Investigation of Comparative Soil Development on Pleistocene and Holocene Geomorphic Surfaces of the Laramie Basin, Wyoming. In *Applied Geology and Archaeology: The Holocene History of Wyoming,* edited by Michael Wilson, pp. 27–33. Geological Survey of Wyoming, Report of Investigation 10.

Rockwell, T. K., D. L. Johnson, E. A. Keller, and G. R. Dembroff
1985　A Late Pleistocene-Holocene Soil Chronosequence in the Ventura Basin,

Southern California, USA. In *Geomorphology and Soils*, edited by K. S. Richards, R. R. Arnett, and S. Ellis, pp. 309–327. George Allen & Unwin, London.

Rutter, N. W.
   1978   Soils in Archaeology. *Geosciences in Canada, 1977*, Annual Report and Review of Soil Science, Geological Survey of Canada. Paper 78–6, 1 p.

Scully, Richard W., and Richard W. Arnold
   1981   Holocene Alluvial Stratigraphy in the Upper Susquehanna River Basin, New York. *Quaternary Research* 15:327–344.

Shlemon, R. J.
   1978   Quaternary Soil-geomorphic Relationships, Southeastern Mojave Desert, California and Arizona. In *Quaternary Soils*, edited by W. C. Mahaney, pp. 187–207. Geo Abstracts, Norwich, UK.

Sjoberg, Alf
   1976   Phosphate Analysis of Anthropic Soils. *Journal of Field Archaeology* 3:447–454.

Solecki, Ralph S.
   1951   Notes on Soil Analysis and Archaeology. *American Antiquity* 16:254–256.

Stafford, Thomas, Jr.
   1981   Alluvial Geology and Archaeological Potential of the Texas Southern High Plains. *American Antiquity* 46:548–565.

Tamplin, M. J.
   1969   The Application of Pedology to Archaeological Research. In *Pedology and Quaternary Research*, edited by S. Pawluk, pp. 153–161. The University of Alberta Printing Department, Edmonton.

Turner, Ellen S., and Thomas R. Hester
   1985   *A Field Guide to Stone Artifacts of Texas Indians*. Texas Monthly Press, Austin.

Weir, Frank A.
   1985   An Early Holocene Burial at the Wilson-Leonard Site in Central Texas. *Mammoth Trumpet* 2:1,3.

Wiant, Michael D., Edwin R. Hajic, and Thomas R. Styles
   1983   Napoleon Hollow and Koster Site Stratigraphy: Implications for Holocene Landscape Evolution and Studies of Archaic Period Settlement Patterns in the Lower Illinois Valley. In *Archaic Hunters and Gatherers in the American Midwest*, edited by J. L. Phillips and J. A. Brown, pp. 147–164. Academic Press, New York.

Yaalon, Dan H.
   1975   Conceptual Models in Pedogenesis: Can Soil-forming Functions Be Solved? *Geoderma* 14:189–205.

Young, Wayne
   1983   The Wilson-Leonard Site (41WM235). *Abstracts of the Paleoindian Lifeways Symposium II*, p. 10. The Museum of Texas Tech University, Lubbock.

4

E. ARTHUR BETTIS III

Soil Morphologic Properties and Weathering Zone Characteristics as Age Indicators in Holocene Alluvium in the Upper Midwest

The present landscape consists of a mosaic of various-aged deposits, erosion surfaces, and soils with predictable distributions. Archaeological remains, being deposits, are subject to the same natural processes of burial, weathering, and erosion that affect the preservation and distribution of noncultural deposits. Although all archaeological deposits have been subject to environmental processes that preserve, alter, or destroy the original depositional context, the impact of these processes on the archaeological record is usually not considered on a landscape scale. In most cases the present landscape is assumed to be reflective of past landscapes and proxy environmental/age indicators such as published soil maps, or landforms determined from topographic maps are used to reconstruct the physical environment of various periods of the past. Such approaches ignore all but the shallow subsurface and are incapable of evaluating archaeological deposits associated with portions of past landscapes not present at the modern surface. These types of paleoenvironmental reconstructions in combination with traditional site locating tech-

Iowa Quaternary Studies Group Contribution No. 30.

119

niques such as pedestrian survey and excavation of shallow test pits result in a bias toward location of shallowly buried or surface archaeological deposits that can produce a skewed perception of the archaeological record (Bettis and Thompson 1982; Hajic 1985; Thompson and Bettis 1981).

The inability of traditional pedestrian survey and shallow testing strategies to adequately sample the archaeological record is a result of two conceptual problems: (1) the belief that the present landscape more or less reflects past landscapes, and (2) failure to consider that the archaeological record has passed through an environmental filter in which burial, alteration, and destruction has occurred. Although both of these concepts are usually discussed in introductory archaeology courses, they usually end up taking a back seat to statistically based environmental or social sampling concepts when strategies for locating archaeological deposits are designed and implemented (e.g., Muller 1975).

Detailed investigations of the alluvial fill sequence in numerous valleys of the Upper Midwest have been accomplished in the last decade (Anderson and Overstreet 1986; Bettis and Thompson 1981; Bettis and Littke 1987; Brakenridge 1981; Hajic 1985; Knox et al. 1981; McDowell 1983; Van Nest and Bettis 1990). These studies, all of which include several radiocarbon-dated geologic sections, demonstrate that modern valley landscapes consist of a mosaic of various-age deposits and geomorphic surfaces. Data from these studies and a literature review of other Midwestern alluvial stratigraphic studies that have reported detailed descriptions of radiocarbon-dated deposits, including Munsell colors, notes on the occurrence of mottles, and the grade and type of soil structure, indicate that some morphologic properties of alluvial deposits and soils developed in the deposits are specific to certain age groupings of the deposits.

This paper presents a first approximation of a model useful for differentiating Historic, late Holocene (LH), and early and middle Holocene (EMH) alluvial deposits in the Upper Midwest. The distinguishing criteria are easily observed properties of deposits and soils that can be recorded by archaeologists with only modest knowledge of soils and geomorphology. Application of this model permits division of the landscape elements comprising modern valleys into three groups: (1) those older than about 3000 to 4000 years (EMH), (2) those younger than that age but prehistoric (LH), and (3) Historic deposits. This will permit incorporation of landscape evolution and environmental filter concepts in archaeological survey design where their previous use has been hampered by the lack of a methodology for easily distinguishing and accurately mapping the various-age deposits present across and beneath the modern landscape. Essential base-line information for assessing the impact that geologic processes have had in shaping the archaeological record will result, allowing archaeologists to focus survey efforts and methods where they are most appropriate in light of the geologic context. The following discussion outlines weathering zones and other morphologic criteria used to distinguish the various alluvial deposits, discusses factors contributing to the morphologic differences, and finally, provides an example of application of the model in an archaeological survey of the central Des Moines River Valley in Iowa.

WEATHERING ZONES IN ALLUVIUM

An easy to use, standardized weathering zone classification scheme for Quaternary deposits in the Upper Midwest has been presented by Hallberg et al. (1978). In this scheme weathering zones in Quaternary sediments are described and differentiated on the basis of interpreted oxidation states as inferred from color, mottling patterns, and matrix carbonate status. For the present analysis only the interpreted oxidation state (color) and mottling pattern of the deposit is used to differentiate weathering zones in alluvium, because the primary matrix carbonate content of alluvial deposits in the Midwest is variable and not necessarily indicative of degree of in situ weathering.

Oxidation of iron is a common weathering phenomenon in alluvial deposits (Carroll 1970). This occurs in an environment where the oxygen supply is high and/or the biological oxygen demand is low. In most cases oxidized sediments indicate that the local water table is or has been at a depth below the oxidized zone. Reduction (deoxidation) occurs in an environment where oxygen supply is limited or where the biological oxygen supply is high. Reduction takes place when either a temporary or permanent water table rise occurs and oxidized sediments enter into an environment of saturation or near-saturation where organic matter and micro-organisms are present. In this environment iron is reduced to a highly mobile ferrous form that may either migrate out of the sediments if there is sufficient ground water movement, migrate to crevices, channels, or other voids in the sediment matrix and be oxidized, or remain in the matrix and react with sulfides in the reduced state (Cate 1964). Data presented by Bradbury et al. (1977) and Daniels et al. (1961) show that progressing from oxidized to deoxidized (reduced) weathering zones, the relative amount of ferrous iron in the sediment increases. Deoxidized zones exhibit low total free iron and the iron, outside silicate mineral structures, is concentrated in secondary segregations of ferric oxides, such as mottles, tubules, and concretions.

The oxides of iron have distinctive optical properties and therefore there is a relationship between the chemical status and distribution of iron (oxidation state) and the matrix colors of sediments. Table 4-1 pre-

TABLE 4-1

Color and Mottling Pattern Criteria for Weathering Zones in Upper Midwestern Alluvial Deposits Used in Table 4-3.

Symbol	Meaning	Description
First Symbol: color reference		
O	oxidized	60% of matrix has hues of 2.5Y or redder (e.g., 10YR, 7.5YR), values of 4 or higher, chroma of 3 or higher, and may have segregation of secondary iron compounds into mottles, tubules, or nodules.
R	reduced	60% of matrix has hues of 2.5Y or 5Y with values from 6 to 4 and chromas of 1 or 2; hues of N, 5GY, 5G, and 5BG with values of 4 or higher. Colors in this zone are usually mixed as weak mottles, diffuse blends of colors, or as discrete bands. This zone may contain considerable segregation of secondary iron compounds (with oxidized colors) into mottles, nodules, or sheets along bedding or joints.
U	unoxidized	matrix color is uniform; has hues of 5Y and N with values of 5 or less; 5GY, 5G, 5BG, 5G with values of 6 or less; with no segregation of iron compounds into mottles, nodules, etc. This zone often contains detrital organic matter.
Second Symbol: if used		
J	jointed	indicates the presence of well-defined subvertical joints in the alluvium. Joint faces have oxidized and reduced colors, may have coatings of clay or secondary iron oxides, and occasionally other secondary minerals such as calcite.
Modifier Symbol: when used precedes first symbol		
M	mottled	refers to zones containing 20–50% contrasting mottles; when used with the unoxidized zone designation it indicates the presence of mottles of reduced colors occupying 20% or *less* of the matrix.

sents the color and mottling pattern criteria used to classify a deposit as oxidized, reduced, or unoxidized in the present analysis. Standard soil horizon designations (Guthrie and Witty 1982; Bettis 1984) and descriptive terminology (Soil Survey Staff 1975) are used to describe properties within the solum.

THE MODEL

Associations of weathering zones (defined on the basis of matrix colors and mottling patterns), organic matter content and distribution, and the nature of soils developed in the alluvium permit the tripartite age grouping of alluvial deposits outlined below.

Early to Middle Holocene (EMH) Alluvium

EMH alluvium was deposited between about 10,500 and 4000 B.P. Where these deposits have not been eroded they often comprise the fill of a single or series of low terraces (Figure 4-1). EMH deposits also make up the bulk of most alluvial fans (Bettis et al. 1984; Bettis and Hoyer 1986; Hajic 1981; Styles 1985; Wiant et al. 1983). Texture of the fine-grained component of these deposits ranges from silt loam to loam. EMH deposits exhibit oxidized colors (Table 4-1) and have red, brown, or gray mottles. The lower portion of many EMH deposits is reduced and in this condition the deposit is light gray and exhibits secondary segregation of iron into brown or reddish brown mottles, tubules, or nodules. In Iowa

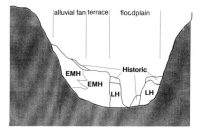

Figure 4-1.   Idealized valley cross section showing spatial relationships among landforms and the alluvial fills described in the text.

123

Ap
E
BE

Bt

Figure 4-2. Exposure of EMH alluvium in eastern Iowa. Surface soil at this location is a Alfisol with an Ap-E-BE-Bt horizon sequence. Note gray mottles in Bt horizon and the absence of bedding in most of the section.

EMH alluvial deposits are the Gunder Member of the DeForest Formation, while those comprising alluvial fans are the Corrington Member (Table 4-2; Bettis and Littke 1987).

Modern surface soils developed in EMH alluvium are Mollisols or Alfisols that usually have subsurface argillic (Bt) horizons. These soils exhibit moderate grade soil structure, brown or dark brown B horizons, few to common argillans, and are well horizonated. Figure 4-2 shows an example of an Alfisol developed in EMH alluvium in eastern Iowa. Archaeological associations and numerous radiocarbon dates indicate that most surface soils on EMH deposits have been developing during the last 2000 to 4000 years (Bettis and Littke 1987; Benn and Bettis 1985; Bettis et al. 1984; Styles 1985).

Late Holocene (LH) Alluvium

LH alluvium was deposited after 3500 B.P. These deposits are usually found within the modern floodplain and can overlap older deposits. The texture of the fine-grained component of LH alluvium is usually loam, silty clay loam, or clay loam. LH deposits are darker colored than EMH deposits, primarily because they contain more organic carbon than the older deposits (Figure 4-3). Most LH alluvial deposits exhibit colors with 10YR hues, values less than 4 and chromas of 3 or less. In most cases prominent red or brown mottles are not present in LH alluvium. LH deposits are assigned to the Roberts Creek Member of the DeForest Formation in Iowa (Table 4-2; Bettis and Littke 1987).

Modern surface soils developed in LH deposits contrast sharply with those developed in EMH deposits. Soils developed in LH deposits are Mollisols or Inceptisols with cambic (Bw) horizons, or Entisols that lack subsurface B horizons. Soils developed in LH deposits usually do not have albic horizons. These soils tend to be dark colored throughout, exhibit weak to moderate grade soil structure, and have weak horizonation (Figure 4-3). These soils have been developing during the last 1500 to 1000 years (Benn and Bettis 1985; Bettis and Littke 1987; Brakenridge 1981; McDowell 1983; Van Nest and Bettis 1990).

Historic Alluvium

The youngest deposits in stream valleys are Historic or very late prehistoric in age. In most cases these deposits began accumulating after Euroamerican settlement. These deposits are characteristically lightercolored than LH deposits, and where greater than about 50 cm in thickness, exhibit prominent stratification in their lower part (Figure 4-4). Often they contain Historic artifacts. Historic alluvium can be found throughout the valley landscape burying all older surfaces. It is thickest in and adjacent to the modern channel belt, at the base of steep slopes,

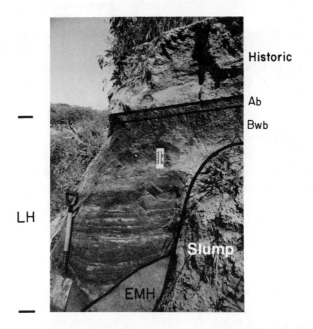

Figure 4-3.   Exposure of Historic deposits overlying a dark-colored Mollisol developed in LH alluvium. The buried Mollisol at this location has a relatively thick Ab-Bwb profile. Note the stratification in the dark-colored LH alluvium beneath the buried soil. Light-colored deposit at the base of the exposure is EMH alluvium that is separated from the overlying LH alluvium by an angular unconformity.

TABLE 4-2

Correlation of Lithostratigraphic Units Used in Iowa with the Regional Age-morphologic Sequence Described in the Text

	Lithostratigraphic Unit	
Age-morphologic group	Member	Formation
EMH	Corrington and Gunder	
LH	Roberts Creek	DeForest
Historic	Camp Creek	

Figure 4-4.   Historic alluvium with very thin, weakly expressed surface soil (Entisol) and bedding at shallow depth beneath the surface.

and along fence lines. In Iowa, Historic deposits are the Camp Creek Member of the DeForest Formation (Bettis and Littke 1987).

Surface soils developed in Historic deposits are Entisols and have A–C soil profiles. These soils have weak to moderate grade structure, weak horizonation, and are thin. Soils may be absent on rapidly aggrading surfaces.

A summary of important criteria for distinguishing the three age-morphologic groups of alluvial deposits outlined above is presented in Table 4-3.

DISCUSSION

An essential aspect of the field application of the model outlined above is to be able to distinguish soil horizons from geologic deposits. Most

Table 4-3

Outline of Criteria Used to Group Upper Midwestern Alluvial Deposits into the Age-morphologic Groups Outlined in the Text

Age-Morphologic Group	Landforms(s)	Bedding	Weathering Zone*	Mottles	Surface Soil (horizon sequence; B horizon color)
EMH	terraces alluvial fans, colluvial slopes	restricted to lower part of section	O; MO; R; or U in part of some sections	common; brown, reddish brown, and/or gray	A-E-Bt A-Bt; brown B horizon
LH	lowest terrace; floodplain	usually restricted to lower part of section	color usually 10YR hue, values 4 or less, chroma 3 or less; disseminated organic carbon imparts dark colors; may be oxidized or unoxidized but matrix colors are dark because of organic carbon content	rare—usually not present	A-Bw; dark-colored B horizon
Historic	floodplain, fencelines, footslopes, buries older surfaces	present throughout section if > 50 cm in thickness	O; MO; R; some sections dark colored because of high organic carbon content	can be present or absent; brown, reddish brown, or gray	A-C; no B horizon

*See Table 4-1 for explanation.

important is the distinction between dark-colored, organic-rich A horizons of soils, and dark-colored, organic-rich LH alluvial deposits. Several criteria are useful for making this distinction including: (1) a gradual or clear lower boundary of A horizons as opposed to an abrupt lower boundary in geologic deposits, (2) absence of bedding in A horizons and its presence in geologic deposits, and (3) the presence of granular, or crumb soil structure in A horizons and its absence or weaker development in geologic deposits.

Almost all of the dated localities used to develop this model are located in Iowa and southwestern Wisconsin. Visits to localities in eastern Nebraska and South Dakota, northeastern Kansas, Missouri, Illinois, Minnesota, and Indiana, however, suggest that the model is also applicable to those areas.

The regional extent of the sequence suggests that temporal variations of regionally occurring phenomena produced these morphologic differences in Holocene alluvial deposits and soils. Two important factors influencing depositional processes, weathering, and soil development that are known to have varied from the early and middle to the late Holocene are vegetation and climate. These two phenomena are linked, but during the entire Holocene vegetation varied across the area in which the morphologic sequence occurs (Webb et al. 1983). The differences between EMH, LH, and Historic deposits occur in areas dominated by prairie as well as those dominated by forest, and both Mollisols and Alfisols have developed on EMH deposits. This indicates that vegetation change alone cannot account for the differences among EMH and LH deposits and associated surface soils. Other climate-influenced phenomena may have played a larger role in the evolution of the sequence.

Knox (1976, 1983) has pointed out that the impact of climatic change on fluvial systems has both direct and indirect components. Direct components include changes in atmospheric circulation patterns, resultant changes in precipitation patterns, and their influence on the hydrology of the fluvial system. The principal indirect component, amount and type of vegetation cover, is seen as a major control on surface runoff, sediment yield, and sediment concentration.

Both direct and indirect impacts of climatic change have influenced the EMH-LH morphologic sequence. The major factors involved are rates of hillslope erosion and sediment delivery to valleys, and water table levels. These factors determined the nature of the original alluvial deposits, and influenced the diagenic and pedogenic processes that modified the deposits.

On a regional scale the highest rates of Holocene slope erosion and valley alluviation occurred prior to 3000 B.P. (Bettis and Hoyer 1986; Brakenridge 1981; Knox 1983; Vreeken 1984; Walker 1966). This phenomenon was a function of decreased vegetation cover combined with increased incidence of high-intensity thunderstorms. During this time surface soils were stripped from many valley slopes, the B and underlying C horizons were eroded, and the resultant oxidized sediment delivered to valleys. Alluviation was rapid with a few intervening periods of slower aggradation during which soils developed on exposed valley surfaces.

A drying trend occurred in the early to middle Holocene, culminating between 6500 and 5000 B.P. (Kim 1986; Van Zant 1979). This decrease in precipitation amount, coupled with rapid runoff during high-intensity storms, resulted in decreased infiltration and lowering of water tables. Lowered water tables promoted oxidation of alluvium and degradation of organic matter present in the alluvium.

After 4000 B.P. increased precipitation amount accompanied by greater infiltration resulting from a decrease in the frequency of high intensity storms fostered greater vegetative cover and expansion of forests (Kim 1986; Van Zant 1979). These climatic and biotic changes brought about lower rates of slope erosion and reduced sediment delivery to valleys. Sediment delivered to valleys during the late Holocene was derived primarily from reworking of older alluvial deposits and erosion of the upper, organic-rich horizons of soils, and may have been higher in organic carbon content than sediment delivered to valleys during the early and middle Holocene. Lower average sedimentation rates during the late Holocene allowed for incorporation of additional organic matter by vegetation growing on exposed surfaces and through the activity of other biota. Higher precipitation amounts and increased infiltration caused water tables to rise after 4000 B.P. Higher water tables inhibited oxidation of organic matter in the alluvium resulting in the dark colors, produced by finely disseminated organic carbon, that are characteristic of LH alluvium.

Most valley surfaces underlain by EMH deposits are, or at one time were, slightly to moderately elevated above the floodplain where LH deposits are found. These elevated surfaces have not been flooded as frequently during the last few millennia as the lower-lying surfaces underlain by LH deposits. This contrast in flooding frequency has produced many of the differences observed in surface soils developed in EMH verses LH deposits. Soils developed in LH deposits are overthickened or cumulic as a result of deposition of overbank alluvium on the soil surface. Such upbuilding inhibits horizonation, fosters thick surface horizons, and limits the development of subsurface B horizons (Johnson 1985; Walker and Coventry 1976). Soils developed in EMH deposits, on the other hand, are flooded less frequently and pedogenesis has not been as interrupted by depositional processes. This has fostered greater horizonation and development of subsurface B horizons in soils developed in EMH deposits. Lowered water tables during the middle Holocene, as well as higher relative elevations of EMH surfaces during the late Holocene, promoted greater overall vertical movement of sediment-free water (precipitation) through the upper part of the EMH deposits. This also acted to produce greater horizonation and development of Bt horizons in soils developed in EMH deposits.

A final factor that could contribute to the differences in morphology of these soils is that they have been developing for different amounts of time. Although time in and of itself exerts no influence on soil development or weathering, the cumulative effect of weathering and pedological processes often differs on surfaces exposed for different amounts of time (Birkeland 1984; Walker and Coventry 1976; Holliday 1988). The EMH-LH morphologic sequence described above at first glance appears to be a generalized chronosequence of soils and weathering zones applicable to alluvial deposits in the Upper Midwest. I would argue, however, that some of the initial conditions of EMH alluvium, particularly the organic matter content, were different than those of LH alluvium and therefore the genetic pathways of soils on EMH alluvium may be quite different than those on LH deposits. Variability in time and space of other factors such as sedimentation history and water table levels have further complicated the genetic pathways of alluvial soils in the Midwest. Finally, soils developed on EMH deposits have formed under different climatic and vegetation conditions than those developed in LH deposits (Webb et al. 1983). The combined effect of these time-independent factors prevent this morphologic sequence from being a chronosequence. Rather, the differences in deposits and soils described in the previous pages result from the combined effect of differences in initial organic matter content, water table history, flood frequency and magnitude, and sedimentation rate. That differential time for pedogenesis has occurred is not debatable, but it cannot be isolated from other factors controlling soil development in this complex system.

Local deviations from the EMH-LH morphologic sequence can occur for several reasons. Dark-colored, organic-rich, unoxidized EMH

131

deposits occur where the water table was not lowered through the thickness of these deposits during the middle Holocene. These occurrences are restricted to the lower part of thick EMH sections and usually have detrital organic matter associated with them (Table 4-3). Oxidized LH deposits may occur in areas of very rapid sedimentation, or where the deposits were derived from oxidized sources, such as dune fields or older, highly oxidized alluvium. In the thick loess regions along the Mississippi and Missouri valleys, an oxidized alluvial fill was deposited between 3500 and 2000 B.P. in 3rd-order and smaller valleys (Bettis and Thompson 1982; Bettis et al. 1986; Daniels and Jordan 1966). This alluvium was derived from erosion of the thick, oxidized loess in the area, and accumulated very rapidly. It is overlain by dark-colored, younger LH deposits. The morphology of EMH and LH alluvium and associated surface soils in 4th-order and larger valleys draining the thick loess areas conforms to the regional pattern previously outlined. In order to avoid interpretation problems caused by these local variations it is essential to obtain radiometric dates on some deposits in a study area to confirm that the morphologic sequence corresponds to the regional age pattern outlined above.

APPLICATION OF THE MODEL TO AN ARCHAEOLOGICAL SURVEY

Knowledge of the distribution of the various-age deposits that comprise present valley landscapes is essential in order to adequately evaluate those landscapes for evidence of past human occupation. The EMH-LH morphologic sequence of alluvium and associated soils can be mapped throughout valleys and provides the baseline information necessary to devise reasoned approaches for assessing the cultural resource potential of an area. This approach was used in an archaeological survey of the central Des Moines River Valley in Iowa (Benn and Bettis 1985; Benn and Rogers 1985; Bettis and Benn 1984; Bettis and Hoyer 1986). A detailed geologic study of the valley was undertaken prior to an intensive archaeological survey and testing program. The geologic study included extensive subsurface drilling, digging of backhoe trenches, examination of cut banks, and radiocarbon dating.

Five major late Wisconsinan to Holocene landform-sediment assemblages (LSA) were recognized, and over 70 radiocarbon and thermoluminescence ages were obtained to provide a temporal framework for the LSAs (Bettis and Hoyer 1986). Each LSA consists of a grouping of genetically and temporally related landforms and deposits comprising the landforms. The highest and oldest LSA consists of a series of late Wisconsinan terraces and benches. Four Holocene LSAs were recognized; a high terrace, alluvial fans and colluvial slopes, a low terrace complex and the modern floodplain. Deposits comprising the high terrace, alluvial fan and colluvial slope LSAs accumulated between 10,500 and 4000 B.P. and have characteristics of the EMH morphologic grouping (Table 4-4). Deposits of the low terrace complex LSA are inset into the high terrace, fan, and colluvial slope deposits. Deposits comprising the low terrace LSA accumulated between 4000 and about 750 B.P. and conform to the LH morphologic grouping. Deposits making up the floodplain LSA are younger than 750 B.P. and are inset into, as well as overlap, older deposits. These deposits are stratified throughout, oxidized, and have little or no pedogenic alteration. The floodplain LSA conforms to the Historic morphologic grouping.

Maps were constructed to show the distribution of the LSAs throughout the valley (Figures 4-5 and 4-6). These maps provide valuable information for locating archaeological deposits and for interpreting the pattern of known sites in the area. Table 4-5 presents an analysis of the geologic potential for the occurrence of buried cultural deposits in the various LSAs. EMH deposits (alluvial fan and high terrace LSA) have high potential for containing buried Paleoindian and Archaic components, but LH deposits (low terrace LSA) are too young to contain these cultural components. On the other hand, LH deposits are likely to contain buried Late Archaic and Woodland components. These components will be at or near the surface of EMH deposits. Historic deposits

TABLE 4-4

Correlation of Landform Sediment Assemblages (LSA) in the Central Des Moines Valley with the Age-morphologic Groups of Upper Midwestern Alluvial Deposits Discussed in the Text

LSA	Age-morphologic group
high terrace	EMH
alluvial fan/colluvial slope	EMH
low terrace complex	LH
floodplain	Historic

133

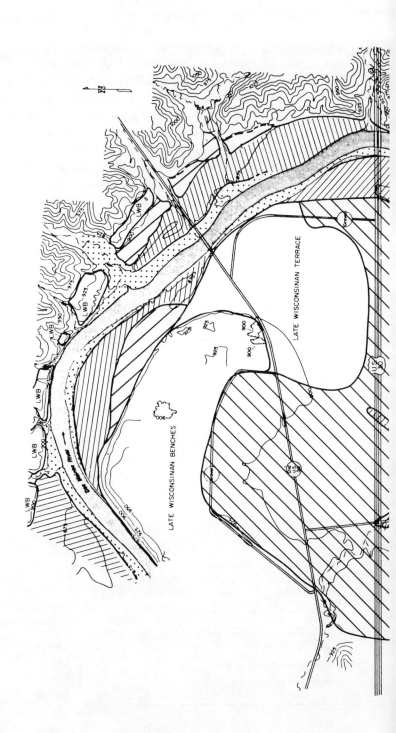

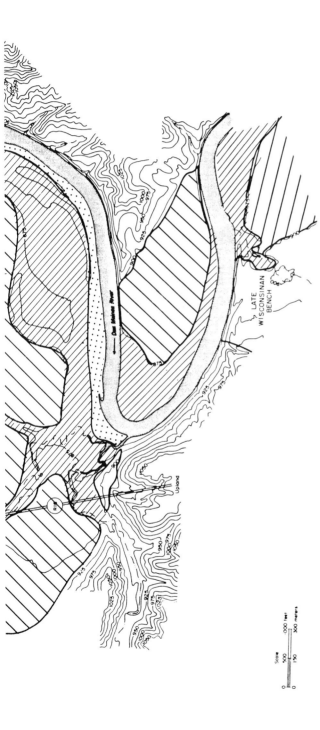

Figure 4-5. Map of the Boone Bottoms area in the central Des Moines Valley showing the distribution of EMH, LH, and Historic deposits. Wide diagonal pattern is EMH, narrow diagonal pattern is LH, and dot pattern is Historic. Note that large tracts of EMH deposits are present in this part of the valley. Many buried Archaic archaeological deposits are potentially present and late prehistoric sites are likely to be near the modern land surface.

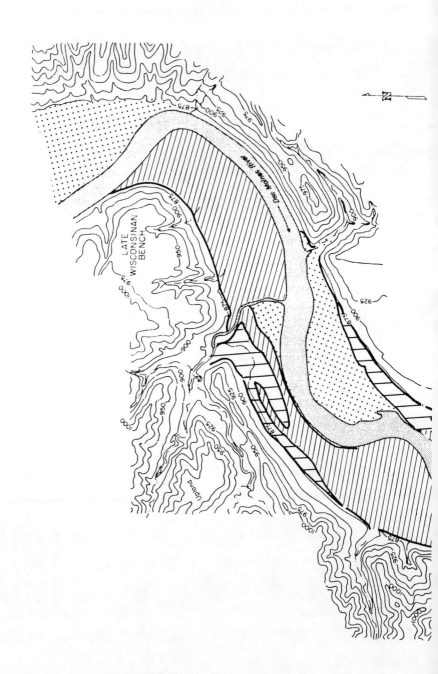

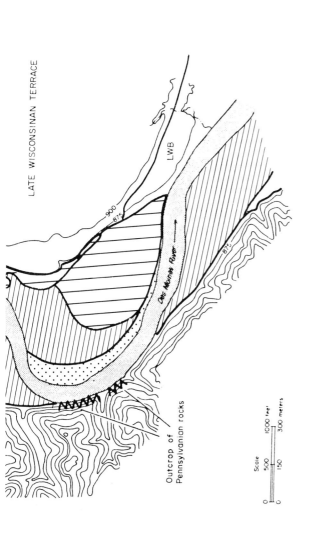

Figure 4-6.   Map of Hubby Bridge area in the central Des Moines Valley showing the distribution of EMH, LH, and Historic deposits. Wide diagonal pattern is EMH, narrow diagonal pattern is LH, and dot pattern is Historic. Note that, in contrast to the Boone Bottoms area, this reach of the valley is dominated by LH deposits. Most of the alluvium in this reach is too young to contain Archaic sites and many late prehistoric sites may be buried in this area.

TABLE 4-5

Preservation Potential for Buried Cultural Deposits in the Central Des Moines Valley
(Assuming All Modern Surfaces Cultivated)

	EMH		LH	Historic
Cultural Period	Alluvial Fans	High Terrace	Low Terrace	Floodplain
Paleoindian	++	+ (late)	−	−
Early and Middle Archaic	++	++	−	−
Late Archaic	++	+	++	−
Woodland	+−	−	++	−
Oneota and Great Oasis	+−	−	++	+−
Historic	−	−	+−	++

−, not possible; +−, low potential; +, moderate potential; ++, high potential
Note: Comparison of this table with Figures 4-5 and 4-6 allows for evaluation of geologic impacts on the archaeological record. This table also indicates where subsurface methods are necessary for locating archaeological sites from the various culture periods.

(floodplain LSA) are too young to contain prehistoric cultural components. Together the maps and Table 4-5 provide the information necessary to devise a plan for sampling the valley landscape for archaeological deposits not detectable using traditional surface survey and shallow test pit site-locating techniques. This approach also allows one to concentrate traditional survey and testing efforts in potentially the most productive parts of the present valley landscape.

If enough subsurface information is available to make accurate estimates of average thicknesses of the various LSAs or EMH-LH-Historic alluvium morphologic groupings, then the next step in devising sampling strategies for buried archaeological deposits is possible; volume estimates of the LSAs or morphologic groupings. Once these estimates are made, the volumes of excavation necessary to sample the valley deposits at the desired level can be determined (see Table 4-4 in Bettis and Hoyer 1986).

Another issue of utmost importance that this approach to assessing the archaeological record brings to light is that the depositional record in valleys is incomplete. Channel activity reworks existing deposits and destroys the context of archaeological materials associated with the deposits. Construction of maps such as those presented in Figures 4-5 and 4-6 permits an assessment of the percentage of past landscapes that have been destroyed by natural processes, and leads to more accurate explanations of the known distribution of archaeological deposits (Bettis and Benn 1989). Comparison of Figures 4-5 and 4-6 reveals that a greater percentage of EMH deposits are preserved in the portion of the valley covered by Figure 4-5 (Boone Bottoms) than that in Figure 4-6 (Hubby Bridge). The archaeological reconnaissance revealed that more Late Archaic and Woodland surface sites are present in the Boone Bottoms area than in the Hubby Bridge area (Benn and Rogers 1985). This could be prematurely interpreted to reflect a settlement pattern with greater preference for the Boone Bottom area during the Late Archaic and Woodland periods. More likely, however, is the probability that the present distribution of surface sites in the area reflects destruction of a higher percentage of EMH deposits and surfaces in the Hubby Bridge area. The net result is that Late Archaic and Woodland surface and near surface archaeological deposits are not as abundant in the Hubby Bridge area as in the Boone Bottoms area where EMH deposits, and associated Late Archaic and Woodland surface sites, are much more well preserved.

Failure to consider the differential preservation of deposits can obviously lead to erroneous conclusions about site distributions and therefore prehistoric culture (Hajic and Bettis 1989). Another aspect of this problem involves apparent gaps in the archaeological record. For example, there is a paucity of reported Middle Archaic cultural deposits in the central Des Moines Valley (Benn and Rogers 1985). Archaeological testing of EMH deposits subsequent to the geological investigations revealed that these sites exist, but are buried and therefore not visible to traditional site-locating techniques (Benn and Rogers 1985). The apparent gap in Middle Archaic occupation of the valley then, may be a geologic phenomenon rather than being reflective of a general lack of occupation during that culture period.

CONCLUSIONS

Associations of several morphologic properties of Upper Midwestern alluvial deposits and surface soils developed in the deposits are age-diagnostic. Well-horizonated surface soils with argillic horizons are developed in oxidized and mottled EMH deposits that accumulated before

4000 B.P. These soils and deposits are found on and beneath terraces in the region. LH alluvium is found beneath low terraces and floodplains in the area and accumulated after 3500 B.P. LH deposits are dark colored and have poorly horizonated surface soils that lack argillic horizons. Historic deposits often bury older alluvium, are oxidized and stratified, and exhibit slight pedogenic alteration.

Differences in the morphology of EMH and LH deposits and their associated surface soils are attributed to various impacts that climatic change has had on the fluvial system. The impacts include both direct and indirect components that influence hydrology, sedimentation, diagenesis, and pedogenesis.

Knowledge of the distribution of EMH, LH, and Historic deposits that comprise modern valley landscapes is essential for developing sampling strategies that are aimed at locating the record of the human past in valleys. An example from the central Des Moines Valley in Iowa shows that apparent Late Archaic and Woodland settlement patterns derived from traditional surface survey and shallow test pit sampling strategies may be more reflective of geological processes subsequent to the occupations than of an actual settlement pattern. Knowing the distribution and thickness of Historic deposits allows archaeologists to concentrate traditional sampling methods where they will be most effective for locating prehistoric sites, and avoid wasted efforts such as extensive surface survey or digging shallow test pits in areas of thick Historic deposits.

Application of the model outlined in this paper to valleys prior to archaeological surveys should result in survey strategies that are more scientifically sound and economically efficient than those relying on traditional methods alone. This will benefit archaeologists, planners, and anyone who uses the information derived from these undertakings.

REFERENCES

Anderson, J. D., and D. F. Overstreet
  1986 *The Archaeology of Coralville Lake, Iowa*, vol. 2, *Evolution of Holocene Landscapes*. Great Lakes Archaeological Research Center, Inc., Wauwatosa.

Benn, D. W., and E. A. Bettis III
  1985 *Archaeology and Landscapes in Saylorville Lake, Iowa*. Field Trip Guide, Association of Iowa Archaeologists Summer Meeting.

Benn, D. W., and L. D. Rogers
  1985 *Interpretive Overview of Cultural Resources in Saylorville Lake, Iowa*. Center for Archaeological Research Project CAR-627-II. Springfield.

Bettis, E. A. III
  1984   New Conventions for the Designation of Soil Horizons and Layers. *Plains Anthropologist* 29(103):57–59.

Bettis, E. A. III, and D. W. Benn
  1984   An Archaeological and Geomorphological Survey in the Central Des Moines River Valley, Iowa. *Plains Anthropologist* 29(105):211–227.
  1989   Geologic Context of Paleoindian and Archaic Occupations in a Portion of the Mississippi Valley, Iowa and Illinois. *Current Research in the Pleistocene* 6:85–86.

Bettis, E. A. III, and B. E. Hoyer
  1986   *Late Wisconsinan and Holocene Landscape Evolution and Alluvial Stratigraphy in the Saylorville Lake Area, Central Des Moines River Valley, Iowa.* Iowa Geological Survey, Open File Report 86-1.

Bettis, E. A. III, B. E. Hoyer, and E. R. Hajic
  1984   Alluvial/Colluvial Fan Development in the American Midwest. American Quaternary Association, Eighth Biennial Meeting, Program and Abstracts. p. 13.

Bettis, E. A. III, and J. P. Littke
  1987   *Holocene Alluvial Stratigraphy and Landscape Development in Soap Creek Watershed, Appanoose, Davis, Monroe, and Wapello Counties, Iowa.* Iowa Department of Natural Resources-Geological Survey Bureau. Open File Report 87-2.

Bettis, E. A. III, J. C. Prior, G. R. Hallberg, and R. L. Handy
  1986   Geology of the Loess Hills Region. *Proceedings of the Iowa Academy of Science* 93(3):78–85.

Bettis, E. A. III, and D. M. Thompson
  1981   Holocene Landscape Evolution in Western Iowa—Concepts, Methods and Implications for Archaeology. In *Current Directions in Midwestern Archaeology*, edited by S. F. Anfinson, pp. 1–14. Occasional Publications in Minnesota Anthropology No. 9. Minnesota Archaeological Society, St. Paul.
  1982   *Interrelations of Cultural and Fluvial Deposits in Northwest Iowa.* Association of Iowa Archaeologist's Fieldtrip Guidebook.

Birkeland, P. W.
  1984   *Soils and Geomorphology.* Oxford University Press, New York.

Brakenridge, G. R.
  1981   Late Quaternary Floodplain Sedimentation along the Pome de Terre River, Southern Missouri. *Quaternary Research* 15:62–76.

Bradbury, K. M., M. J. Graham, and R. V. Ruhe
  1977   *Monroe Reservoir, Indiana. Part I: Hydrologic Circulation, Sedimentation, and Water Chemistry.* Indiana University, Water Resources Research Center. Technical Report No. 87.

Carroll, D.
1970   *Rock Weathering*. Plenum Press, New York.

Cate, R. B., Jr.
1964   New Data on the Chemistry of Submerged Soils. *Economic Geology* 59:161–162.

Daniels, R. B., and R. H. Jordan
1966   *Physiographic History and the Soils, Entrenched Stream Systems, and Gullies, Harrison County, Iowa*. U.S. Dept. of Agriculture—Soil Conservation Service. Technical Bulletin 1348.

Daniels, R. B., G. H. Simonson, and R. L. Handy
1961   Ferrous Iron Content and Color of Sediments. *Soil Science* 191:378–382.

Guthrie, R. L., and J. E. Witty
1982   New Designations for Soil Horizons and Layers and the New Soil Survey Manual. *Soil Science Society of America Proceedings* 46:443–444.

Hajic, E. R.
1981   Geology and Paleopedology of the Koster Archaeological Site, Greene County, Illinois. Unpublished M.S. thesis, University of Iowa, Iowa City.
1985   Landscape Evolution and Archaeological Contexts in the Lower Illinois River Valley. *American Archaeology* 5(2):127–136.

Hajic, E. R., and E. A. Bettis III
1989   Settlement Patterns or Sediment Patterns?—A Stratigraphic Model for Interpretation of the Archaeological Record of the Upper Mississippi River Basin. Geological Society of American Annual Meeting, *Abstracts with Programs* 21:A214.

Hallberg, G. R., T. E. Fenton, and G. A. Miller
1978   Standard Weathering Zone Terminology for the Description of Quaternary Sediments in Iowa. In *Standard Procedures for Evaluation of Quaternary Materials in Iowa*, edited by G. R. Hallberg, pp. 75–109. Iowa Geological Survey, Technical Information Series No. 8.

Holliday, V. T.
1988   Genesis of a Late-Holocene soil chronosequence at the Lubbock Lake Archaeological Site, Texas. *Annals of the Association of American Geographers* 78(4):594–610.

Johnson, W. C.
1985   Revision of Terrace Chronologies along the Kansas River and Tributaries. *Proceedings of the Institute for Tertiary-Quaternary Studies*, 1985 Meeting, p. 21, Lawrence.

Kim, H. K.
1986   *Late-glacial and Holocene Environment in Central Iowa: A Comparative Study on Pollen Data from Four Sites*. Unpublished Ph.D. dissertation, University of Iowa, Iowa City.

Knox, J. C.
 1976 Concept of the Graded Stream. In *Theories of Landform Development,* edited by R. Flemal and W. Melhorn, pp. 169–198. Binghamton, State University of New York, Publications in Geomorphology.
 1983 Responses of River Systems to Holocene Climates. In *Late Quaternary Environments of the United States,* vol. 2, *The Holocene,* edited by H. E. Wright, Jr., pp. 26–41. University of Minnesota Press, Minneapolis.

Knox, J. C., P. F. McDowell, and W. C. Johnson
 1981 Holocene Fluvial Stratigraphy and Climatic Change in the Driftless Area, Wisconsin. In *Quaternary Paleoclimate,* edited by W. C. Manhaney, pp. 107–127. Geo Abstracts, Norwich, England.

McDowell, P. F.
 1983 Evidence of Stream Response to Holocene Climatic Change in a Small Wisconsin Watershed. *Quaternary Research* 19:100–116.

Muller, J. W. (editor)
 1975 *Sampling in Archaeology.* University of Arizona Press, Tucson.

Soil Survey Staff
 1975 *Soil Taxonomy: A Basic System of Soil Classification for Making and Interpreting Soil Surveys.* U.S. Department of Agriculture, Agriculture Handbook No. 436. Washington, D.C.

Styles, T. R.
 1985 *Holocene and Late Pleistocene Geology of the Napolean Hollow Site in the Lower Illinois Valley.* Kampsville Archaeological Center, Research Series vol. 5.

Thompson, D. M., and E. A. Bettis III
 1981 Out of Sight, Out of Planning: Assessing and Protecting Cultural Resources in Evolving Landscapes. *Contract Abstracts and CRM Archaeology* 2:16–22.

Van Nest, J., and E. A. Bettis III
 1990 Postglacial Response of a Stream in Central Iowa to Changes in Climate and Drainage Basin Factors. *Quaternary Research* 33:73–85.

Van Zant, K. L.
 1979 Late Glacial and Postglacial Pollen and Plant Macrofossils from Lake West Okoboji, Northwestern Iowa. *Quaternary Research* 12:358–380.

Vreeken, W. J.
 1984 Soil-landscape Chronograms for Pedochronological Analysis. *Geoderma* 34:149–164.

Walker, P. H.
 1966 *Postglacial Environments in Relation to Landscape and Soils on the Cary Drift, Iowa.* Agriculture and Home Economics Experiment Station, Research Bulletin 549, Iowa State University, Ames.

Walker, P. H., and R. J. Conventry
1976   Soil Profile Development in Some Alluvial Deposits of Eastern New South Wales. *Australian Journal of Soil Research* 14:305–317.

Webb, T. III, E. J. Cushing, and H. E. Wright Jr.
1983   Holocene Changes in the Vegetation of the Midwest. In *Late Quaternary Environments of the United States*, Vol. 2, *The Holocene*, edited by H. E. Wright, Jr., pp. 142–165. University of Minnesota Press, Minneapolis.

Wiant, M. D., E. R. Hajic, and T. R. Styles
1983   Napolean Hollow and Koster Site Stratigraphy: Implications for Holocene Landscape Evolution and Studies of Archaic Period Settlement Patterns in the Lower Illinois River Valley. In *Archaic Hunters and Gatherers in the American Midwest*, edited by J. L. Phillips and J. A. Brown, pp. 147–164. Academic Press, New York.

5

PAUL GOLDBERG

Micromorphology, Soils, and Archaeological Sites

Most soils, whether or not they are associated with archaeological sites, are studied with traditional laboratory techniques that include granulometry (grain-size, or particle-size analysis), chemical analyses (e.g., pH, calcium carbonate, organic matter, and iron content), and mineralogical investigations of the heavy mineral and clay mineral fractions. An excellent illustrative example of the stratigraphic and palaeoenvironmental study of soils, some associated with archaeological finds, can be found in Cremaschi (1987). While no doubt these methods provide valuable and useful results, most of these techniques make use of bulk samples collected from a particular horizon or layer. Consequently, their ability to pick up subtle textural or chemical variations within the sample resulting from a combination of pedogenic, geologic or anthropogenic events—commonly spatially and temporally superimposed upon one another—is limited.

A technique that is capable of discriminating such events or sequence of events is that of micromorphology, the study of undisturbed soil (or sediment) material in thin section. The purpose of this paper is to illustrate the use of micromorphology in the study of soils and apparent soils from three archaeological sites in the Old World, and to demon-

145

strate its capability of sorting out an often complicated mixture of pedological, geological, and anthropogenic events. Conclusions based from such studies have implications that concern not only the development of the soil itself but also larger issues related to paleoclimatic reconstruction, stratigraphic correlation, and past human activities.

TECHNIQUE

The technique of micromorphology made its debut about 50 years ago when Kubiena (1938) illustrated how microscopic observations using petrographic thin sections could be used to make inferences concerning the processes involved in the formation of soils. Though petrography was a well-established discipline in geology at the time, Kubiena was the first to apply the concept of petrography to the soil context. The idea was slow to catch on, and it was not until the mid-1960s that it received a renewed boost with the appearance of Brewer's (1964) *Fabric and Mineral Analysis of Soils*. This book provided a wealth of descriptive terms that could be used to describe and interpret soils and their formation processes. Since publication of Brewer's volume the study and use of micromorphological techniques dramatically increased, but it became increasingly clear that in Brewer's scheme, description and interpretation (genesis) were in some cases too closely intertwined. This lead to the publication of the *Handbook for Soil Thin Section Description* (Bullock et al. 1985) which introduced new and different micromorphological terms that emphasized objective descriptive criteria, independent of genetic connotations.

The use of micromorphology in archaeological contexts—including soils, sediments, and archaeological materials, such as pottery and plaster—has been even slower to get off the mark, as shown by only the handful of papers on such subjects, many of them devoted to the petrographic analysis of pottery (see Goldberg 1983). The dearth of information on archaeological uses of micromorphology should be at least partially remedied with the publication of Courty et al. (1989), which provides details about the practice and application of micromorphology in archaeology, as well as several case studies.

Thin-section preparation techniques of soils and soft sediments differ somewhat from those used in petrography, where rocks are generally indurated and can be easily cut. Soft materials must be first hardened and essentially transformed into a rock before a thin section can be made. Thus a thin section from soft material is generally prepared from a block

(~10 × 5 × 7 cm) collected in the field, and transported to the laboratory where it is oven-dried for several days at ~60° C. It is then impregnated with either polyester resin or epoxy under vacuum, and sliced with a rock saw, using kerosene. The block is finally mounted on a glass slide and polished to the standard thickness of 30 μm. (For methods, see Brewer 1976; Murphy 1986.)

EXAMPLES

The following presents three examples of the application of micromorphology to the study of soils and sediments associated with archaeological sites in order to show how such analyses can contribute to a fuller understanding of the formation of these soils and sediments. This information also has important archaeological ramifications relating to site function and palaeoenvironments. Although these examples were chosen from sites of different ages and geographic site settings, the ability of the technique to answer pedological, geological and archaeologically related questions should be clear.

Berekhat Ram, Golan Heights

The Acheulean site of Berekhat Ram (Figure 5-1) is situated on the volcanic plateau of the Golan Heights, inside an extinct volcanic crater which is now filled by a natural lake. Excavations at the site as well as a geological trench to the north of it exposed two basalt flows and a red clayey layer, with two subunits, between them (Figure 5-2; see Goren-Inbar 1985 for details). This red clay is 1 to 3 m thick and contains a level of Acheulian artifacts ~25 cm thick, about 95 cm below the top of the clay.

At the top of the profile is the Upper Kramim Basalt which yielded a $^{40}Ar/^{39}Ar$ date of 233,000 ± 3000 yr B.P. (Feraud et al. 1983). Directly underlying it is the upper subunit of the clay layer, from which four samples were collected from an exposure ~25 m to the north of the excavation, and one from the lower subunit in the area of the excavation itself (Goldberg 1987). This latter unit, the lowermost in the clay layer, is not exposed in the northern profile (Table 5-1). The clay layer overlies the locally weathered Lower Kramim Basalt that was dated to ~800,000 yr B.P. (Goren-Inbar 1985).

147

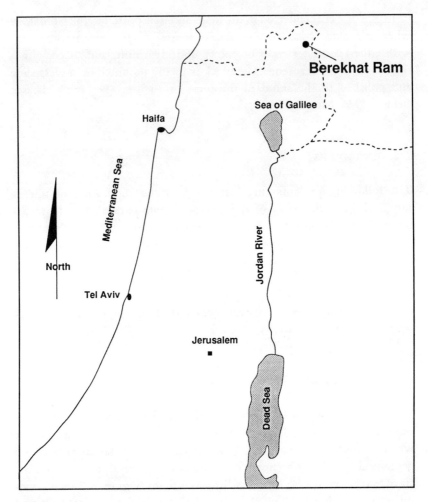

Figure 5-1. Map of northern Israel showing location of Berekhat Ram.

Of principal concern here is the origin of this red clay layer—whether it is a soil, a zone of hydrothermal alteration, a sediment, or all of the above—and its relation to the archaeological materials. Though previous analyses had been performed by Singer (1983), his results were not definitive with respect to several of these aspects.

Figure 5-2. Berekhat Ram, exposure north of excavation area, showing clay layer and Upper Kramim Basalt; Lower Kramim Basalt is concealed in this photograph.

Micromorphology. The five samples described above were examined and briefly described using the nomenclature of Bullock et al. (1985). (For complete descriptions, see Goldberg 1987).

The coarse fraction of sample 5 (lowermost sample of clay; from excavation) consists of rounded sand-size grains of quartz and iron pisolites, and lesser amounts of angular quartz silt and fragments of volcanic glass, tuff and angular chert (Figure 5-3a). The fine fraction consists of red- and orange-brown clay with a weakly developed, granostriated, b-fabric (see Glossary for explanation of terms).

Pedological features are expressed by two types of argillans (clay coatings) on voids. The most evident is the filling of irregular cracks by microlaminated reddish brown clay. The second type, which overlies the first, is made up of thin discontinuous films of bright yellow, limpid clay.

Samples 2, 3 and 4 (from profile north of archaeological excavation) are by and large similar to each other but are quite different from sample 5, which they overly; they are described as an ensemble. These samples contain only traces of quartz sand; quartz silt is much more

TABLE 5-1

Summary of Stratigraphy at Berekhat Ram

I. UPPER KRAMIN BASALT (233,000 ± 3000 yrs B.P.)

II. CLAY LAYER:

Profile north of archaeological site:

Sample No.	Depth	Color (dry)	Description
1	0–30	5YR5/1	Crumbly weathered basalt, with small pieces (−2cm) of fresher basalt
2	30–45	5YR5/1	Hard, coarse, gritty, crumbly clay
3	45–60	5YR4/6	Hard, coarse crumbly to massive, slightly gritty clay with fresh basalt pebbles and scoria fragments
4	60–110	5YR5/6	Clay, similar to that in no. 3 but slightly more massive

Profile from archaeological site:

5		5YR3/6	Sandy clay containing sandstone and limestone fragments and iron pisolites (this unit not exposed in profile north of site)

III. LOWER KRAMIM BASALT (~800,000 yrs B.P.)

abundant as are weathered fragments of scoria, basalt, and tuff (Figure 5-3b). They also contain rounded sand-size grains of red-brown papules similar to the matrix in the lower subunit. The fine fraction of these three samples is also strikingly different from the first sample and is composed of fine silt-size grains of weathered volcanic materials mixed within a dark red-brown clay, with an undifferentiated b-fabric. Clay coatings are very prominent and consist of well oriented and moderately birefringent, non-laminated to regularly- and cross-laminated limpid, light yellow-brown and dusty, dark yellow-brown clay; the red-brown type of clay coating is absent.

Sample no. 1, the uppermost sample, is composed of exfoliated vesicular and massive basalt from the Upper Kramim Basalt. Conspicuous is the abundance and distribution of clay coatings and infillings, which not only fill vesicles within the basalt but also cracks between

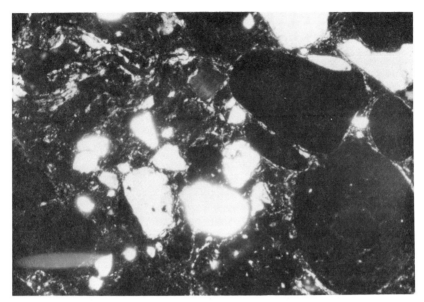

Figure 5-3a. Photomicrograph of lower unit (sample no. 5) from Berekhat Ram. Note the rounded sand size grains of quartz and iron pisolites as well as finer quartz silt fraction. The light areas between grains are illuviated red-brown clay. Cross-polarized light (XPL); field length = 1.7 mm.

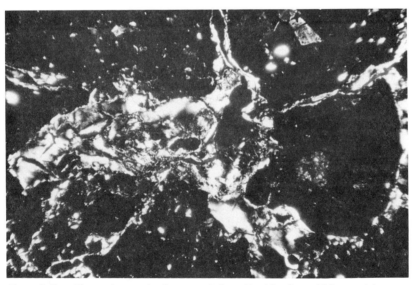

Figure 5-3b. Photomicrograph of upper unit from Berekhat Ram. This material contrasts sharply with that of sample no. 5 as illustrated by the absence of quartz sand and pisolites, and the abundance of weathered volcanic fragments (large dark grain on right) in a more abundant, clayier matrix. Also striking are the prominent clay coatings (center of photograph) consisting of laminated light yellow-brown limpid clay. XPL; field length = 1.7 mm.

151

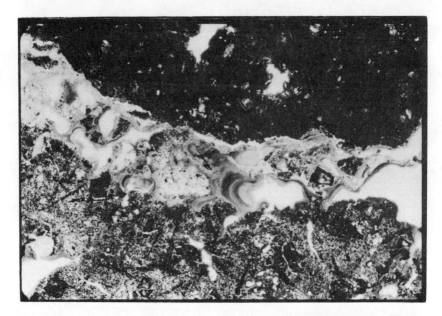

Figure 5-3c. Sample no. 1 from Berekhat Ram exhibiting well-oriented yellow clay filling voids between exfoliation shells of the Upper Kramim Basalt. Note the darker and
fresher basalt at the top and the weathered exfoliation shell at the base of the photograph. Plane-polarized light (PPL); field length = 1.4 mm.

exfoliation shells (Figure 5-3c). These coatings are identical to those in
samples 2, 3, and 4 and are composed of bright yellow, limpid well-
oriented, microlaminated clay.

Interpretation and Discussion of Berekhat Ram Profile. These micromorphological observations demonstrate that the clay layer is in fact
composed of two markedly different lithological units. The lower unit
(sample no. 5; Figure 5-3a) is composed of quartz sand and ferruginous
pisolites in a red-brown matrix, which point to colluviation of materials
derived from the nearby slopes of Mt. Hermon, ~0.5 km to the north
where pisolitic sandstone crops out. The absence of sedimentary structures, such as bedding, suggests that alluviation was not the mode of
deposition, though pedogenesis might have obliterated some primary
structures. The quartz silt is ubiquitous in Israeli soils (Yaalon and Ganor
1973) and is ultimately of aeolian origin. The illuvial red-brown clay

voids, infillings, and the grano-striated fabric also indicate that this lower unit is partially pedogenic in origin, though at present the paleoenvironmental significance of these pedological features is not clear.

Micromorphological analyses also demonstrate the sedimentary origin of the upper portion of the profile, represented by the upper clay subunit: the markedly different composition of primarily weathered basaltic materials in a homogeneous brown clay indicates that it is not a weathering product of the underlying layer but that it was formed from a different volcanic source in the area. It is most probably of local colluvial origin as shown by rounded quartz sand and red-brown clay papules that have been reworked from the lower layer.

The abundant yellow argillans also attest to post-depositional modification of the upper clay subunit. Though these were originally thought to result from pedological processes, this interpretation was abandoned because of the presence of the limpid clay infillings in both the clay layer and in between the weathered exfoliation leaves of the Upper Kramim Basalt (Figure 5-3c). These features demonstrate that the infilling must have occurred after this upper basalt flow was emplaced and is most probably related to the presence of groundwater concentrated at the contact between the clay and basalt (cf. Singer 1983). In sum, the clay layer profile at Berekhat Ram depicts a complex sequence involving two sedimentary units and postdepositional modification by pedogenesis and groundwater.

In addition to the pedological and geological arguments, an understanding of the origin of such a profile should permit the archaeologist to better evaluate and interpret the lateral and vertical distribution of the artifacts. The overall colluvial nature of the clay and pedologic activity in the lower unit could explain the distribution of the artifacts through a band ~25 cm thick as well as suggest that their present-day positions may not exactly correspond to their original ones.

The Bronze Age/Neolithic Site of Fort Harrouard
(Eure et Loir), France

The site of Fort Harrouard (Figure 5-4), situated on a chalk plateau along the Eure River, was excavated during the 1930s by Abbé Philippe who uncovered Neolithic and Bronze Age remains, associated metallurgy and large rampart constructions, and Iron Age and Roman occupations (Philippe 1936, 1937). The plateau is partly covered with Tertiary "flint with

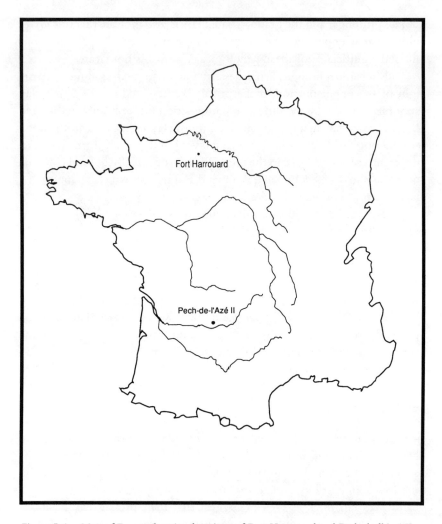

Figure 5-4.   Map of France showing locations of Fort Harrouard and Pech-de-l'Azé II.

clays" and in local patches, the Fountainebleau sands and Pleistocene loess, the latter occurring particularly along slopes (Dewolf 1981).

The studied profile is located in Area II (Mohen and Villes 1984) which consists of soft, loessial sediment at the base (units Y1 and Y2, see below), capped by a dark brown silty layer (Middle Neolithic) (unit Y3) and abruptly truncated by a chalky talus construction (Late Neo-lithic)(Table 5-2; Figure 5-5). Micromorphology was used to clarify

TABLE 5-2

Stratigraphic Units at Fort Harrouard, France

Unit	Depth (cm)	Color (dry)	Description
Y3 (upper)	0–15	10YR5/4 to 4/4	Coarse silt with abundant coarse fragments of flints, many mm-sized charcoal fragments and sherds. Massive structure, many fine pores. Flat, sharp, regular boundary resulting from truncation by the Late Neolithic talus construction; generally no effervescence with HCl but top shows penetration of lime to a depth of 1 cm from the overlying talus
Y2 (middle)	15–60	10YR5/6 to 6/4	Silt with a few coarse flint fragments, massive structure, abundant fine pores and tubules filled with darker material (10YR5/4), no effervescence with HCl; flat, regular, clear boundary, characterized by a change in color. A few sherds and bones occurred throughout; some charcoal in the upper part
Y1 (bottom)	60–75	10YR7/4	Fine silt, massive structure, fine porosity with well expressed whitish coatings on pores (pseudomycelium) and strong effervescence with HCl; flat, regular, sharp boundary characterized by a change in color

whether the dark layer represented a soil, an anthropic feature or possibly both. For a more complete discussion of this study, see Courty et al. (1989).

Micromorphology. Unit Y1 (bottom loess) displays a massive to spongy and crumbly structure. The coarse fraction consists mostly of

Figure 5-5.   Fort Harrouard, Area II showing white, Late Neolithic rampart in lower half of photograph, truncating dark layer of unit Y3; higher Bronze Age rampart is visible to the right of the standing figures.

calcareous and quartz silt (30 μm) and some quartz sand (200–300 μm) mixed with a dusty fine fraction consisting of calcitic clay (Figure 5-6a). Pedofeatures are expressed by coatings of needle-shaped calcite and micritic hypocoatings (see Glossary). No signs of illuvial clay were found. Both pedological and anthropogenic features are poorly developed indicating that this lowermost unit is essentially a weakly weathered loess with micromorphological characteristics similar to those from late glacial loesses in the area (Fedoroff and Goldberg 1982).

Unit Y2 (middle loess) is represented by the following characteristics. The structure is homogeneous and massive to spongy. The very coarse fraction (coarse silt and sand) is more abundant and contains some flints and abundant charcoal; silt is heterogeneously mixed in with the fine fraction, which is reddish brown to yellowish brown and distributed as aggregates (100 μm) with low birefringence. It is completely noncalcareous and contains abundant microcontrasted particles (see Glossary) that produce a dusty appearance or aspect. Pedofeatures are expressed by dusty, reddish brown clay coatings which are moderately integrated into the groundmass (see Glossary) as well as localized around voids or irreg-

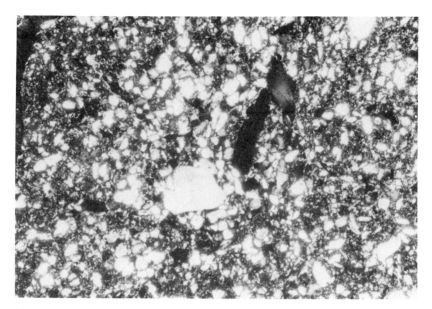

Figure 5-6a. Fort Harrouard, bottom loess unit showing quartz silt mixed with dusty fine matrix composed of calcareous clay. The sparkly aspect of this sample is due both to the presence of quartz silt and the calcareous groundmass. XPL; field length = 1.4 mm.

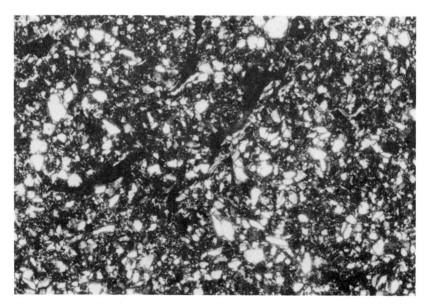

Figure 5-6b. Fort Harrouard, upper decalcified unit with disaggregated charcoal fragments. Note also the darkness of the sample in comparison to Figure 5-4a and the abundance of micro-contrasted particles which furnish the dark color of the unit in the field. XPL; field length = 1.4 mm.

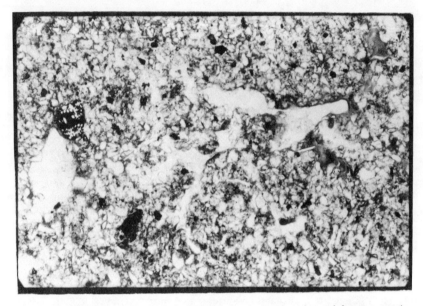

Figure 5-6c.   Fort Harrouard, upper decalcified unit showing charcoal fragments, microcontrasted particles and void coatings composed of dusty, non-laminated clay (void in upper right part of photograph). PPL; field length = 1.4 mm.

ularly distributed around the surface of aggregates and fine sand grains.

Y3 (upper unit) exhibits a massive to spongy microstructure, slightly fissured. The coarse fraction is composed of very coarse elements (0.2 to 10 mm) represented by numerous grains of flint (from "flint with clays") and abundant pieces of disaggregated charcoal (Figures 5-6b,c) as well as quartz sand, traces of bone, fine sand and fine silt. The fine fraction is darkish brown, dusty, and contains abundant, very fine (<5 μm) phytoliths. The dusty part of the fine fraction comprises poorly sorted charcoal and microcontrasted particles (Figure 5-6c), mixed with eluviated portions of the groundmass. Pedological features include insect excrements, and reddish brown, dusty, non-laminated clay coatings in voids (Figure 5-6c); thin, dark grey calcitic textural coatings also occur in this same area.

Interpretation of Fort Harrouard Profile. The above observations illustrate that the darker layer at the top of the profile unit (unit Y3) represents a soil developed on a natural deposit of originally calcareous loess (unit Y1) at the base that has been partially affected by anthropogenic activity. In the first stages of development, the upper part of the then extant loess was simultaneously undergoing decalcification and reworking by biological activity. This is well illustrated by the decalcified nature of the middle loessial sample (Y2) and the well-developed spongy and crumbly microstructure and channels. This initial phase was soon followed by clay illuviation that is well expressed in Y2. However, the clay coatings displayed here are too poorly expressed and the manifestations of biological activity are too abundant in comparison to those of a typical Holocene soil profile that forms under forest cover in this area (N. Fedoroff, personal communication, 1985). Two interpretations are possible. In the first case, the soil could have developed under more of a grassland environment, with some trees but predominantly grasses, rather than under a forested one. In the second case, the soil may be only in its initial stages of formation, and well-developed clay coatings might not have had time to form. However, the spongy microstructure and abundant organic matter are more in line with the first interpretation.

Toward the end of pedogenesis anthropic effects modified the soil as shown in Y3 by the abundance of charcoal and the mixing of both eluviated and illuviated horizons (not illustrated here, see Courty et al. 1989). In addition, the fine fragmentation of the charcoal and its dispersion throughout the unit points to biological activity of plants (e.g., roots) and animals (e.g., worms, and insects). Moreover, the occurrence of dusty illuvial clay within the groundmass and voids, as well as around some of the charcoal grains and aggregates demonstrates that illuviation took place after the episodes of burning and biological activity. These various biogenic and anthropogenic features may be related to cultivation of the leveled soil but as yet there is no other evidence to support this hypothesis. Translocation of calcitic silt marks the end of the evolution of the sequence and is most probably related to water percolation after the overlying talus was built.

Rockshelter of Pech-de-l'Azé II, Southwestern France

The Dordogne region in southwestern France is rich in prehistoric cave and rockshelter sites (Laville et al. 1980). These are commonly filled with coarse bedrock debris (*éboulis*), generally of cryoclastic origin. Within these layers are beds that are redder in color and richer in clay than the

Figure 5-7. Photograph of Section 2 from Pech-de-l'Azé II Rockshelter. In this profile only the reddened layer of Bed 8 is visible and is expressed as an irregular dark band in the lower quarter of the photograph above a basal stony layer. Measure is 50 cm long.

surrounding layers, which has lead researchers to interpret them as paleosols with abundant illuvial clay that formed during weathering intervals associated with warmer (either interstadial or interglacial) conditions
(Laville et al. 1980:73).

The rockshelter of Pech-de-l'Azé II (Figure 5-4) is situated about 5
km from the town of Sarlat. Though the sediments are relatively im-
poverished in *éboulis*, they do contain reddened units (Beds 8, 6, and 4;
Figure 5-7) of which only Beds 8 and 6 are discussed here. These were
studied micromorphologically in order to assess the extent of pedological
development (see Goldberg 1979, for details). Field descriptions of these
units are presented in Table 5-3 (freely translated from Laville 1973).

Micromorphologically, the material from Bed 8 consists predominantly of quartz sand and bedrock fragments in a clayey groundmass
with a gefuric (see Glossary) to close porphyric (see Glossary) related
distribution (Figure 5-8a). In addition, the upper part of the bed contains
several bone fragments and exhibits a weakly developed banded fabric,
consisting of fine laminae of coarser and finer material (a result of alternate freezing and thawing). Most notable however, is the absence of
illuvial clay which would be expected if this were indeed a true paleosol
developed under temperate conditions.

A similar situation exists for Bed 6 where samples were collected
from two localities in the rockshelter. Although there are lateral variations, a similar picture is obtained in both areas. In its upper part Bed 6 is
composed principally of quartz grains, bedrock fragments, and occasional pieces of bone in a reddish brown clay matrix, commonly rich in iron

TABLE 5-3

Description of Selected Reddened Units from Pech-de-L'Azé II Rockshelter
(modified from Laville 1973)

Bed No.	Age	Description
8	Riss I; Riss I/II	Contains abundant, well-rounded *éboulis* in a brown clayey sand matrix
6 (upper)	Riss II; Riss II/III	Consists of brown-red sandy clay with altered *éboulis*, and clay coatings on ped surfaces
6 (lower)		Composed of red-yellow silty sandy clay becoming dark brown clayey somewhat silty sand at the base with some rounded *éboulis*

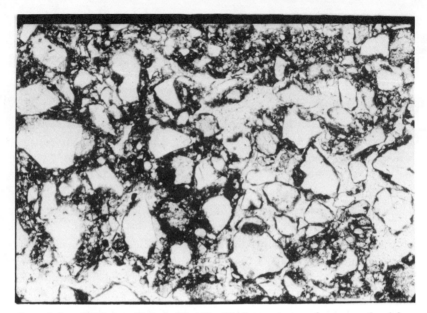

Figure 5-8a. Bed 8 from Pech-de-l'Azé II exhibiting a mixture of quartz sand and finer clayey groundmass. PPL; field length = 1.4 mm.

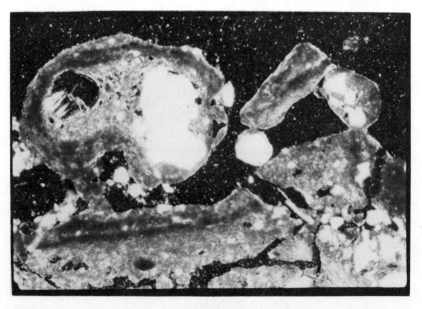

Figure 5-8b. Bed 6 from Pech-de-l'Azé II illustrating thick, dusty clay and silt coatings, both in voids and around grains. XPL; field length = 1.4 mm.

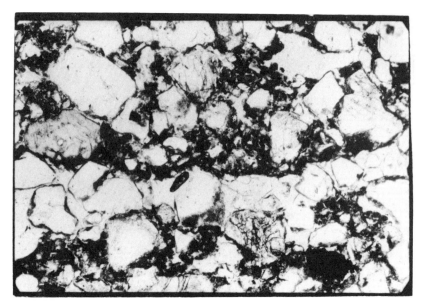

Figure 5-8c.   Bed 6 from Pech-de-l'Azé II showing development of banded fabric in its lower part. This is generally ascribed to result from freeze-thaw activity. PPL; field length = 1.4 mm.

oxides. In addition, Bed 6 contains sand–size aggregates (not originally described by Goldberg 1979) comprised of the same clay as in the matrix, as well as sandy detritus from the breakdown of the bedrock. Surrounding both the aggregates and individual grains are coatings (~50–100 μm thick) of coarse, moderately oriented, dusty red-brown clay, with traces of fine quartz silt (Figure 5-8b); this same red-brown clay also partially fills intergranular voids. In the lower part, as in Bed 8, a weakly developed banded fabric can be observed (Figure 5-8c).

While such clay coatings and infillings superficially resemble cutans, their thickness, poor sorting and geometry (they completely coat grains and aggregates) suggest that they are more likely a result of translocation of coarse clay and silt associated with turbation and movement of grains under saturated, poorly drained and possibly cold conditions, such as a mud slurry or solifluction deposit (Courty et al. 1989). This interpretation fits well with the occurrence of banded fabric in the lower part of both beds (Figure 5-8c) and the occurrence of rounded aggregates

163

in the upper part which probably result from cryoturbation phenomena (Fedoroff and Goldberg 1982).

In sum, the micromorphological evidence for soil development in these reddish layers appears to be lacking since there are no signs of true pedological clay illuviation. Similar conclusions have been reached for thicker and more pronounced red layers at the site of La Micoque, based on the observation of tens of large thin sections (Courty, personal communication; Goldberg, personal observation of the Micoque thin sections). There, solifluction of red, clay-rich Tertiary weathering products (*sidérolithique*) seems responsible for the origin of these layers.

CONCLUSIONS

These examples were chosen to illustrate the occurrence of soils and soil-like features affiliated with archaeological sites and contexts, and to show how micromorphology can be used to interpret them. Although similar types of micromorphological studies of soils and sediments exist (e.g., Courty and Nørnberg 1985; Fisher and Macphail 1985; Macphail 1986; Macphail et al. 1987), their total number is small in comparison to the number of archaeological sites in the world. Moreover, other than the variety of the settings and situations, these particular examples attempted to show how micromorphology can provide refinements or avenues of interpretation that other methodologies are less successful or capable of doing.

In the case of Berekhat Ram, micromorphology clearly revealed the presence of a complex profile of combined sedimentary and pedological origin with additional modification by groundwater. Although Singer (1983) alluded to such a potpourri, his analyses were less than conclusive, especially those of grain size. At Fort Harrouard the dark layer was found to be a result of both anthropic and pedogenic effects as demonstrated by the clay coatings around charcoal fragments. Such evidence would have gone unrecognized in most routine soil analyses. Finally, at Pech-de-l'Azé micromorphology demonstrated a diminished role of pedogenesis in the formation of the reddish soil units which, until recently, figured strongly in the chronological and paleoenvironmental definition of the Pleistocene sequence in southwestern France: although these beds are red and relatively enriched in clay, there is no micromorphological evidence to suggest that they are soils; deposition of reworked Tertiary plateau clays seems a better alternative hypothesis.

Finally, the intent of this note is not to deride the genuine and valuable efforts and contributions of my colleagues. Rather it is to show that micromorphology is a sensitive technique that can be used to make inferences about the origin, depositional and post-depositional processes associated with soils and soil-like features in archaeological contexts. Moreover, it can help to critically evaluate the results of other analyses which are less sensitive in detecting the evidence for pedogenesis. Micromorphology is obviously not a technique that by itself can unequivocally answer all questions, but when used in conjunction with other analytical techniques (e.g., SEM, Edax) it represents an excellent first step in dealing with such problems.

ACKNOWLEDGMENTS

I thank several of my colleagues who in one way or another helped with the individual research projects cited above: Prof. François Bordes, M.-A. Courty, N. Fedoroff, N. Goren-Inbar, H. Laville, and J.-P. Mohen. The comments from V. Holliday and anonymous reviewers are gratefully acknowledged. M. Horton helped with the photographs.

REFERENCES

Brewer, R.
  1964   *Fabric and Mineral Analysis of Soils.* J. Wiley and Sons, N.Y.
  1976   *Fabric and Mineral Analysis of Soils,* 2d ed. Krieger, Huntington, N.Y.

Bullock, P., N. Fedoroff, A. Jongerius, G. Stoops, and T. Tursina
  1985   *Handbook for Soil Thin Section Description.* Waine Research Publications, Wolverhampton.

Courty, M. A., and P. Nørnberg
  1985   Comparison between Buried Uncultivated and Cultivated Iron Age Soils on the West Coast of Jutland, Denmark. *ISKOS* 5:57–69.

Courty, M. A., P. Goldberg, and R. I. Macphail
  1989   *Soils, Micromorphology and Archaeology.* Cambridge University Press.

Cremaschi, M.
  1987   *Paleosols and Vetusols in the Central Po Plain (Northern Italy).* Milano, Edizioni Unicopli.

Dewolf, Y.
1981   Le contact Ile-de-France, Basse-Normandie. Evolution géodynamique, *Mém. et Docts. de Géogr.* Editions CNRS, Paris.

Fedoroff, N., and P. Goldberg
1982   Comparative Micromorphology of Two Late Pleistocene Palaeosols in the Paris Basin. *Catena* 9:227–251.

Feraud, G., D. York, C. Hall, N. Goren, and H. P. Schwarcz
1983   40Ar/39Ar Age Limit for an Acheulean Site in Israel (Sample Site: Berekhat Ram). *Nature* 304:263–265.

Fisher, P. F., and R. I. Macphail
1985   Studies of Archaeological Soils and Deposits by Micromorphological Techniques. In *Palaeoenvironmental Investigations: Research Design, Methods and Data Analysis*, edited by N. R. J. Fieller, D. D. Gilbertson, and N. G. A. Ralph, pp. 93–12. British Archaeological Reports, International Series 258.

Goldberg, P.
1979   Micromorphology of Pech de l'Azé II Sediments. *Journal of Archaeological Science* 6:17–47.
1983   Applications of Micromorphology in Archaeology. In *Soil Micromorphology*, edited by P. Bullock and C. P. Murphy, pp. 139–150. A B Academic Publishers, Berkhamsted.
1987   Soils, Sediments and Acheulian Artifacts at Berekhat Ram, Golan Heights. In *Micromorphologie des Sols—Soil Micromorphology*, edited by N. Fedoroff, L. M. Bresson, and M. A. Courty, pp. 583–589. Association Française pour l'Etude du Sol (A.F.E.S.), Plaisir.

Goren-Inbar, N.
1985   The Lithic Assemblage of the Berekhat Ram Acheulian site, Golan Heights. *Paléorient* 11:7–28.

Kubiena, W. L.
1938   *Micropedology.* Collegiate Press, Ames, Iowa.

Laville, H.
1973   *Climatologie et chronologie du Paléolithique en Périgord: étude sédimentologique de depôts en grottes et sous abris.* Thèse de Doctorat d'Etat ès Sciences Naturelles, Université de Bordeaux I.

Laville, H., J.-P. Rigaud, and J. Sackett
1980   *Rockshelters of the Perigord: Geological Stratigraphy and Archaeological Succession.* Academic Press, New York.

Macphail, R. I.
1986   Paleosols in Archaeology: Their Role in Understanding Flandrian Pedogenesis. In *Paleosols: Their Recognition and Interpretation*, edited by V. P. Wright, pp. 263–290. Blackwell, Oxford.

Macphail, R. I., J. C. C. Romans, and L. Robertson
1987   The Application of Micromorphology to the Understanding of Holocene Soil

Development in the British Isles; with Special Reference to Early Cultivation. In *Micromorphologie des Sols—Soil Micromorphology*, edited by N. Fedoroff, L. M. Bresson and M. A. Courty, pp. 647–657. Association Française pour l'Etude du Sol (A.F.E.S.), Plaisir.

Mohen, J.-P., and A. Villes
   1984   La Reprise des Fouilles au Fort-Harrouard à Sorel-Mousel (Eure-et-Loir). *Bulletin de la Societé Amis d'Anet et Syndicat d'Initiative*, Serie Nouvelle, no. 8.

Murphy, C. P.
   1986   *Thin Section Preparation of Soils and Sediments*. A B Academic Publishers, Berkhamsted.

Philippe, J.
   1936   Le Fort-Harrouard. *L'Anthropologie* 46:257–301; 541–612.
   1937   Le Fort-Harrouard. *L'Anthropologie* 47:253–308.

Singer, A.
   1983   The Paleosols of Berekhat Ram, Golan Heights: Morphology, Chemistry, Mineralogy, Genesis. *Israel Journal of Earth-Sciences* 32:93–104.

Yaalon, D., and E. Ganor
   1973   The Influence of Dust on Soils during the Quaternary. *Soil Science* 116:146–155.

6

BRUCE G. GLADFELTER

Soil Properties of Sediments in Wadi Feiran, Sinai: A Geoarchaeological Interpretation

For nearly a century northern Sinai and the adjoining Negev have been important areas for an understanding of Levantine prehistory during the late Pleistocene (Bar-Yosef 1984). However, nothing was known about the Paleolithic of southern Sinai until this decade when an Upper Paleolithic site was reported in the upper drainage of Wadi el Sheikh (Belfer-Cohen and Goldberg 1982) at the oasis of Tarfat el Quidrein (Figure 6-1). Subsequent excavation of three, large Upper Paleolithic sites in the small basin of Wadi Abu Noshra, a tributary to Wadi el Sheikh at Tarfat el Quidrein, has uncovered extensive surfaces of occupation sealed within a thick aggradation of fine alluvium and other deposits (Phillips 1987a, 1987b, 1988). This paper examines soil properties of these sediments as this evidence contributes to an interpretation of the archaeology.

Archaeological models of hunter-gatherer adaptations have been proposed which focus on strategies of exploitation, and social organization and mobility (see Phillips 1987a:174–177 and references). They are based on the temporal and spatial availability of resources that would characterize different environments. Briefly, a model of "residential mobility" depicts highly mobile foragers in arid or semiarid environments who are engaged in well-developed gathering activities and practice for-

169

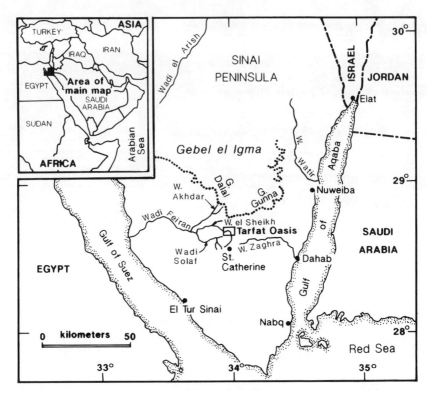

Figure 6-1. Map of selected locations in southern Sinai. Figure 6-3 is an enlargement of the segment of Wadi el Sheikh outlined by a rectangle in the central portion of the map.

tuitous hunting occasioned by scarce resources, including water. Alternatively, seasonally mobile collectors who exploit highly nutritious staples requiring intensive processing, develop a "logistic mobility" approach which maximizes the exploitation of a wide variety of resources and which involves storage facilities. This system should not be found in arid or semiarid environments.

The lithic assemblages of the excavated sites in Wadi Abu Noshra include a very high proportion of blades and bladelets as opposed to flakes; such assemblages characterize the Ahmarian techno-complex of the Levantine Upper Paleolithic (Phillips 1988). The pristine condition of the abundant tools renders them suitable for edgewear analysis; this information and refitted cores provide an exceptional opportunity for anal-

170

ysis of intrasite and intersite functional variability and also, consequently, of the alternative models that have been proposed.

The Ahmarian techno-complexes of the Upper Paleolithic from northern and southern Sinai are comparable, but the sedimentary sequences in which they are found are not. A synthesis of sedimentological information in northern Sinai and the adjoining Negev (Goldberg 1986) recognizes four wetter phases in the late Quaternary characterized by net aggradation, each separated by periods of erosion during generally drier conditions. The wetter stages occurred prior to 70,000 B.P. and between about 45,000 and 22,000 B.P., 15,000 and 12,000 B.P., and since 6000 B.P. The sedimentary record preserved in Wadi el Sheikh, on the other hand, is one that indicates more constant or uniform environmental conditions for this period. The faunal assemblage of the sites in Wadi Abu Noshra, which includes herbivores, carnivores, rodents, birds and fish (see Phillips 1988), some macrobotanical remains recovered archaeologically, and marls within the sedimentary sequence, attest to a wetter climatic environment during the late Pleistocene than is the case today in the highlands of southern Sinai.

The reconstruction of a particular prehistoric environment clearly is fundamental to an evaluation of the models of subsistence strategies, and a record of ancient pedogenesis provides input for such a reconstruction. A few soil properties do occur in the Pleistocene deposits that contain the Upper Paleolithic sites, and this discussion evaluates these properties. A fundamental problem in the interpretation of certain paleosols that is illustrated here is the difficulty of distinguishing geochemical or diagenic properties from pedogenic ones.

THE SETTING AND LATE PLEISTOCENE DEPOSITS

The contemporary arid landscape of southern Sinai is dominated by the mountainous terrain of an uplifted segment of the Arabo–Nubian shield. Dike-laced uplands of granite and gneiss today are barren of vegetation and soil cover, and virtually all traces of prehistoric occupation have been eroded from upland surfaces of bedrock. The few exceptions are protected recesses weathered into the bedrock, and Neolithic structures beneath immense boulders. However, archaeological sites have survived on and within remnants of the late Pleistocene deposits in larger wadi systems such as Wadi el Sheikh (Figure 6-1) and in a few small tributary wadis. Wadi Abu Noshra is one such tributary, and the Upper Paleolith-

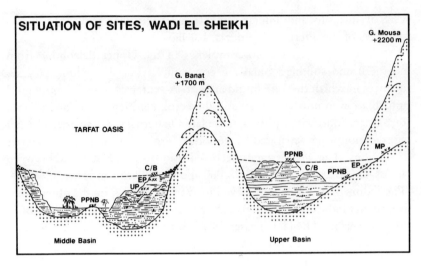

Figure 6-2. Composite cross section illustrating the geomorphic and stratigraphic settings of archaeological sites in Wadi el Sheikh. This schematic reconstruction is based on a surface survey of the drainage basin in 1982 (from: Phillips and Gladfelter 1990) and on the excavation of certain sites. The upper basin of Wadi el Sheikh encompasses the reach of the wadi between Ouatia Pass (Figure 6-3) and St. Catherine (Figure 6-1). Dashed lines approximate the level of valley fill in the late Pleistocene; sites located on surfaces at elevations lower than this indicate that a certain amount of degradation had occurred by the time of the respective occupation. Key: MP, Middle Paleolithic Mousterian; UP, Upper Paleolithic; EP, Epipaleolithic; PPNB, Prepottery Neolithic B; C/B, Chalcolithic-Bronze Age.

ic sites are found within a thick deposit of late Pleistocene sediments in its small basin. Elsewhere in the drainage system of Wadi Feiran, additional Upper Paleolithic and Epipaleolithic sites are sealed in primary contexts within these deposits, and Neolithic and Chalcolithic sites are found on top of them as well as on lower surfaces that have been re-exposed by erosion (Figure 6-2; Phillips and Gladfelter 1989).

Wadi Feiran, including Wadi El Shiekh, is the principal drainage system on the western flank of the Precambrian shield of southern Sinai (Figure 6-1). Lake deposits are described in the upper basin by Awad (1951, 1953), Barron (1907), De Martonne (1947), Issar and Eckstein (1969), Nir (1970), and Walter (1988). These descriptions and the maps that they include refer to all remnants of Pleistocene alluvial deposits as "marl," but only the highly calcareous, fine-textured sediments within these exposures are marl in the strict sense (Gladfelter 1988). In addition to the marly, paludal facies, the Pleistocene deposits include: (1) very coarse, clastic colluvial fan sediments found at the margins of basins and in piedmont settings; (2) prisms of medium-to-coarse, fluviatile gravels derived from this colluvium; (3) beds of stratified and in some cases crossbedded fluviatile gravel, sand, and silt, and (4) beds of finer sand and silt. All of these units are interlayered and one can grade laterally into another demonstrating that the sedimentary facies of the deposits are explained by horizontal variations of paleohydraulic conditions.

Observations at the oasis of Tarfat el Quidrein in the upper drainage of Wadi el Sheikh (Figure 6-1) indicate that major episodes of downcutting and infilling did not occur during the late Pleistocene. The alluvial terraces at the mouth of Ouatia Pass (Figure 6-3) have been formed

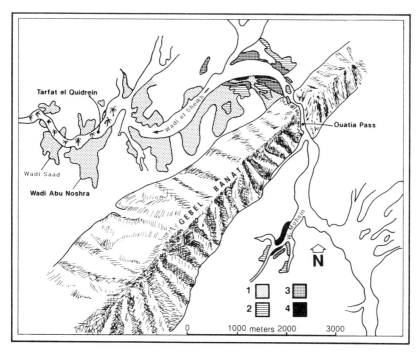

Figure 6-3.   Map of Pleistocene deposits and Holocene cut-terraces in the vicinity of the oasis at Tarfat el Quidrein. The Holocene erosional terraces are cut into late Pleistocene alluvium. In places, such as in Wadi Abu Noshra, paludal sediments are sealed within the alluvium. Key: (1) late Pleistocene alluvium, (2) High Terrace of alluvium, (3) Middle Terrace surface, (3) Low Terrace surface.

by incision of a single body of fill that aggraded during the late Pleistocene. The terraces here, and elsewhere in the upper basin of Wadi el Sheikh such as at Wadi Mohsin (Figure 6-3), were incised in stages of unknown age during the Holocene. Desert pavements of varnished lag have developed on these terraces but aside from the morphologic sequence, there is no information of any sort to permit these surfaces to be absolutely dated.

At the Oasis of Tarfat el Quidrein, incision during the Holocene has sculpted a terrain of badlands rather than terraces, and the several residual knolls in Figure 6-6 represent that terrain. Absolute dates that are presently available show that the aggrading of sediments at Tarfat el Quidrein began about 65,000 B.P. (Th/U), terminated by 12,000 B.P., and by about 9000 B.P. these deposits were already extensively incised and degraded (Gladfelter 1990). Consequently, for a period of at least 50,000 years that was contemporaneous with the last glacial, valleys in the upper basin of Wadi Feiran were filled with appreciable thicknesses of sediment, most of which was flushed away during the Holocene. Preserved within the surviving deposits, however, are the many marls that denote ancient bodies of perennial surface freshwater.

The Sedimentary Sequence

Pleistocene deposits near the oasis of Tarfat el Quidrein, consisting of interbedded alluvial, palustrine, and colluvial sediments along the course of Wadi el Sheikh, are at least 50 m thick. A major portion of the original sequence has been eroded away and badland terrain occurs where extensive remnants of the beds are found. A complete stratigraphic or sedimentary column of aggradation is not preserved at a single location, but within Wadi Abu Noshra (Figure 6-4a), an unusually thick occurrence of the deposits is preserved along with the Upper Paleolithic sites that are sealed within them (Phillips 1987a, 1987b). The upper part of this Pleistocene alluvium and marl is shown in Figure 6-4b. Wells at the mouth of this wadi penetrate at least 15 m of coarse alluvium, but it is not known whether these deposits are a lower part of the late Pleistocene sedimentary column or they are fill of Holocene age.

Marl in the Pleistocene deposits (Figure 6-4c) typically is very pale brown (10YR 8/4) calcareous silty or clayey fine sandy mud, usually containing between 30% and 60% total carbonate (percentage of total weight). Marls 1, 2, and 3 (Figure 6-5) contain mollusca, ostracoda, and

Figure 6-4. Photographs of Wadi Abu Noshra: (a) View to the south toward Gebel Banat with Wadi el Sheikh in the middle foreground. Dissected, late Pleistocene deposits at the mouth of Wadi Abu Noshra are seen in the right middle foreground. (b) Part of the sedimentary sequence of Section II (Figure 6-5), including marls 1 through 5. Note figure of person to the right of marl 5 for scale. (c) Marl 4; scale is approximately 50 cm long.

Figure 6-4. (*Continued*)

charaphyta species from habitats of freshwater ponds that existed in shallow depressions on the alluvial bottoms (Gladfelter et al. n.d.). These molluscan assemblages as well as fish bone recovered archaeologically indicate that the ponds were perennial features. The sedimentary sequence at the oasis at Tarfat el Quidrein contains at least 15 separate strata of marl (Figure 6-6). Radiocarbon assays obtained from certain marl units establish the late Pleistocene age of these deposits: Marl 4, 29,110 ± 460 B.P. (SMU 1845); Marl 7, 18,910 ± 200 B.P. (B-13895). These dates as well as those from archaeological associations are discussed by Gladfelter et al. (n.d.). At present the time control is inadequate to assess intervals of marl formation; probably just a few millennia separate these palustrine phases. The apparent rhythm of marl formation was uneven, judging from the thicknesses of the marl sediment that vary between about 20 cm and 50 cm, and from the thicknesses of the sediment separating them, which is as little as 95 cm (Marls 5 and 6) and as much as 400 cm (Marls 6 and 7).

During the aggradation of the sediments, there was very little relief on the ancient surface as shown by the broadly horizontal attitude of depositional units within the deposits and by fine texture indicative of the

WADI ABU NOSHRA, Section II

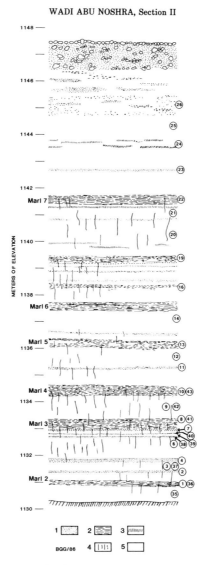

Figure 6-5.   Section II at Wadi Abu Noshra. Meaning of symbols: (1) Lenses of well-sorted, fine–medium sand. (2) Marls and marly units. (3) Fine sandy silt lenses. (4) Fossilized root casts. (5) Massive silty sand matrix with lenses of coarser sediment. Circled numbers locate samples in Table 6-1.

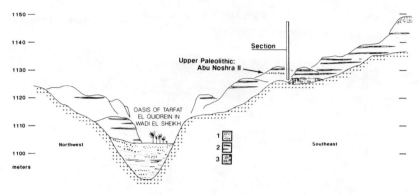

Figure 6-6. Vertical succession of marl beds at Tarfat Oasis. Shown schematically are the several marl strata in Wadi Abu Noshra and immediately opposite it. Additional strata of marl occur within other remnants of late Pleistocene deposits at the oasis of Tarfat el Quidrein. The general level of Abu Noshra II, the largest of three Ahmarian sites excavated in the deposits, is illustrated as is the overall sedimentary column encompassed by Section II (Figure 6-5), but there are no sites or artifacts in Section II. Key: (1) Alluvial sands and gravel. (2) Marl. (3) Coarse gravel, in places conglomeratic. No horizontal scale.

low energy sedimentation that sealed and preserved the integrity of the Upper Paleolithic sites. In addition, there is no evidence of fill within the sequence that would denote channels cut into the deposits and the establishment of significant relief on the aggrading surface. The evidence from southern Sinai does not support a model of climatically forced, sedimentological periodicity (i.e., swings between erosional and depositional phases) wherein spates of alluviation were separated by periods of "stability" and soil formation.

SOIL DEVELOPMENT

It is fair to say that "Quaternary paleosol studies . . . have tended to support the ingrained concept that pedogenesis is coincident with periods of landscape stability that alternate with larger, more normal periods of more or less continuous deposition or erosion" (Kraus and Bown 1986:182). This concept is not always the case, as at the oasis of Tarfat el Quidrein where it would be inappropriate to infer that the sparse record of paleosols in the alluvial sequence connotes geomorphic instability throughout the late Pleistocene.

In situations where organic constituents build rapidly or where aerosols are significant contributors (e.g., Yaalon 1987), the development of soil is an accretionary process. Additions of alluvium to a surface also build a solum. In these cases the process of accretion must be reconciled with the notion that soil formation requires a "stable" surface, and for soils in alluvium, the question of stability must include a consideration of the relative rates of pedogenesis and alluviation, as the ongoing nature of the latter arrests the former (see, for example, Kraus and Bown 1986:184; Ferring, this volume). While alluvial deposition may be a discrete event, the formation of soil requires an interval of time so that thick deposits might represent a short time (decades or centuries), but soil on an alluvial surface may denote longer periods of non–deposition (centuries or millennia) (see Ferring 1986, and Holliday, this volume). For alluvial settings: if the rate of pedogenesis was greater than the rate of alluviation, a paleosol should be evident; if the rates of pedogenesis and alluviation were comparable, thick horizonation may be expected such that the "alluvial soil" is a composite of superimposed profiles (see Kraus and Bown 1986); if the rate of alluviation was greater than that of soil development, a record of pedogenesis would not persist even though the environmental (climatic) conditions were suitable for the formation of soil.

In Wadi Abu Noshra, these relative rates are expressed in a given sedimentary sequence in terms of alluviation and non–alluviation (= potential pedogenesis): when alluviation occurred, sands and clayey silts accumulated in the sedimentary column; when non–alluviation prevailed, marls developed and pedogenesis could have progressed on exposed lateral surfaces. Deductively, it would be expected that some indication of ancient soil development would be discernible because moisture was available, as indicated by the presence of marls and of vegetation as shown by root casts and macrobotanical remains. But sustained alluviation or heightened rates of sedimentation could preclude the development of soil, in which case the subsurface formation of concretions of calcite would connote geochemical rather than pedochemical weathering (e.g., Buol et al. 1980:86; Carroll 1970). In this situation the spatial pattern of subsequent aggradation would have eclipsed the physical evidence of soil development. Pedogenesis that could have occurred on inter-channel surfaces on the aggrading valley-floor may have been erased by the pattern of shifting erosion within the period of net deposition. As veneers of fresh alluvium were scattered across the floodplain by short-lived depositional events, soil formation was arrested by the sediments that buried incipient entisols while the surface of the floodplain aggraded.

The striking aspect of the alluvial sequence (sensu lato) in Wadi Abu Noshra, and in the environs of Tarfat el Quidrein, is the absence of well-developed pedogenic profiles, which might suggest that rates of pedogenesis were surpassed by rates of sedimentation. Yet with respect to alluvial sequences, Kraus and Bown (1986:186) have observed that "sedimentation and erosion are highly episodic and together occupy very little of the time represented by any alluvial sequence. Therefore, it matters not whether the fluvial system was in a net aggradational or a net degradational regime because stasis, and its corollary pedogenesis, are the dominant processes in developing an alluvial sequence and occupy the vastly greater proportion of time." This is difficult to reconcile with the information in Wadi Abu Noshra discussed below.

Evidence for Paleosols

A relevant question here is, when is a sediment a soil and, therefore, when is a sediment a paleosol? This is worth noting because of the difficulty in distinguishing products and processes of pedogenesis from diagenesis. Valentine and Dalrymple (1976:210) observed that "there are very few features that are unique to terrestrial soils as opposed to sediments." Many authors have addressed this question (Catt 1987; Fenwick 1985; Jenkins 1985; Valentine and Dalrymple 1976; Yaalon 1971) and the concensus seems to be that those properties that characterize contemporary soils (color, texture, structure, cutans, consistency, special features, reaction, boundaries) should be recognizable also in buried paleosols and, additionally, a paleo-catena should be developed to discern a paleo-surface (Valentine and Dalrymple 1976). In situations where burial has occurred, particular emphasis on the chemistry and mineralogy of the matrix is warranted (Jenkins 1985).

Dissection and denudation of the late Pleistocene deposits in the small basin of Wadi Abu Noshra during the Holocene has exposed the buried archaeological sites, but it also has removed an appreciable proportion of the sedimentary record so that the complete vertical succession of deposits is preserved only at one location. Two sections through this sequence were described in the field and representatively sampled;

properties from one of these sections (Figure 6-5) are presented in Table 6-1. Nine of the samples in Table 6-1 were obtained from marl strata (keyed with a superscript); the remaining samples are from alluvial deposits. All of the sediments include a significant component of calcium and magnesium that was imported as atmospheric dust or as solute in rain water. These minerals can not be autocthonous because the entire drainage basin of Wadi el Sheikh consists of igneous rocks; the minerals are derived from Cretaceous limestone in Gebel el Igma to the north. Calcium is the dominant soluble salt and the high content of soluble salts in all of the sediments, as well as the high levels of Ca and Mg cations, and the weakly alkaline pH values show that the deposits have not been leached. High concentrations of cations of Ca, Mg, Na and K can occur under conditions of high evapotranspiration in settings with a high ground water table (e.g., Bridges and Burnham 1980).

The marl sediments indicate that pools of water occupied ancient alluvial surfaces for periods of time. Elsewhere on these surfaces alluviation continued during these periods, which is shown by changes of facies in the sediments. Therefore, some alluvial deposits within the sedimentary column of Section II (Figure 6-5), can be lateral depositional equivalents of marl facies that existed simultaneously someplace else in the basin, and comparison of properties of samples from marl and from alluvium within this vertical sequence may be taken to represent different settings on the ancient, aggrading surface. Comparison of the percentage content of organic matter in marl and alluvial sediments, for example, shows that the average content is slightly higher in the marls (statistically significant at .05) than in the alluvial deposits. This is the case, too, for soluble salts (statistically significant at .02), calcium being the most important salt. But the Mg/Ca ratio is lower in the marl deposits which is the expected case for bodies of water that are open systems (Eugster and Kelts 1983: 328). Aside from these small differences, most properties of the samples in Table 6-1 do not vary significantly between the marl and alluvial sediments, and inspection of multiple samples from the same sediment shows horizontal variability of certain properties, commonly organic matter, soluble salts and texture, within the respective deposit. Horizontal comparisons can be made between the following pairs of samples (see Figure 6-5 for location of sample): 10 and 43, 9 and 42, 8 and 41, 3 and 37, 1 and 36. These internal differences may obscure vertical changes in properties that could denote the translocation of clay or mineral constituents, yet concretionary nodules have formed in these deposits (see below).

TABLE 6-1

Properties of Samples in Section II (Figure 6-5)

Sample Number	K (ppm)	NA (ppm)	MG (ppm)	CA (ppm)	Soluble Salts	Organic Matter (%)	CEC	pH	Eh	CaCO3 (%)	Munsell Color	Gran. (%)	Sand (%)	Silt (%)	Clay (%)
1[a]	259	366	719	8150	918	0.8	23.7	7.5	350	5.5	10YR 7/4	7.3	87.3	2.4	2.5
2	123	265	372	3760	322	0.2	11.1	8.2	326	3.9	10YR 7/6	0.2	89.2	10.0	6.5
3	212	308	489	4805	451	1.3	14.3	7.9	328	5.7	10YR 8/4	1.7	97.0	—	—
4	139	282	427	3590	284	0.4	10.9	7.3	319	5.2	10YR 8/2	0.2	99.5	—	—
6	181	286	582	4870	548	1.4	14.8	7.4	311	6.2	10YR 8/4	3.2	60.1	27.6	8.7
7	139	263	422	3640	321	0.4	11.0	7.7	315	5.8	10YR 8/4	—	86.5	9.1	4.3
8[a]	190	392	710	5380	811	0.8	16.6	7.6	314	5.6	10YR 8/4	1.7	94.7	1.9	1.7
9	254	369	734	4875	499	0.3	15.5	7.8	325	6.1	10YR 8/4	1.6	75.0	14.2	9.2
10[a]	269	306	679	4260	428	0.8	13.8	7.9	321	4.8	10YR 8/4	0.2	87.4	8.4	4.1
11	179	252	424	3180	307	0.9	9.9	8.0	338	4.5	10YR 8/4	2.4	82.6	10.9	4.2
12	282	312	673	4615	503	1.1	14.6	7.8	310	3.9	10YR 8/4	0.4	99.4	—	—
13[a]	210	319	551	3630	367	0.9	11.6	7.9	318	4.3	10YR 8/3	1.2	98.0	—	—
14[a]	185	449	339	4005	544	1.8	11.6	7.7	318	4.4	10YR 8/3	1.0	98.7	—	—
16	291	418	001	6300	814	0.6	20.2	7.5	318	3.3	10YR 8/3	0.3	91.0	2.8	5.9
19	232	363	792	5650	837	0.6	17.7	7.7	322	4.7	10YR 8/3	0.1	73.1	18.7	8.1
20	275	363	903	5600	748	0.5	18.1	7.8	325	5.7	10YR 8/3	1.4	68.7	4.7	15.2
21	275	342	762	4605	538	0.7	15.0	8.0	320	4.9	10YR 8/4	0.4	75.2	1.5	12.9
22[a]	415	359	654	3690	427	0.7	12.4	8.2	318	5.8	10YR 8/3	0.6	90.0	4.3	5.2

23	310	381	879	4990	062	0.5	16.5	7.7	327	5.4	10YR 8/4	—	77.8	15.5	6.7
24	419	306	773	4420	447	0.7	14.8	8.0	328	5.3	10YR 8/4	1.9	85.8	3.8	8.7
25	226	319	742	3795	297	0.5	12.8	8.2	335	5.5	10YR 7/6	1.2	73.2	12.2	13.4
26	203	309	745	3550	245	0.7	12.2	8.5	342	4.2	10YR 7/6	0.4	78.8	14.3	6.5
35	213	326	672	3720	282	0.4	12.3	8.0	320	6.1	10YR 8/4	0.6	66.1	21.6	11.5
36ª	234	314	602	3640	242	0.8	11.9	8.0	322	6.1	10YR 8/2	9.0	77.8	7.0	6.2
37	217	318	642	4235	345	0.7	13.5	8.0	324	5.6	10YR 7/2	2.5	59.7	23.2	14.6
38	313	385	879	5550	629	0.5	17.9	7.4	318	6.3	10YR 7/3	5.6	68.9	18.0	7.4
39	144	372	530	3780	262	0.3	11.8	7.8	319	6.2	10YR 7/4	0.1	74.3	19.1	6.4
40	270	405	898	6800	630	0.8	21.0	7.7	314	6.1	10YR 8/2	0.7	83.1	11.5	3.7
41ª	142	399	704	4920	373	0.9	15.4	8.0	318	5.9	10YR 8/2	5.0	91.4	1.3	2.3
42	225	414	918	5650	451	1.0	18.2	8.0	318	6.0	10YR 8/3	2.6	58.4	13.4	25.6
43ª	186	402	837	5350	794	1.0	17.1	7.8	325	5.6	10YR 8/2	2.4	85.0	9.0	2.9

ª Sample from marl.

Analyses performed by the State Soils Laboratory, University of Wisconsin, Milwaukee. Procedures followed "Wisconsin Procedures for Soil Testing, Plant Analysis and Feed and Forage Analysis," Soil Fertility Series, No. 6. Madison: Department of Soil Sciences, University of Wisconsin-Extension (1980 Revision). Analysis of these data included eight additional samples from a comparable section. Those results are omitted from this table because their provenance cannot be shown in Figure 6–6. Contents of K, Ca, Mg and Na are available amounts and were used to calculate CEC. Munsell colors are for dry samples. The bulk of the sand content usually is in the fine sand and very fine sand fractions (<2Phi and >4Phi).

The only "soil" properties that occur within the sedimentary column are apparent pedogenic structure and concretions, but neither may be related to ancient pedogenesis. The marls have platy or prismatic structure and the intervening, usually massive, fine-textured sediments in places also have developed blocky or prismatic structure. However, about one meter beneath the present surface in freshly excavated exposures, the sediment is highly indurated and does not exhibit pedogenic structure at all. Pedogenic structure in the marls and other sediments comprising the contemporary surface has formed since their exposure by erosion of the overlying deposits. Thus, no systematic horizonation of structural change can be demonstrated in buried deposits.

Many of the properties enumerated by Fenwick (1985) that are needed to recognize a paleosol do not occur in the sequence in Wadi Abu Noshra (Figure 6-5): (1) there is very little evidence for organic enrichment; (2) vertical color differences of significance (increase in redness) are absent; (3) vertical trends in change of granulometry (ratio of fine clay [<1 μm] to total or coarse clay [>1 μm] are masked or no more significant that horizontal variations; (4) gross mineral assemblages of calcite, quartz, dolomite and feldspars are remarkably comparable for samples that have been analyzed; (5) disruption of original (primary) sedimentary structure is unrecognizable and, as noted above, beyond about one meter beneath the exposed modern surface, pedogenic structure is absent; (6) "boundaries" that ignore inherent primary sedimentary units have not developed. These properties would not support an inference of paleosol development even though fossil root casts that are abundant in many of the sediments indicate that plants did colonize the ancient, aggrading lowland. At some levels, these root canals terminate at the top of a sedimentary unit (e.g., marls 1 through 4, Figure 6-5) showing that a vegetation cover was able to gain hold on a surface before it was buried by renewed alluviation.

The malacology of the marl deposits shows that the ponds were freshwater and the virtual lack of gypsum or other evaporites in the sediments shows that rates of evaporation were less than the rates of water input. The improved moisture availability, compared to today, undoubtedly permitted soil development on interfluves and in alluvium of the floor of valleys. But evidence for these paleosols is meagre; it is gone from the denuded uplands and that preserved in the sedimentary record is open to alternative interpretations.

Concretions

Calcic soils, an informal term meaning soils with appreciable amounts of secondary, allogenic carbonate (Machette 1985), can be confused with nonpedogenic accumulations of carbonate. In northern Sinai and the southern Negev, calcic paleosols are described (Bruins and Yaalon 1979; Goodfriend and Magaritz 1988) in which the form of carbonate is dissimilar from that in Wadi Abu Noshra. Calcium carbonate in the former areas forms small, soft nodules but in Wadi Abu Noshra the calcium carbonate is in the form of much larger, very hard and brittle, cemented calcite. This difference can be attributed, at least in part, to the greater precipitation at Wadi Abu Noshra due to the orographic effect of nearby Gebel Banat.

In the upper basin of Wadi el Sheikh, to the south and in the leeward of this mountain, Quaternary deposits have negligible contents of calcium carbonate. Because both areas consist of igneous bedrock it is apparent that the calcium was imported as eolian dust from the plateau of Cretaceous limestone to the north. Loess-laden storms are thought to have been prevalent during the wetter late Pleistocene in northern Sinai (Issar and Bruins 1983) and these sediments are significant constituents of many soils (Yaalon 1987). In south-central Sinai, eolian dust was trapped on the windward flank of Gebel Banat; the effects of mountain ranges on local climatic gradients and the concentration of calcium carbonate in soils and sediment of arid lands has been documented, for example, in the American Southwest (Gile 1975, 1977).

Concretionary carbonate occurs throughout most of the deposits; in a few strata its formation assumes the appearance of a "layer," but there are no zones of concretionary forms within the vertical sequence indicative of a K horizon. In freshwater an increase in the concentration of ammonia from decomposing plants, such as charaphytes, causes strong akaline conditions around the plants and an increase in pH so that carbonate precipitates. This reaction will continue until ammonia or dissolved calcium carbonate is no longer available (see Müller 1967). The former would seem to be the case here because calcium carbonate is present through most of the sedimentary column and certain concretions are found in sediments other than the marls. The primary contributor to this process is the escape of CO_2; very active bacteria increase CO_2 in interstitial water and carbonate is put into solution. When the content of CO_2 decreases, as in the alluvial deposits, and more escapes the calcium carbonate achieves a solid state.

There are three distinct types of carbonate concretions in the late Pleistocene deposits, each of which denotes a particular genetic condition. The first kind is massive, without consistent shape (other than never being truely concentric), and ranges in size from a few millimeters to several centimeters in maximum dimension (Figure 6-7). These are found commonly in the alluvium and occasionally in the marls but they do not occur in horizontal bands, perceptible zones, or horizons. They formed in a subsurface environment but they are not pedogenic because (1) "horizons" of concretions do not erase primary sedimentary structure or sedimentary boundaries, (2) the concretions are very hard calcite, as opposed to chalky pellets, which could mean protracted migration of interstitial groundwater to centers of formation, a circumstance compatible with water availability indicated by the ponds, and (3) concretions are in marls as well as the intervening alluvium and as such they occur irrespective of "surfaces" of potential soil development. This variety of concretion can be referred to as polymorphous because it occurs in any shape, but mostly it is more nodular than filament-like. These concretions are the principal component of the clastic lag that litters the eroded deposits.

A second type of concretion is skeletal in form, reminding some previous observers such as Awad (1953), Issar and Eckstein (1969) and Nir (1970), of plant casts. These most commonly appear as interwoven, thick, dendritic-like tubular or platy filaments or solid shafts about 1 cm in diameter but they are not root casts. They are without layers of concretionary banding and seem to occur as diagenic forms at the boundary of marked change in the texture of the alluvium. Since porosity improves along the boundary of textural changes from fine to coarser strata, precipitation is prone to occur there because of the improved ability of CO_2 to escape.

The third kind of concretion is syngenetic; sponge-like structure typifies the generally flat or tabular morphology of this more whitish type. This variety approaches tufa in structural appearance, although true casts of reed or sedge stems are absent in all but a very few cases. When found in situ, these concretions are along the edges of marl sediments showing that they formed originally at the margins of standing water.

The basal gravels (Figure 6-5) in places are cemented to form a conglomerate. Such conglomerates occur throughout the Wadi el Sheikh system and elsewhere in southern Sinai where the calcite is thought to be an inorganic, freshwater precipitate (Bogoch and Cook 1974). In Wadi Abu Noshra the infiltrating calcium carbonate was imported as an aero-

Figure 6-7.   Photograph of concretions. Pictured are the first type of concretion referred to in the text. The nodules are exposed here on the eroded face of a collapsed
block of sediment.

sol; its precipitation was likely due to a phase change caused by the increased porosity of the matrix.

Calcic accumulations found in unconsolidated material of non-calcareous geologic provinces depend upon the relative rates of supply of calcium carbonate and of moisture to the soil/sediment matrix. Because the sedimentary column is calcareous through most of its thickness, calcium influx apparently was sustained for much of the late Pleistocene and calcic enrichment was not, therefore, supply-limited. This conclusion is substantiated further by the data in Table 6-1; available cations, particularly Ca, are high for all of the sedimentary column without apparent leached layers that would implicate a depletion of calcium influx (e.g., Machette 1985: 13). And since calcite concretions do not occur preferentially in layers or zones within the deposits, translocation of calcium carbonate was not moisture-limited.

DISCUSSION AND CONCLUSIONS

Marls developed at only two places within the massif of southern Sinai during the late Pleistocene because of the orographic effect of nearby mountains which produced locally favorable water yields. Ponds sustained by atmospheric water directly and by slope runoff indirectly were hydrologically open, freshwater systems with charaphytic growth. A particular pool probably was an element of the landscape for a short period, a matter of centuries or perhaps longer. The now denuded interfluves of bedrock most likely supported vegetation that trapped wind-borne dust from the north and modulated the delivery of sediment and runoff to the lowlands. Soil structure in some sediments is not primary, and carbonate concretions are thought to be diagenic rather than pedogenic. Thus, while soil properties are observed in some of the deposits, the development of soil on ancient surfaces can not be demonstrated. And while the aggrading alluvial surfaces were "stable" in the sense that rates of alluviation seem to have been slow, Entisols are presumed to have characterized the alluvial surfaces.

The reconstruction that is proposed here means that water and associated resources were available in the area probably on a continual basis in the late Pleistocene, which fulfills the conditions for a logistic mobility model of hunter-gatherer social organization and subsistence. This is consistent with the conclusion reached on the basis of the archaeological record alone (Phillips 1988). If, on the other hand, the reoccurrence of marl units in the sediments and the soil properties in some deposits were regarded as indicating a rhythm of climatic change in this setting, the alternative model of residential mobility would be more appropriate because of periods of restricted availability of resources. The swings between wetter and drier conditions interpreted for northern Sinai, by way of contrast, could have fostered a subsistence strategy of residential mobility.

The reconstruction for the sites in Wadi Abu Noshra holds that the environment supported an exploitable biomass throughout the late Pleistocene rather than just at those times represented by marl in the sedimentary sequence. The environment attracted hunter-gatherer populations on many occasions, but the archaeological record that survives is one fragmented by accelerated erosion which followed the shift to hyperarid conditions in the Holocene.

ACKNOWLEDGMENTS

Fieldwork was conducted under the aegis of the Egyptian Antiquities Organization and with the cooperation of James L. Phillips, Director of the University of Illinois at Chicago Southern Sinai Research Expedition. Critical comments on the manuscript by anonymous reviewers, and by W. R. Farrand both in the field and during revision, were very helpful. I thank the editor of this volume, Vance T. Holliday, for his patience, persistence, and perspicacity in guiding the manuscript to its final form, in spite of the fact that I was unable to present the original version at the Symposium. I also thank Lawrence Keeley for assuming that role in my place. Siim Soot, Department of Geography at U.I.C., offered valuable, critical discussion of the management of the data in Table 6-1. Cartographic services were provided by Ray Brod, Cartographic Laboratory, in the Department of Geography at U.I.C. This research was supported by NSF grant BNS 8409021.

REFERENCES

Awad, Hassan
  1951   Lés Depôts Lacustrine de l'Ouadi el Sheikh et de l'Ouadi Solaf. In *Le Montagne du Sinai Central*, pp. 151–154. Société Royale de Géographie d' Egypte, Cairo.

1953   Signification morphologique dés depôts lacustres de la Montagne du Sinai Central. *Bulletin Société Royale de Géographie d'Egypte* XXV:23–28.

Barron, T.
1907   *The Topography and Geology of the Penninsula of Sinai* (Western Portion). National Printing Department, Cairo.

Bar-Yosef, O.
1984   Near East. In *Neue Forschungen zur Altsteinzeit*, Band 4: Forshungen zur Allegemeinen und Vergleichenden Archaologie, edited by H. Muller-Karpe, pp. 233–298. C. H. Beck, Munich.

Belfer-Cohen, A., and P. Goldberg
1982   An Upper Paleolithic Site in South Central Sinai. *Israel Exploration Journal* 32:185–189.

Bogoch, R., and P. Cook
1974   Calcite Cementation of a Quaternary Conglomerate in Southern Sinai. *Journal of Sedimentary Petrology* 44(3):917–920.

Bridges, E. M., and C. P. Burnham
1980   Soils of the State of Bahrain. *Journal of Soil Science* 31:689–707.

Bruins, H. J., and D. H. Yaalon
1979   Stratigraphy of the Netivot Section in the Desert Loess of the Negev (Israel). *Acta Geol. Acad. Sci. Hung.* 22:161–169.

Buol, S. W., F. D. Hole, and R. J. McCracken
1980   *Soil Genesis and Classification.* 2nd edition. Iowa State University Press, Ames, Iowa.

Carroll, D.
1970   *Rock Weathering.* Plenum Press, New York.

Catt, J. A.
1987   Paleosols. *Progress in Physical Geography* 11(4):487–510.

Eugster, H. P., and K. Kelts
1983   Lacustrine Chemical Sediments. In *Chemical Sediments and Geomorphology: Precipitates and Residua in the Near-surface Enviroment*, edited by A. S. Goudie and K. Pye, pp. 321–368. Academic Press, London.

Fenwick, I. M.
1985   Paleosols: Problems of Recognition and Interpretation. In *Soils and Quaternary Landscape Evolution*, edited by J. Boardman, pp. 3–21. John Wiley and Sons, Chichester, England.

Ferring, C. R.
1986   Rates of Fluvial Sedimentation: Implications for Archaeological Variability. *Geoarchaeology: An International Journal* 1(3):259–274.

Gile, L. H.
  1975   Holocene Soils and Soil-geomorphic Relations in an Arid Region of Southern
          New Mexico. *Quaternary Research* 5:321–360.
  1977   Holocene Soils and Soil-geomorphic Relations in a Semi-arid Region of
          Southern New Mexico. *Quaternary Research* 7:112–132.

Gladfelter, B. G.
  1988   Late Pleistocene Lakes within the Mountains of Southern Sinai: Observations
          at the Tarfat Oasis. *Bulletin, Société de Géographie d' Egypte* Tomes LXI–
          LXII:29–49.
  1990   The Geomorphic Situation of Upper Paleolithic Sites in Wadi el Sheikh,
          Southern Sinai. *Geoarchaeology: An International Journal*, in press.

Gladfelter, B. G., H. Haas, and E. Tchernov
  n.d.   Radiocarbon Ages and Mollusca of the Late Pleistocene Marshes of Southern
          Sinai. Ms. in preparation.

Goldberg, P.
  1986   Late Quaternary Environmental History of the Southern Levant. *Geoarchaeol-
          ogy: An International Journal* 1(3):225–244.

Goodfriend, G. A., and M. Magaritz
  1988   Paleosols and Late Pleistocene Rainfall Fluctuations in the Negev Desert. *Na-
          ture* 332:144–146.

Issar, A., and H. Bruins
  1983   Special Climatological Conditions in the Deserts of Sinai and the Negev during
          the Latest Pleistocene. *Palaeogeography, Palaeoclimatology, Palaeoecology* 43:63–72.

Issar, A., and Y. Eckstein
  1969   The Lacustrine Beds of Wadi Feiran, Sinai: Their Origin and Significance. *Is-
          rael Journal of Earth Sciences* 18:21–27.

Jenkins, D. A.
  1985   Chemical and Mineralogical Composition in the Identification of Paleosols. In
          Soils and Quaternary Landscape Evolution, edited by J. Boardman, pp. 23–43.
          John Wiley and Sons, Chichester, England.

Kraus, M. J., and T. M. Bown
  1986   Paleosols and Time Resolution in Alluvial Stratigraphy. In *Paleosols, Their
          Recognition and Interpretation*, edited by V. P. Wright, pp. 180–207. Blackwell,
          London.

Machette, M. N.
  1985   Calcic Soils of the Southwestern United States. In *Soils and Quaternary Geol-
          ogy of the Southwestern United States*, edited by D. I. Weide, pp. 1–21. Special
          Paper 203. Geological Society of America, Boulder.

De Martonne, E.
  1947   Reconnaissance geographique au Sinai. *Annales de Géographie* LVI:241–264.

Müller, G.
  1967   Diagenesis in Argillaceous Sediments. In *Diagenesis in Sediments*, edited by G. Larsen and G. V. Chillingar, pp. 127–178. Elsevier, Amsterdam.

Nir, D.
  1970   Les lacs Quaternaires dans la region de Feiran (Sinai Central). *Revue de Géographie Physique et de Géologie Dynamique* (2) XII (4):335–346.

Phillips, J. L.
  1987a   Upper Paleolithic Hunter-gathers in the Wadi Feiran, Southern Sinai. In *The Pleistocene Old World*, edited by O. Soffer, pp. 196–182. Plenum, New York.
  1987b   Sinai during the Paleolithic: The Early Periods. In *Prehistory of Arid North Africa: Essays in Honor of Fred Wendorf*, edited by A. E. Close, pp. 105–121. Southern Methodist University Press, Dallas.
  1988   The Upper Paleolithic of the Wadi Feiran, Southern Sinai. *Paleorient* 14(2):183–200.

Phillips, J. L., and B. G. Gladfelter
  1989   A Survey in the Upper Wadi Feiran Basin, Southern Sinai. *Paleorient* 15:113–122.

Valentine, K. W. G., and J. B. Dalrymple
  1976   Quaternary Buried Paleosols: A Critical Review. *Quaternary Research* 6:209–222.

Walter, J. K.
  1888   Die Korallenriffe der Sinaihalbinsel. *Abn. d. Kon. Sachs. Ges. de Wiss.* (Leipzig) XIV (10):439–505.

Yaalon, D. H.
  1971   Soil Forming Processes in Time and Space. In *Paleopedology*, edited by D. H. Yaalon, pp. 29–40. University Press, Jerusalem.
  1987   Saharan Dust and Desert Loess: Effect on Surrounding Soils. *Journal of African Earth Sciences* (4) 6:569–571.

7

JULIE K. STEIN

Organic Matter in Archaeological Contexts

Organic matter refers to all living organisms, as well as to all the dead residues of plant and animal tissues. Organic matter has been used in archaeological research primarily as evidence for reconstruction of diet, climate, landscape reconstruction, and a signature of occupation. As people inhabit a landscape, organic matter accumulates on the surface in the form of discarded food refuse, excreta, and the debris of fire-building activity, shelter construction, and tool manufacture. These activities enrich the surface in organic matter, the decomposed remains of which are detected by archaeologists. Organic matter is also used in archaeology to define intrasite structures or features (e.g., post molds, hearths, storage pits, animal burrows), to discern stratigraphic layering, to date deposits, and to reconstruct landscapes.

Not all archaeologists who analyze organic matter in their research understand the complex nature of the material. Using organic matter in archaeological research requires an understanding of the source from which it came, and how it was transported, deposited, and altered after deposition. Organic matter originates from two very different sources, one related to sediments and the other to soils. After organic matter is deposited it is subjected to complex chemical reactions associated with decomposition. The chemical reactions that occur depend on local chemical conditions and are not entirely understood (Bohn et al. 1985; Kumada 1987; Lindsay 1979; Sposito 1989; Stevenson 1986), yet they control the fate of organic matter and affect what archaeologists observe in sites and what is interpreted about prehistory.

In this paper I explore the role played by organic matter in archaeological interpretations. Initially, the source of organic matter is considered, noting the difference between organic matter deposited as sedimentary particles and organic matter accumulated as part of soil formation processes. Secondly, the post-depositional alteration of organic matter is discussed, with special emphasis given to how organic matter is lost from a sediment or soil. Finally, examples of the use of organic matter in archaeological interpretations are provided. These discussions and examples clarify the problems associated with the source and alteration of organic matter.

SOURCE OF ORGANIC MATTER

Organic matter associated with prehistoric occupations comes from two very different sources, one related to sediments and the other to soils. Organic matter associated with sediments is transported from one place to another by a transport agent. Organic matter associated with soils is part of a biological community that is involved with the weathering of parent material on a stable surface, and is transported below the surface with other products of weathering. The difference between these two sources causes confusion in archaeology.

Definitions of Sediment and Soil

In the English language, the terms *sediment* and *soil* have a variety of meanings, some of which are different from the formal definitions of the terms used in sedimentology and pedology. In English, a sediment is "matter that settles from a liquid (often associated with wine), or matter deposited by water." In English, a soil is "the earth or ground, the portion of the earth's surface in which plants grow, or a country or foreign place." The difference between sediment and soil in English involves such considerations as whether water (or wine) is involved, or whether plants will grow. According to these English definitions, sediment would not be an appropriate name for most archaeological material, and soil would be. Yet these definitions are not the ones used in scientific research.

In sedimentology, a *sediment* is defined as "particulate matter that has been transported by some process from one location to another" (Stein 1987:339). When an archaeologist describes site material as a sediment, the implicit focus is placed on the fact that the material has been transported. It came from a source, was carried to this site, and was deposited (Hassan 1978; Stein 1985). A *soil* can mean many things, depending on the focus of the researcher (Holliday 1990, and in this volume). To an agricultural soil scientist, soil is a medium for plant growth. To an engineer and some geologists, soil is unconsolidated sediment, including loose or weathered rock or regolith. To pedologists, a soil is a product of weathering consisting of a layer(s) or horizon(s) of mineral and/or organic constituents of variable thicknesses, occurring at the immediate surface of the earth in sediment and/or weathered rock (modified from Birkeland 1984 and Holliday 1990). When an archaeologist describes site material as a soil, the meaning could be any one of these definitions depending on the archaeologist's focus, or it could be the meaning implied in nonformal English usage.

Sedimentary Sources of Organic Matter. The majority of particles found in archaeological contexts are clastic sediments (transported by an agent), as opposed to biological sediments (transported by the organism's own locomotion), or chemical sediments (transported in solutions). The most significant agents involved in transporting archaeological clastic sediments are people who carry animals and plants to habitation sites for subsistence and construction needs, as well as carnivores and scavengers that purposely carry organic remains to their lair or inadvertently drop them in a particular location.

Organic clastic sediments (e.g., bones, charcoal, shells, seeds, or decomposed residues) in archaeological sites can be described and interpreted in a manner similar to other clastic sediments (Shackley 1975). Attributes such as texture (size distributions), composition (taxa, and element frequencies), and orientation are used to interpret the depositional history of organic sediments (i.e., sources, transport agents, and environment of deposition) just as they are used for mineral clastic sediments (Stein 1987). The attribute of surface features (e.g., tooth marks, butchering marks) is also of special interest to the study of organic clastic sediments, having a role that is as significant as the surface features of mineral clastic sediments (e.g., pitting, rounding).

Like all sediments, these organic sediments are also subject to post-depositional alterations. Animal tissue can decompose, while bone mineral can change as elements in the surrounding matrix equilibrate with the bone (Whitmer et al. 1989). Plant tissue can be repeatedly wetted and dried until stress breaks it into unidentifiable fragments (Brady 1989). These post-depositional alterations are associated with decomposition, and result in the alteration of large-sized organic clasts into small-sized amorphous organic clasts. These small-sized clasts are usually reduced to the state of humus and often aggregate into larger clasts or coat the outer surfaces of larger particles.

Pedogenic Sources of Organic Matter. To consider organic matter as part of a soil it has to be involved with weathering processes taking place on a surface, which result in the in situ alteration of the parent material. The surface must be a stable one, where neither deposition nor erosion is taking place or is very slow, and which allows weathering to proceed for a long time. Organic matter associated with soils is usually refered to as soil organic matter (SOM). SOM is defined by pedologists as the accumulations of dead plant and animal matter, partially decayed and partially resynthesized plant and animal residues, as well as the completely decayed residue called humus, which is a complex and rather resistant mixture of brown to dark brown amorphous and colloidal substances (Bohn et al. 1985:135). Soil organic matter accumulates on a stable landscape. It is part of a biological community, controlled by the availability of seeds, nutrients, water, heat, and light. The biological organisms are not necessarily transported to the location, but rather usually grow and live on and within the parent material. Over time, decomposed organic matter mixes with the parent material to produce the A horizon, then is sometimes transported downward into the parent material and accumulates in subsurface horizons. The form of the organic matter that is transported is either root mass or is fine-grained humus, which coats the outer surfaces of larger grains, attaches itself to clay and silt particles as well as to other organic molecules, and accumulates along pathways created by plant roots or organisms.

Confusion in Archaeology over Sources of Organic Matter

The confusion in archaeology over the source of organic matter (organic sediments as opposed to soil organic matter) stems from the fact that soil organic matter accumulates in sediments (some of which are organic clastic sediments), and that archaeologists often use the commonplace English definitions of sediment and soil, rather than the scientific definitions of the terms. Although some archaeologists may consider the accumulation of soil organic matter at the surface as a depositional event, technically it is not. Soils, and the organic matter associated with them, are formed in sediments (parent material) after their deposition. Some organic matter is brought to the site by people during occupation, and some of it is added later when weathering begins and vegetation takes root on the stable surface. These two sources are more clearly identified if archaeologists are aware of the sedimentological and pedological definitions of sediment and soil, and use them appropriately. Three fictitious examples of the formation of the archaeological record will illustrate possible sources of organic matter, and the confusion that can result if the terms sediment and soil are used imprecisely.

Initially, consider the case where only a small amount of artifactual material (including all material associated with occupation; some organic, some nonorganic) is deposited on a stable surface (with a well-developed soil). Deposition of artifactual material in this case does not result in the accumulation of an easily identified deposit (with boundaries and discernible thickness), but rather adds small amounts of organic and inorganic sedimentary particles to the surface of an existing sediment. Under these circumstances the source of the organic matter in the deposit is primarily from soil processes.

In another case, artifactual material is deposited in large quantities, continuously or sporadically over time, resulting in thick deposits. The objects in these deposits are organic and inorganic sediments and are buried well below the surface, because deposition was rapid or continuous. Eventually artifact deposition ceases at the location, and only the upper portion of the deposit acts as a parent material for a new soil. The majority of the deposit below the zone of weathering is therefore removed from the post-depositional effects of surface conditions and processes of soil formation. Under these circumstances the source of the organic matter in the deposit is primarily from sedimentological processes.

Lastly, artifactual material is deposited in moderate quantities on a stable surface. Eventually artifact deposition ceases at the location, and the new archaeological sediment acts as parent material for a new soil developing on its upper surface. However, in this case the entire thickness of the archaeological sediment is affected by pedogenic processes. Under these circumstances the source of the organic matter in this deposit is originally from sedimentological processes, but with contributions at a later time of soil organic matter. Some of the organic matter is a sediment, transported by people from some other location and deposited at this new location. Some of it is soil, incorporated into the parent material by the growth and decay of plants and animals that inhabited the upper surface of the deposit. Finally, the portion of it that began as sedimentary organic matter and the portion that was added later through additional vegetation growth at the surface is decomposed and homogenized through weathering.

These examples demonstrate that the source of organic matter in an archaeological site can be from a combination of *sediments* and *soils*. If additions of cultural organic matter are small and added to stable surfaces, then most of the organic matter in the site is soil organic matter. For these cases, any artifacts deposited with the organic matter will remain close to the surface, and the amount of soil organic matter found near the artifacts will be comparable to the amounts found in adjacent nonartifact bearing stable surfaces. If additions of cultural organic matter are large, most of the organic matter in the deposit is organic sediment. In these deposits the levels of organic matter may be higher than levels of organic matter on the surrounding nonartifact bearing surfaces. The amount of organic matter is related to the amount that was deposited culturally.

DECOMPOSITION OF ORGANIC MATTER

From the moment after death occurs organic matter begins to decompose, whether the organic particle was a clastic particle in a sediment or a part of soil formation. Almost instantaneously, tissues are attacked by microbial organisms that utilize for their metabolism the energy produced during oxidation. For material added after deposition of the sediment, the majority of the initial decomposition of large objects is carried out by mammals, termites, and earthworms. Many plants and organisms obtain their energy from this partially decomposed plant matter, and in turn reduce the organic compounds into residues and humus. As the organic matter becomes more finely divided, the size of the decomposing organisms decrease. Although deeply buried sedimentary organic matter is protected from the destructive effects of some types of mammals and plants, it can still be attacked by organisms that inhabit the subsurface, and eventually be decomposed (Mahaney and Boyer 1986). All decomposition is affected by environmental factors, especially temperature, moisture, and available oxygen. As temperature, moisture, and available oxygen increases, so does the rate of decomposition (Birkeland 1984).

The organisms involved in decomposing organic matter, and the residues that are created during decomposition, are composed of many elements (Figure 7-1), primarily carbon, hydrogen, and oxygen, with smaller amounts of nitrogen, phosphorus, and sulfur (Ahlrichs 1972; Andreux 1982; Kumada 1987; Limbrey 1975; Stevenson 1986; Tate 1987). The term "organic matter" refers to various combinations of these elements and should not be confused with references to organic carbon, which is a measurement of just the carbon atoms in the organic matter (Nelson and Sommers 1982). The elements in organic matter are joined in various compounds such as proteins, glucose, carbohydrates, fats, tannins, and lignin in the fresher organic matter. As decomposition proceeds, these compounds are transformed into humus, a substance composed of humin, humic acid, and fulvic acid (Kumada 1987).

At every stage of this reduction, carbon dioxide gas is released and escapes from the soil (Kumada 1978; Stevenson 1986). Molds and spore-forming bacteria are especially active in consuming the proteins, starch-

		proteins	CARBON
	Dead plant and	glucose	
	animal tissue	carbohydrates	Hydrogen
		tannins	
		fats	Oxygen
ORGANIC	Partially decayed	lignin	
MATTER	residues	etc.	traces of:
			N
			P
	Completely decayed	humin	S
	humus	humic acid	K
		fulvic acid	Ca

Figure 7-1. Composition of organic matter, showing the relationship between organic matter and organic carbon.

es, and cellulose of fresh organic matter, and they release carbon dioxide, water, ammonia, hydrogen sulfide, sulfur dioxide, and organic acids as by-products. Further reduction by other micro-organisms results in the creation of humus, and the further release of carbon dioxide. The carbon that is released as carbon dioxide is transferred from the sediment to the atmosphere or dissolved in soil water to produce carbonic acid and low pH. In temperate regions half of the organic carbon produced during soil genesis is lost to the atmosphere in the first 3–4 months, and in the tropics half is lost in only 3–4 weeks (Bohn et al. 1985). Thus, the organic carbon content of the soil organic matter or organic sediment is lowered through decomposition.

In the context of soils, organic matter is not only lost, new organic matter is added annually to replace the 50 percent to 80 percent of organic matter lost from most temperate soils every year. As more organic matter is added, more microorganisms can be supported. This increased population will decompose the organic matter at a rate faster than the previous population, because more organisms are processing the material. If the supply of organic matter is decreased, the microorganism population will be similarly reduced. The decomposition rate of organic matter in soils is proportional to the accumulation rate. The more added, the more rapidly it disappears. Thus, prevailing conditions result in a steady state of organic matter cycling. The time required to reach this state ranges from 200 to 10,000 years, depending on local conditions and the magnitude of change (Birkeland 1984:203–204). A steady state will be maintained as long as the surface is stable, even when surface climates shift and amounts of organic matter increase and decrease. The steady-state condition will be maintained until the source of the organic matter is eliminated (by burial), or the parent material (sediment) is removed (by erosion). Once the organic matter supply is cut off the decomposition and accumulation rates are no longer in equilibrium.

In the context of sediments, deposition of organic matter is a single event. The organic matter will support a microorganism population that is related to the amount of organic matter originally deposited. Lacking a continuing source of organic matter, a steady state is not reached. The microorganism population will be supported until the original organic sediments decompose (i.e., until all the carbon dioxide is lost to the atmosphere, and the other byproducts reduced to humus). As decomposition occurs, the microorganism population will change. If the process occurs for millennia the organic matter will be reduced to only the most resistant humus. On the other hand, if the organic sediment is buried by repeated deposition, then the rate of decay and the size of the microorganism population will depend on the conditions within the buried deposits. Decomposition is slowed when oxygen or water are not available, or in places experiencing extreme acidity or cold. In these circumstances animal and plant material can survive for millennia (and no soil organic matter is added from the surface), and in certain cases (wet sites, desert sites, bog sites, frozen sites) can be almost perfectly preserved (e.g,. Purdy 1988).

ORGANIC MATTER AND ARCHAEOLOGY

In archaeological contexts, organic matter can have two possible sources, each of which experiences decomposition. However, the organic matter from these two sources can lead to different interpretations when used in archaeological research. The uses of organic matter having the greatest potential in archaeology are here divided into three categories: its potential as a datable material, its potential in landscape reconstruction, and its potential for defining archaeological sites.

Dating Organic Matter

Once organic matter is at a location, either from a pedogenetic or a sedimentologic source, it can be used to date a deposit. Using radiometric dating techniques, the age of an organic substance is determined on either large-sized particles, or on the fine-grained amorphous by-products of decomposition.

The most frequently dated materials in archaeological contexts are large-sized organic sedimentary particles, most notably wood, charcoal, shell, and bone (Burleigh 1974; Michels 1973; Taylor 1987). The age reflected by the radiometric age of these particles is the moment of the organism's death. For example, the age of a piece of charcoal is the time of the death of that wood within the tree. However, most archaeologists do not want to know when the tree died or when the wood died, but rather want to know the date of the depositional event that created the deposit in which the charcoal was found. For this reason, the organic sedimentary particles used for dating are selected so as to maximize the probability that the age of the organism's death will be the same as the age of the depositional event. To insure this, the particle to be dated is selected from the deposit only after certain interpretations have been made, including reconstruction of its source (was the charcoal from the inside or outside of a 1000-year-old cedar?), of its transport agent (was the charcoal floated to the sites or moved by rodents?), of its environment of deposition (was the burning of the charcoal contemporary with deposition and not an event that occurred in another location at another time?), and of its post-depositional alterations (was the charcoal contaminated by mixing with groundwater or coal?). In other words, the particle is described in sedimentological terms and its depositional history interpreted before the analysis is completed.

In addition to dating the large-sized organic matter, archaeological sites contain fine-grained organic matter that can also provide ages for the deposits in which they are found. Organic matter that has decomposed can persist for a very long time, in microbial metabolites and cell walls, and in organo-mineral complexes (Bruckert 1982). This resistant organic matter contains organic carbon that can be used for radiometric dating, and will be discussed after considering the problems associated with determining the radiometric age of SOM.

Dating Organic Matter in Soils. Most of the research on the use of fine-grained organic matter for determining ages of horizons has occurred in soil science, and focuses on only the organic matter added during pedogenesis (Alexander and Price 1980; Campbell et al. 1967; Geyh et al. 1971; Goh and Malloy 1978; Matthews 1980; Scharpenseel 1971, 1979; Sheppard et al. 1979). The radiocarbon age of fine-grained organic matter reflects a mixture of organic matter that has been added recently to a stable surface, and organic matter that has been re-synthesized over hundreds to thousands of years. Radiometric ages of such organic matter are referred to as apparent mean residence times (AMRT) of organic components (Matthews 1985; Scharpenseel and Schiffmann 1977; Stout et al. 1981). The absolute age of the surface soil, defined as the period of time since the beginning of soil formation, will always be older than the AMRT of the uncontaminated soil organic matter within in. The oldest carbon, held in resistant humic acid and humin, is often located in the subsurface horizons, where it has been transported and stored over years of illuviation. Stored with it is younger illuviated carbon (and carbon from in situ decay of roots) that dilutes the isotopic age of the older carbon (Guillet 1982). Organic carbon in surface horizons is dominated by younger carbon, stored as both partially decomposed organic tissues and stabilized carbon held in cell walls and microbial structures. Mixing this young organic carbon with organic carbon from earlier stages of pedogenesis, yields a radiocarbon age that is older than the age of the most recent accumulation of organic matter. The age of the organic carbon in surface horizons reflects the mean annual rate of turnover of the easily biodegradable organic matter, also described as the rate of rejuvenation of the soil organic matter. The carbon that becomes stabilized can have a half-life of 5 to 25 years, and resistant fractions within the humus can range in age from 250 to 2500 years (Bohn et al. 1985).

On the other hand, the radiocarbon age from the top of an A horizon of a buried soil represents the approximate age of the burial. If burial occurs quickly and terminates the addition of young organic matter (rejuvenation), then the radiocarbon age of the organic carbon in the buried soil is a combination of the AMRT of the soil prior to burial and the time that has elapsed since burial (Matthews 1985). The age is approximate because not only is the AMRT of organic matter in surface horizons always older than the age of the burial event, but also the less-resistant organic components of the surface horizon can be slowly lost from the buried soil surface horizon after burial (Birkeland 1984; Catt 1986). The rate of loss of the biodegradable fraction is controlled by the original type of soil, the diagenetic environment, the AMRT of the surface horizon, and the length of exposure of the sample (Haas et al. 1986). Thus, attempts to date the time of burial of the soil are approximate and must be evaluated for local conditions (Ruhe 1983). One way to minimize the error of this date is to sample from only the uppermost portion of the buried surface, because the AMRT of soil organic carbon increases with depth.

Problems associated with organic matter in soils affect the accuracy of determining age of soils with radiocarbon methods (Geyh et al. 1983). The complex nature of soil organic matter and problems with fractionation procedures are the most crucial concerns (Haas et al. 1986; Matthews 1985). Soil organic matter contains many contaminants that are difficult to remove during the procedures used to process radiocarbon ages. Young carbon compounds, bonded in complex ways to older carbon, are difficult to separate in soil aggregates. In addition, contamination of buried soil horizons with modern carbon can occur either while the soil is forming (i.e., contamination associated with the notion of AMRT) or after the soil has been buried. Soils buried below thin deposits, exposed in artificial cuts or valley walls, or within the zone of groundwater penetration are especially prone to such contamination (Haas et al. 1986). Careful selection of appropriate pretreatment procedures and sampling localities, as well as removal of roots and carbonates, and concentration of fine organic particles can control for some of these problems (Scharpenseel 1971).

Dating Organic Matter in Archaeological Sites. Determining the age of fine-grained organic matter is not frequently used in archaeology. Fine-grained organic matter in archaeological sites does not only come from the accumulation of organic matter on the surface, as is the case in pedogenesis. As discussed in the three examples used to illustrate the sources of organic matter in archaeological sites, the fine-grained organic matter in archaeological contexts can come from a combination of decomposing soil organic matter and decomposing sedimentary organic clasts (e.g., humanly transported animal carcasses, seaweed, berries, nuts, and water or wind transported organic clasts). These decomposing organic sediments contain carbon atoms with radiometric signatures corresponding to the moment of the organism's death. If, for example, the source of some fine-grained organic matter was a decomposing deer carcass, then the age of the fine-grained organic matter corresponds to the moment of death of the deer. The fine-grained organic matter from the decomposing tissue of the deer may mix with the products of other decomposing organic tissue, such as seaweed, berries or nuts. The radiometric age of the mixture of decomposed tissue would represent the ages of all the organisms and plants that were transported to the site and that decomposed in the same vicinity. Thus, the fine-grained organic matter in an archaeological site will be a mixture of the age of death of all organic sedimentary clasts brought to the site.

Determining the age of organic matter can be complicated when organic matter comes from two sources, a combination of decomposing sedimentary organic matter (derived from the organisms in the archaeological deposit) and of organic matter associated with soil formation that formed near the upper boundary (stable surface) of the archaeological (sedimentary) deposit. The age of the organic matter in the deposit will reflect a combination of the age of death of all transported organisms and the AMRT of the soil organic matter added at the upper boundary. In such cases the radiometric date of the fine-grained organic matter from the site will be younger than the real age of the depositional event (the occupation). The dilution of the age occurs when younger organic matter, associated with soil formation near the upper boundary of the archaeological deposit and transported downward into the existing archaeological sediments, is mixed with the older organic matter in the sediments.

Perhaps the best way to interpret dates obtained from fine-grained organic matter in archaeological sites is to separate the sources of the organic matter. This can be done by measuring the ages of large-sized organic objects (wood, charcoal, or bone), the ages of fine-grained organic matter located near the surface of the deposit (and supposedly associated with soil formation), and the ages of fine-grained organic matter located near the bottom of the deposit (and supposedly of sedimentological origin and removed from the effects of soil formation). Of course, this comparison would be meaningful only if rates of sedimentation (rates of accumulation of occupational debris) are rapid, and the age of the top and bottom of the deposit (before soil formation) were similar (Ferring 1986). At the Lubbock Lake site, wood, charcoal, humic acid, and humin were dated to compare the age of the objects in the deposit and the date of the formation of the soils (Haas et al. 1986). Although the archaeological deposits at Lubbock Lake were not sufficiently thick to form a layer that was beyond the effects of soil formation, the results of the Lubbock Lake research indicate that deposition of the wood and charcoal was contemporaneous with (and slightly older than) the formation of the soil, and that the A horizon of the buried soil provides a maximum age for the time of burial and an estimate for the beginning of pedogenesis (Holliday et al. 1983).

Using the age of fine-grained organic matter from archaeological sites also has great potential in other situations. In sites on the Northwest Coast, where large cedar trees were used extensively in house and canoe construction and tool manufacture, the age of a single tree can vary by 1000 years from the inside to the outside of a tree. One archaeological deposit could therefore contain wood charcoal from a single tree and single depositional event, but with a great range in ages. In such situations, where wood charcoal is not an appropriate single-source for age determination of archaeological material, the age of fine-grained organic matter could be used to narrow the range of dates for the deposit. Another example concerns situations where construction material containing organic remains are reused over millennia. To determine the age of the mudbrick the organic component of the mudbricks is analyzed. The age of the bricks might be much older than the period in which the structure (where they were found) was made, which in turn may be older

205

than the period in which the structure was last occupied. The organic content of the mudbricks might provide a more detailed history of the occupation and construction practices.

Reconstructing Ancient Landscapes

"Landscapes" are "stretches of country as seen from a particular vantage point" (Harris 1968). Landscapes are not the sediments in the substrates, or the soils developing on the surface (Hole and Campbell 1985). They are "stretches of country," or surfaces (Roberts 1987). Reconstructing ancient landscapes is of interest to archaeologists because the old landscapes are the surfaces on which prehistoric people lived, and in some fashion affected the activities and decisions of prehistoric peoples (Butzer 1971, 1982). Landscapes are not environments, which are subdivisions of the landscape based on physical, chemical and/or biological criteria (Hassan 1985), and they are not landforms, which are distinct surface features resulting from a particular geomorphic phenomenon (Davidson 1985).

Landscapes are classified, according to the dynamic processes that dominate their surfaces, as having *erosional* surfaces if their shape depends on what is left after material has been transported, and as having *depositional* surfaces if their shape depends on the size and shape of the material deposited. Landscapes are classified as *stable* if weathering is the dominant process, and material is neither being transported nor deposited (Gerrard 1981; Tuttle 1980). Landscapes have also been classified by the assemblage of soil bodies on a land surface in a particular landscape, and referred to as soilscapes (Buol et al. 1989; Soil Survey Staff 1975).

Although soils can form in deposits making up any landscape, organic matter is not distributed evenly over these three possible types of landscapes. Soil organic matter is restricted in distribution to stable landscapes. On erosional and depositional landscapes soil organic matter is minimal, even though on depositional surfaces sedimentological organic matter can make up a large proportion of the sediment being deposited. Stable landscapes, on the other hand, are locations where soil organic matter thrives. Encouraged by weathering processes operating at the surface (i.e., in the presence of water and atmosphere), the vast majority of the world's soil organic matter is found on stable landscapes.

Archaeologists interested in landscape reconstructions are generally restricted to areas dominated by depositional sequences of sediment (stratified deposits), and searching for buried surfaces (ancient landscapes) that were at one time stable, especially buried surfaces with well-developed soils (Fenwick 1985). The preoccupation with buried soils in landscape reconstruction represents a search for unconformable discontinuities in the depositional regime (i.e., a search for places in the depositional record when deposition ceased, stability occurred, and soils developed). Unconformable discontinuities are surfaces of contact between vertically successive deposits where a period of nondeposition or erosion has occurred between adjacent units (Krumbein and Sloss 1963; Stein 1987, 1990). These unconformable surfaces represent places in the stratigraphic sequence that are observable over a distance (the scale of which depends on the research). The unconformable surface is a marker in time that is essential for stratigraphic correlation of deposits across any geographic region. Unconformities are often difficult to recognize in stratigraphic sequences. Buried soils are recommended geologically as a criterion for defining an unconformity, and are thus the focus of research involving reconstructions of ancient landscapes from depositional sequences.

Archaeological research, where landscape reconstruction using soil organic matter has been crucial, depends on correlating buried soils (some of which contain artifactual material) from location to location (Macphail 1986). The buried soil is originally described at the location where artifacts are found, carefully noting the stratigraphic relationship between the artifacts and the buried soil horizons. Using these descriptions, other localities are examined and correlations noted. As discussed by Holliday (1990, and the chapter in this volume), correlating a buried soil across a landscape is most reliable when the two soils being compared are in similar landscape positions (topographic positions) and of similar parent material. These factors exert strong influences on soil morphology and will affect the comparisons. Once a soil, which reflects an unconformity or stable surfaces, is correlated across space it can be used to reconstruct the "paleotopography" of the area (Stein 1986). This use in landscape reconstruction of soil organic matter, as it relates to buried soils, has been very successful in archaeological research, as noted in the discussion by and references within Holliday (1990) and other chapters in this volume.

Defining Archaeological Sites

Organic matter has frequently been used to define some aspect of an archaeological site, especially the boundaries of occupation (horizontally and vertically), the presence of features, the source of the deposits, or the presence of post-depositional alterations (see Stein 1984). The source of the organic matter discussed in such studies may be both sedimentary and pedogenic, the difference of which is usually implied rather than specified.

Three examples are discussed. Although others exist, these three represent some of the potential uses of organic matter in archaeological research, and some of the problems that archaeologists encounter when they use organic matter without explaining some of its complexities. One of the best examples is the work done by Heidenreich and Narratil (1973), who measured a suite of chemical elements on samples collected from the surface to determine the perimeter of the Robitaille site, Ontario. They examined many chemical compounds, and expected to find (among other things) the highest organic matter values in the samples taken from within the village confines. Instead they found that organic matter values did not change significantly from within the village to beyond it. Their expectations were based on the assumption that greater amounts of organic matter were deposited by the occupants within the village boundaries (in the form of sediments), and that the deposition of sedimentary organic matter would raise the level of organic matter within the village to levels higher than found associated with the surrounding soils (soil organic matter). To me, their findings suggest that the deposition of sedimentary organic matter, associated with occupation of the village, was not sufficiently large to change the overall amount of organic matter on the surface within the village (and associated with a soil that must have existed there before occupation). Any increase in the deposition of organic matter, caused by activities associated with occupation, was accompanied by an increase in microorganism activity, an increase in the rate of decomposition, and an increase in the loss of carbon dioxide. Thus, the authors found the levels of organic matter to be the same inside and outside the site boundaries. A similar study was done by Griffith (1980, 1981) at the Benson site, Ontario, where again organic matter levels were found to be the same within and outside a village boundary.

Another example of the use of organic matter in defining archaeological sites is the analysis of a site feature conducted by Goffer et al. (1983), at the tell site of Ancient Beer-Sheba, Israel. Two large pits (radius 3 m, depth 6 m and volume over 100 cu m) were discovered that were filled with very dark sediment. The large size and organic-rich content of the pits lead the authors to suggest that the pits were used for making compost. The percentages of organic carbon, nitrogen, and phosphorus were determined for samples from pit fill, from the tell, from a soil located off the tell, and from compost found in the modern town. The largest percentages of carbon were found in the sample from the modern compost, with decreasing values found in the pit fill, the tell sediment, and the lowest percentages in the soil located off the tell. The highest values of phosphorus were found in the pit fill, which lead the authors to suggest that originally the percentages of carbon were also higher in the pit fill, but had been lowered through decomposition and leaching. Although the loss of the organic matter is an assumption of the authors and not a condition that was proven, the authors' conclusions identify correctly one of the limitations associated with using organic matter for identifying features, i.e., the loss of organic matter during decomposition (through escaping carbon dioxide and soil solutions). Interestingly, even if the assumed loss of organic matter through time was correct, the percentages of organic matter in samples from the pit fill were higher than the levels in samples from the tell or the soil in the surrounding area. Only in the modern compost were the percentages of organic matter higher than the values found in the pit fill samples. Thus, decomposition had resulted in the loss of organic matter in the form of carbon dioxide. However, the percentages of organic matter in the pit fill were elevated above those expected by occupation or pedogenesis alone. Perhaps the decomposition rate was depressed by some factor involved with burial, or perhaps there had not been enough time for large amounts of carbon dioxide to be released. Although this research is an excellent example of an imaginative use of organic matter in an archaeological investigation, it is also an example of imprecise usage of the terms soil and sediment. The reader must be careful to realize that the source of the organic matter in the pit fill discussed in the article is sedimentological, yet it is compared to organic matter associated with soils of the surrounding landscape, as well as to organic matter from the tell, which could be either sedimentological or pedological.

The last example to be discussed represents the use of organic matter in defining a buried soil, published well before most archaeologists considered chemical studies of value (Mattingly and Williams 1962). At the Roman earthwork at Winterslow, near Salisbury, England, a soil was discovered below a Roman amphitheater. Samples of this buried soil were chemically analyzed and compared to other samples, among which was one sample collected from a nearby modern cultivated surface. The results indicate that the chemistry of the buried soil is similar to the chemistry of the surrounding surface soil, with the expected deficiencies in carbon, nitrogen and organic phosphorus. The interesting aspect of this research is the authors' attempt to estimate the percentage of carbon, nitrogen, and organic phosphorus that was lost since Roman times. Using the assumption that the soil, before it was buried, had ratios of carbon, nitrogen, and organic phosphorus that were about the same as those found in the surface soil today, and the assumption that the percentage of total phosphorus had not changed since burial, the authors estimated the chemical composition of the soil in Roman times and the percentages lost since that time. What the authors assume, but do not state, is that these estimates are based on the fact that the source of the organic matter is from pedogenesis only, and that decomposition occurred even after burial (i.e., decomposition was not inhibited by the overlying amphitheater). These assumptions are difficult to accept, given that Neolithic artifacts are found on the surface where the soil was formed, and that the construction of an amphitheater would certainly affect the ability of moisture to penetrate to the location of the buried soil. In any event, the study represents an interesting use of organic matter, and one published well before its time.

CONCLUSIONS

Organic matter has been frequently used in archaeological research, and in fact has great potential to enhance archaeological interpretation. Organic matter has two sources, sedimentologic and pedogenic. Organic matter found in archaeological sites, which is associated with sedimentation, has to be transported from one place to another by a transport agent. Organic matter found in archaeological sites, which is associated with soil formation, has to be added to the deposits after deposition through weathering and growth of organisms on a stable surface, or it has to be already on the stable surface before the occupation occurred. Whether from a sedimentological or pedological source, organic matter decomposes from fresh tissue into amorphous humus, releasing carbon dioxide into the atmosphere at each stage of reduction.

Organic matter can be used in archaeological research in the context of dating, landscape reconstruction, and definition of archaeological sites. A new area of research involving organic matter examines the values of stable isotopes of carbon ($^{13}C/^{12}C$) in soil organic matter as indicators of the parent floral community (Schwartz et al. 1986). Stable carbon isotopes have been used in archaeological research to detect subsistence remains (Sillen et al. 1989), but as yet their use as indicators of floral communities in archaeological landscape reconstruction is just beginning.

Although organic matter has been utilized to some extent in archaeological investigations for the last two decades, it has not been utilized fully. With a clearer understanding of its potential, the study of organic matter can make significant contributions to the discipline.

ACKNOWLEDGMENTS

This essay is dedicated to my geoarchaeology class of spring 1988. I wish to thank them for their confusion and their inspiration to write this paper. I would like to acknowledge Stanley E. Chernicoff, Robert C. Dunnell, William R. Farrand, Donald K. Grayson, Vance T. Holliday, Angela R. Linse, Nancy Sikes, and two anonymous reviewers for their helpful comments. I also thank Vance T. Holliday for the opportunity to participate in the Fryxell Symposium at the annual meeting of the Society for American Archaeology, Phoenix, Arizona.

REFERENCES

Ahlrichs, J. L.
    1972   The Soil Environment. In *Organic Chemicals in the Soil Environment*, edited by C. A. I. Goring and J. W. Hamaker, pp. 3–46. Marcel Dekker, Inc., New York.

Alexander, C. S., and L. W. Price
    1980   Radiocarbon Dating of the Rate of Movement of Two Solifluction Lobes in the Ruby Ranges, Yukon Territory. *Quaternary Research* 13:365–379.

Andreux, F.
    1982   Genesis and Properties of Humic Molecules. In *Constituents and Properties of Soils*, edited by M. Bonneau and B. Souchier, pp. 109–139. Academic Press, New York.

Birkeland, P. W.
    1984   *Soils and Geomorphology*. Oxford University Press, New York.

Bohn, H. L., B. L. McNeal, and G. A. O'Connor
    1985   *Soil Chemistry*. John Wiley & Sons, New York.

Brady, T. J.
  1989   The Influence of Flotation on the Rate of Recovery of Charcoal from Archae-
         ological Sites. *Journal of Ethnobiology* 9:207–227.

Bruckert, S.
  1982   Analysis of the Organo-mineral Complexes of Soils. In *Constituents and Prop-
         erties of Soils*, edited by M. Bonneau and B. Soucheir, pp. 214–237. Academic
         Press, New York.

Buol, S. W., F. D. Hole, and R. J. McCracken
  1989   *Soil Genesis and Classification*. 3d ed. Iowa State University Press, Ames.

Burleigh, R.
  1974   Radiocarbon Dating: Some Practical Considerations for the Archaeologist.
         Journal of Archaeological Science 1:69–87.

Butzer, K. W.
  1971   *Environment and Archaeology: An Ecological Approach to Prehistory*. Aldine,
         Chicago.
  1982   *Archaeology as Human Ecology: Method and Theory for a Contextual Approach*.
         Cambridge University Press, New York.

Campbell, C. A., E. A. Paul, D. A. Rennie, and K. J. McCallum
  1967   Factors Affecting the Accuracy of the Carbon-dating Method in Soil Humus
         Studies. *Soil Science* 104:81–85.

Catt, J. A.
  1986   *Soils and Quaternary Geology: A Handbook for Field Scientists*. Clarendon Press,
         Oxford.

Davidson, D. A.
  1985   Geomorphology and Archaeology. In *Archaeological Geology*, edited by G.
         Rapp, Jr. and J. A. Gifford, pp. 25–55. Yale University Press, New Haven.

Fenwick, I.
  1985   Paleosols: Problems of Recognition and Interpretation. In *Soils and Quaternary
         Landscape Evolution.*, edited by J. Boardman, pp. 3–21. John Wiley & Sons,
         New York.

Ferring, C. R.
  1986   Rates of Fluvial Sedimentation: Implications for Archaeological Variability.
         Geoarchaeology 1:259–274.

Gerrard, A. J.
  1981   *Soils and Landforms*. Allen & Unwin, London.

Geyh, M. A., J. H. Benzler, and G. Roeschman
  1971   Problems of Dating Pleistocene and Holocene Soils by Radiometric Methods.
         In *Paleopedology: Origin, Nature and Dating of Paleosoils*, edited by D. H.
         Yaalon, pp. 63–75. International Society of Soil Scientists and Israel Univer-
         sity Press, Jerusalem.

Geyh, M. A., G. Roeschmann, T. A. Wijmstra, and A. A. Middeldorp
1983   The Unreliability of ^{14}C dates Obtained from Buried Sandy Podzols. *Radiocarbon* 25:409–416.

Goffer, Z., M. Molcho, and I. Geit-Arieh,
1983   The Disposal of Wastes in Ancient Beer-Sheba. *Journal of Field Archaeology* 10:231–235.

Goh, K. M., and B. P. J. Malloy
1978   Radiocarbon Dating of Paleosols Using Soil Organic Matter Components. *Journal of Soil Science* 29:567–573.

Griffith, M. A.
1980   A Pedological Investigation of an Archaeological Site in Ontario, Canada: An Examination of the Soils in and Adjacent to a Former Village, (part 1). *Geoderma* 24:327–336.
1981   A Pedological Investigation of an Archaeological Site in Ontario, Canada: An Examination of the Soils in and Adjacent to a Former Village, (part 2). *Geoderma* 25:27–36.

Guillet, B.
1982   Study of the Turnover of Soil Organic Matter Using Radio-isotopes. In *Constituents and Properties of Soils*, edited by M. Bonneau and B. Souchier, pp. 238–257. Academic Press, New York.

Haas, H., V. Holliday, and R. Stuckenrath
1986   Dating of Holocene Stratigraphy with Soluble and Insoluble Organic Fractions at the Lubbock Lake Archaeological Site, Texas: An Ideal Case Study. *Radiocarbon* 28:473–485.

Harris, S. A.
1968   Landscape Analysis. In *The Encyclopedia of Geomorphology*, edited by R. W. Fairbridge, pp. 626–629. Reinhold, New York.

Hassan, F. A.
1978   Sediments in Archaeology: Methods and Implications for Paleoenvironmental and Cultural Analysis. *Journal of Field Archaeology* 5:197–213.
1985   Paleoenvironments and Contemporary Archaeology: A Geoarchaeological Approach. In *Archaeological Geology*, edited by G. Rapp, Jr. and J. A. Gifford, pp. 85–102. Yale University Press, New Haven.

Heidenreich, C. E., and S. Narratil
1973   Soil Analysis at the Robitaille Site, Part 1, Determining the Perimeter of the Village. *Ontario Archaeology* 20:25–29.

Hole, F. D., and J. B. Campbell
1985   *Soil Landscape Analysis*. Rowman & Allanheld Publ., Totowa, New Jersey.

Holliday, V. T.
1990   Pedology for Archaeologists. In *Archaeological Geology in North America*, edited by N. P. Lasca and J. Donahue, pp. 525–540. Geological Society of America, Centennial Special Volume 4, Boulder, Colorado.
1992   Soil formation, time, and archaeology. This volume.

Holliday, V. T., E. Johnson, H. Haas, and R. Stuckenrath
  1983   Radiocarbon Ages from the Lubbock Lake Site, 1950–1980: Framework for
         Cultural and Ecological Change on the Southern High Plains. *Plains An-
         thropologist* 28(101):165–182.

Krumbein, W. C., and L. L. Sloss
  1963   *Stratigraphy and Sedimentation.* Freeman, San Francisco.

Kumada, K.
  1987   *Chemistry of Soil Organic Matter.* Elsevier, New York.

Limbrey, S.
  1975   *Soil Science in Archaeology.* Academic Press, London.

Lindsay, W. L.
  1979   *Chemical Equilibria in Soils.* John Wiley & Sons, Inc.

Macphail, R. I.
  1986   Paleosols in Archaeology: Their Role in Understanding Flandrian Ped-
         ogenesis. In *Paleosols: Their Recognition and Interpretation,* edited by V. P.
         Wright, pp. 263–290. Princeton University Press, Princeton.

Mahaney, W. C., and M. G. Boyer
  1986   Microflora Distributions in Quaternary Paleosols on Mount Kenya, East Af-
         rica. *Catena* 13:155–167.

Matthews, J. A.
  1980   Some Problems and Implications of ^{14}C Dates from a Podzol Buried Beneath
         an End Moraine at Haugabreen, Southern Norway. *Geografiska Annales* 62A
         (3–4):185–208.
  1985   Radiocarbon Dating of Surface and Buried Soils: Principles, Problems and
         Prospects. In *Geomorphology and Soils,* edited by K. S. Richards, R. R. Arnett,
         and S. Ellis, pp. 269–288. Allen & Unwin, London.

Mattingly, G. E. G., and R. J. B. Williams
  1962   A Note on the Chemical Analysis of a Soil Buried Since Roman Times. *Jour-
         nal of Soil Science* 13:254–258.

Michels, J. W.
  1973   *Dating Methods in Archaeology.* Seminar Press, New York.

Nelson, D. W., and L. E. Sommers
  1982   Total Carbon, Organic Carbon, and Organic Matter. In *Methods of Soil Anal-
         ysis (part 2): Chemical and Microbiological Properties,* 2d edition, edited by A. L.
         Page, R. H. Miller, and D. R. Keeney, pp. 539–579. Agronomy monograph
         number 9, American Society of Agronomy, Inc. and Soil Science Society of
         America, Inc. Madison, Wisconsin.

Purdy, B. A. (editor)
  1988   *Wet Site Archaeology.* Telford Press, Caldwell, New Jersey.

Roberts, B. K.
   1987   Landscape Archaeology. In *Landscape and Culture: Geographical and Archaeological Perspectives*, edited by J. M. Wagstaff, pp. 77–95. Basil Blackwell, Oxford.

Ruhe, R. V.
   1983   Aspects of Holocene Pedology in the United States. In *Late Quaternary Environments of the United States*, vol. 2, *The Holocene*, edited by H. E. Wright, Jr., pp. 12–25. University of Minnesota Press, Minneapolis.

Scharpenseel, H. W.
   1971   Radiocarbon Dating of Soils: Problems, Troubles, Hopes. In *Paleopedology: Origin, Nature and Dating of Paleosoils*, edited by D. H. Yaalon, pp. 77–88. International Society of Soil Scientists and Israel University Press, Jerusalem.
   1979   Soil Fraction Dating. In *Radiocarbon Dating*, edited by R. Berger and H. E. Suess, pp. 277–283. University of California Press, Berkeley.

Scharpenseel, H. W., and H. Schiffmann
   1977   Radiocarbon Dating of Soils, a Review. *Zeitschrift Pflanzanernaehr Bodenkunde* 140:159–174.

Schwartz, D., A. Mariotti, R. Lanfranchi, and B. Guillet
   1986 $^{13}C/^{12}C$ Ratios of Soil Organic Matter as Indicators of Vegetation Changes in the Congo. *Geoderma* 39:97–103.

Shackley, M. L.
   1975   *Archaeological Sediments*. John Wiley & Sons, New York.

Sheppard, J. C., S. Y. Ali, and P. J. Mehringer, Jr.
   1979   Radiocarbon Dating of Organic Components of Sediments and Peats. In *Radiocarbon Dating*, edited by R. Berger and H. E. Suess, pp. 284–305. University of California Press, Berkeley.

Sillen, A., J. C. Sealy, and N. J. van der Merwe
   1989   Chemistry and Paleodietary Research: No More Easy Answers. *American Antiquity* 54:504–512.

Soil Survey Staff
   1975   *Soil Taxonomy*. U.S. Department of Agriculture, Agriculture Handbook 436.

Sposito, G.
   1989   *The Chemistry of Soils*. Oxford University Press, New York.

Stein, J. K.
   1984   Organic Matter and Carbonates in Archaeological Sites. *Journal of Field Archaeology* 11:239–246.
   1985   Interpreting Sediments in Cultural Settings. In *Archaeological Sediments in Context*, edited by J. K. Stein and W. R. Farrand. Center for the Study of Early Man, Institute for Quaternary Studies, University of Maine, Orono.
   1986   Coring Archaeological Sites. *American Antiquity* 51:505–527.
   1987   Deposits for Archaeologists. *Advances in Archaeological Method and Theory*, vol. 11, edited by M. B. Schiffer, pp. 337–395. Academic Press, Orlando, Florida.

1990　Archaeological Stratigraphy. In *Archaeological Geology in North America*, edited by N. P. Lasca and J. Donahue, pp. 513–523. Geological Society of America, Centennial Special Volume 4, Boulder, Colorado.

Stevenson, F. J.
1986　*Cycles of Soil: Carbon, Nitrogen, Phosphorus, Sulfur, Micronutrients*. John Wiley & Sons, New York.

Stout, J. D., K. M. Goh, and T. A. Rafter
1981　Chemistry and Turnover of Naturally Occurring Resistant Organic Compounds in Soil. In *Soil Biochemistry*, vol. 5, edited by E. A. Paul and J. N. Ladd, pp. 1–73. Marcel Dekker, New York.

Tate, R. L., III
1987　*Soil Organic Matter: Biological and Ecological Effects*, John Wiley & Sons, New York.

Taylor, R. E.
1987　*Radiocarbon Dating: An Archaeological Perspective*. Academic Press, New York.

Tuttle, S. D.
1980　*Landforms and Landscapes*. Wm. C. Brown Co., Dubuque, Iowa.

Whitmer, A. M., A. F. Ramenofsky, L. J. Thibodeaux, J. Thomas, S. D. Field, and B. J. Miller
1989　The Role of Diffusion in Diagenesis of Buried Bone. In *Archaeological Method and Theory*, vol. 1. edited by Michael B. Schiffer, pp. 205–272. University of Arizona Press, Tucson.

8

JONATHAN A. SANDOR

Long-term Effects of Prehistoric Agriculture on Soils: Examples from New Mexico and Peru

Knowledge about soils at prehistoric agricultural sites can be applied to problems of mutual interest in archaeology, agriculture, and the earth sciences. Case studies of prehistoric agricultural soils are used in this paper to explore the interaction between agriculture and the physical environment, with emphasis on the identification of changes in soils and landscapes resulting from prehistoric agriculture. Archaeologists can use this type of research to better understand past agricultural land use and its impact on the environment (Butzer 1982), as well as to infer strategies for agricultural production. Prehistoric agriculture is also relevant to agriculture today. Concern about soil degradation and its effect on agricultural productivity and environmental quality has led to major research efforts to develop sustainable agricultural systems that are not only productive, but that also conserve soil resources (e.g., Douglass 1984; Stinner and House 1989). A key limitation in this research is incomplete knowledge about environmental effects of agricultural land use over long time periods. The archaeological record can provide that long-term perspective.

The research presented here comes from two sites of extensive prehistoric terrace agriculture in semiarid, mountainous regions of New Mexico and Peru. Because of fundamental differences in cultural and

217

environmental contexts between these regions, the inclusion of these particular sites here is not for comparative purposes, but rather to indicate the wide range of possible effects of agricultural land use on soil. One study was conducted in the Mimbres area of southwest New Mexico, where agricultural terraces were farmed sometime between A.D. 1000 and 1150, and then abandoned. The second study is continuing in the Colca Valley, Peru, where terrace agriculture has been practiced for the past 1500 years or more.

An important aspect of both studies is the parallel investigation of natural and agricultural soils. There are several reasons for this approach. Natural soils and landscapes, relatively unmodified by human use, provide a reference against which changes resulting from agriculture can be measured. Along with other environmental factors such as climate, natural soil and geomorphic properties largely determine the agricultural potential of an area and continue to influence agricultural land use throughout its history. Also, the response of soil to agricultural land use can vary greatly in pathway, magnitude, and duration depending on a soil's natural characteristics and sensitivity to disturbance.

Because much of the material from these studies has already been published, the approach here is to summarize findings considered most relevant to archaeologists. Additional information on methods, data, and supporting literature is in the cited references.

STUDIES IN NEW MEXICO

Location and Cultural Background

The archaeological sites studied are located in a semiarid mountainous region of southwest New Mexico in the Sapillo Valley and adjacent Mimbres Valley (Figure 8-1). Work was concentrated in the Sapillo Valley because of the extensive terracing there and the presence of undisturbed soils suitable as reference points for changes in agricultural soils. These prehistoric agricultural terracing sites are typical of many such sites in the southwest U.S. and northern Mexico that date to between A.D. 1000 and 1500 (Donkin 1979). Similar runoff agriculture techniques are still used by Pueblo groups and other traditional agriculturalists (e.g., Hack 1942; Donkin 1979). The sites, ranging from 2 to 30 ha, consist of series of small rock dams built across gentle hillslopes or small, ephemeral streams (Figures 8-2 and 8-3). Sediment accumulation upslope

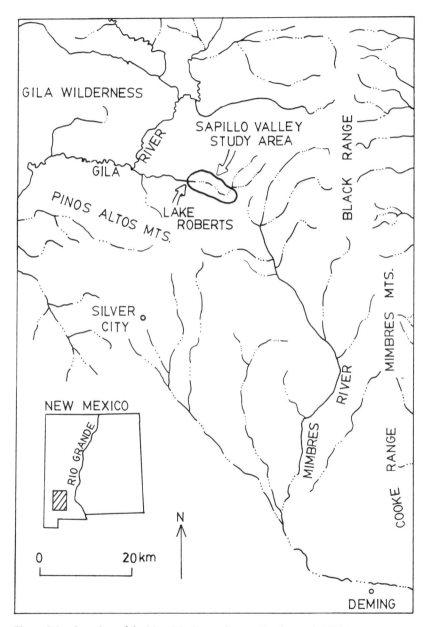

Figure 8-1.   Location of the New Mexico study area (Sandor et al. 1986a).

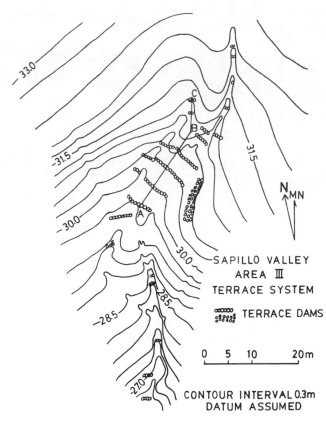

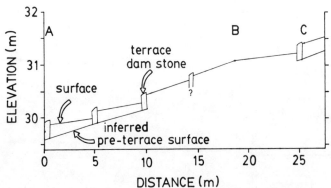

Figure 8-2.   Map and longitudinal profile of some prehistoric agricultural terraces (Sandor et al. 1986a).

Figure 8-3.   Aerial photo of terraced area III (see Figures 8-2 and 8-4). White strip across dams is 10 m long and points north toward upper left.

of each dam, probably by alluvial and colluvial processes (Sandor 1983), resulted in the terraced landscape. Evidence for the direct agricultural function of the terraces, rather than the possible hydrological use proposed by Doolittle (1985), is given in Sandor (1983).

Small surface rooms and pottery at these sites correlate with nearby tree-ring dated pueblos of the Mimbres Classic period, which lasted from about A.D. 1000 to 1150 (Anyon et al. 1981; Minnis 1985). The specific duration of use within this period is uncertain. This period represents the population zenith for the area and there is evidence for intensive land use and alteration of the natural vegetation and faunal populations during that time (Minnis 1985). Terracing was probably supplemental to irrigation agriculture on the major floodplains and botanical evidence from pueblo sites indicates that corn (*Zea mays* L.) was the principal crop (Minnis 1985). Tree-ring data from near the study area indicate generally moister and more stable climatic conditions during this period, particularly in the latter half of eleventh century A.D. (Minnis 1985). Similar findings were made in the Colorado Plateaus area using tree-ring, pollen, faunal, and geologic data (Euler et al. 1979).

221

Placement and Function of Agricultural Terraces

Location of the agricultural terracing sites within a narrow range of geomorphic settings and soils suggests that a set of placement criteria was used to achieve favorable conditions for runoff agriculture (Figures 8-2 and 8-4; Sandor 1983). Compared to a regional elevation range of 1400 to 3200 m, the terracing sites occur between 1800 and 2000 m. Placement of fields at these elevations would maximize the probability of obtaining sufficient water for crop needs, while allowing for a margin of safety in the variable frost-free period. Topographic placement characteristics include gentle slopes, mostly 3–10 percent, and small drainage areas of 1 to 8 ha. These gentle slopes and small watersheds allow runoff but reduce the possibility of high runoff velocities that may damage crops. Hydrologists have demonstrated that small watersheds also have a relatively greater frequency of runoff events and runoff yield per unit area in arid regions (Osborn and Renard 1970; Evenari et al. 1982). No locational pattern with respect to slope aspect was observed.

An important topographic function of terracing includes further reduction of runoff velocities by decreasing slope angle (average terraced slope angle is 0.65 that of original) and slope length (Figure 8-2). In this way, terracing encourages trapping of runoff for crop use. Soil moisture measurements taken before and after a runoff event suggest increased available water in terraced soils relative to unterraced soils in similar landscape positions (Sandor 1983).

Most of the agricultural terraces in the study area were found to occur on or just downslope from soils with shallow, strongly developed argillic horizons in which much clay has accumulated. These soils are the oldest of the study area, weathered from volcanic alluvium on stepped valley-border surfaces of Pleistocene age (Figures 8-4 and 8-5; Sandor 1983; Sandor et al. 1986a). Deliberate placement of fields with respect to these soils is implied because the soils occupy only a small percentage of the area and no fields were found in several areas with similar elevation and topographic settings that lacked the argillic horizons (Sandor 1983). These soils are effective runoff producers and promote higher moisture in the crop root zone because water is detained above the slowly permeable argillic horizon. In this context, terracing would also serve to thicken the naturally thin loamy A horizon overlying the argillic horizon to meet soil volume requirements for crop roots. Runoff derived from unterraced soils with argillic horizons would benefit terraced fields placed directly downslope. The strategy of using the argillic horizons is

LEGEND:

Alluvium

ay *Younger alluvium;* channel and floodplain deposits, wide variation in texture, up to 10–15m thick. Soils with no or little development, various Entisols and some Haplustolls.

ao *Older alluvium;* thin (2–5m) Pleistocene alluvium on valley border and upland erosion surfaces and alluvial terrace deposits, wide variation in texture. Deep soils with mostly strongly-developed argillic horizons, mainly Paleustolls and Argiustolls with clayey-skeletal or fine families.

ao-y *Older alluvium – soils without argillic horizons;* alluvium with characteristics similar to ao, surfaces contiguous with ao. Soils mostly Haplustolls with loamy-skeletal or loamy families.

Colluvium

c1 *Colluvium – thin soils with argillic horizons;* Lithic Argiustolls with mostly clayey-skeletal families; about 40–50cm to bedrock.

c2 *Colluvium – moderately deep soils with cambic horizons;* Typic Ustochrepts with loamy-skeletal families; 50–100cm to bedrock.

Rock

Sedimentary:

Tg‡ *Gila Group* (Miocene-Pliocene); lower member well-bedded, lithic (volcanic) sandstone cemented mainly with zeolite (clinoptylolite); contains interbedded clay lenses and pebble congolmerate; loamy and uncemented in some areas; about 120m thick; grades vertically into upper member. Upper member massive fanglomerate about 140m thick.

Volcanic:

Tbm *Bearwallow Mountain Formation;* alkaline olivine basalt (21 million yr); interbedded with lower part of Tg.

Tba *Alum Mountain Formation* (mid-Tertiary); mainly andesite to basalt.

Other Symbols

I, UII, LIV, V uncultivated sample areas (L = lower, U = upper)

II, III, IV Prehistoric cultivated areas

P Classic Mimbres pueblo site

---

† Map compiled from USDA-FS (1973) and geologic maps (see references in Sandor, 1983), with modifications based on authors' work.

Map base from USGS 7.5-min quads.

‡ Tg members undifferentiated on Fig. 4. Deposits are underlain by Tg unless otherwise noted.

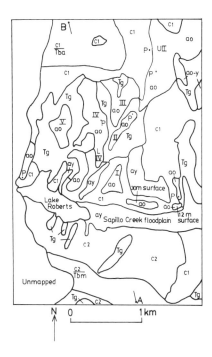

Figure 8-4. Surficial geology and general soil map of part of the Sapillo Valley (Sandor et al. 1986a).

223

Figure 8-5. Aerial photo of main part of the Sapillo Valley study area (see Figure 8-4).

analogous to placement of cornfields by the Hopi Indians downslope from areas with shallow, nearly impermeable shale (Hack 1942) and to placement of prehistoric gridded fields over a duripan in Arizona (Alan Kosse, personal communication 1975). Herbel and Gile (1973) monitored soil moisture in the arid Rio Grande Valley and found relatively favorable conditions for plant growth in areas with similar characteristics.

Soil Changes Resulting from Terrace Agriculture

Changes in prehistoric agricultural soils were inferred from comparisons with nearby, similarly developed, uncultivated soils that serve as reference points or controls for the cultivated soils (Figure 8-4; Sandor et al. 1986a). Human disturbance to the sites since abandonment is thought to be minimal because the agricultural terraces and associated archaeological features are intact and artifacts from later periods are absent. Historic land use within this part of the Gila National Forest has been limited mainly to some cattle grazing controlled by the U.S. Forest Service.

Before discussing soil changes, evidence for vegetation change and accelerated erosion initiated by cultivation is presented because these factors are considered major contributors to the long-term soil changes. In contrast to more grass-covered uncultivated areas, some cultivated areas are nearly devoid of grass cover and apparently have been since they were cleared for agriculture. A possible reason for the failure of grass, mainly blue grama (*Bouteloua gracilis*), to better reestablish itself after abandonment comes from research done on a similar problem on the Great Plains. There, Wilson and Briske (1979) observed only a few blue grama plants growing back on cultivated land abandoned for the past 40 years and reported that attempts to reestablish blue grama from seed seldom succeeded. They attributed the problem to the rare occurrence of special climatic conditions required for seedling development in the present climate. Their findings suggest that the grassland in the New Mexico study area is essentially relict from the Pleistocene or early Holocene, having become established under moister conditions. Maintenance of existing blue grama cover continues because once established, blue grama is hardy and drought-resistant.

Other possible factors contributing to sparse grass cover may involve sedimentation following dam construction, and accelerated erosion. Hubbell and Gardner (1944) concluded from studies of rangeland in New Mexico that sedimentation, in amounts similar to that resulting from agricultural terracing, was especially detrimental to blue grama. Subsequent erosion of agricultural fields, discussed in the next paragraph, could have perpetuated adverse conditions for reestablishment of grass.

Sparse grass cover is associated with cultivated areas exhibiting sheet and gully erosion. Incisions range in size from rills up to gullies 1.2 m deep and 4 m wide. In many places gullies cut through argillic horizons that required a stable landscape and thousands of years to form. The network of gullies, especially pronounced at cultivated Area IV (Figure 8-6), contrasts with the smooth, ungullied, uncultivated surfaces. The following evidence indicates that accelerated erosion began during cultivation: (1) gullies cut through agricultural terraces and associated fills that contain archaeological artifacts, showing that cultivation preceded gullying; and (2) dams built within some gullies, commonly near broken terrace dams, indicate attempts to repair gullies. Stewart and Donnelly (1943) reported that the Zuni used similar measures to stop gullies in agricultural fields. Evidence that erosion has continued intermittently to the present includes observations of renewed gully incision during storms and exposure of tree roots in gully banks. Besides the erosive

Figure 8-6. Aerial photo of terraced area IV. Note erosion and lack of grass cover (trees are juniper and pinyon pine). White strip is 10 m long and points north toward top.

effect of rainsplash on cultivated surfaces exposed by reduced grass and surface stone cover, gullies may have been initiated by runoff scouring soils at terrace dam bases.

Three kinds of soils were compared to investigate long-term changes in the prehistoric agricultural soils. Uncultivated soils in geomorphic settings similar and adjacent to agricultural sites provided reference points for measuring changes in cultivated soils. Although a number of complete profiles from uncultivated and cultivated soils were analyzed, soil horizons above the Bt horizon were sampled more intensively after finding that Bt horizons were not physically disturbed by prehistoric agriculture (except where gullied). The A and BAt horizons were thought to represent the main cultivated zone. Uncultivated and cultivated A horizons were also compared with sediment (local, reworked soil) accumulated upslope of small trees which had recently fallen across uncultivated surfaces. These deposits, referred to as "recent-sediment deposits," are similar in thickness and texture to cultivated A horizons (Sandor et al. 1986a). The recent-sediment deposits, considered analogous to terraced but uncultivated A horizons, were used to distinguish those soil changes resulting from cultivation from those changes which could result from terracing alone.

The most visible change in the prehistorically cultivated soils is increased A horizon thickness resulting from deposition within agricultural terraces. The deposit within an agricultural terrace, a wedge-shaped body of soil upslope of each dam (Figure 8-2), varies in thickness depending on dam height, distance upslope from the dam, and original and depositional slopes (Leopold and Bull 1979). Whereas uncultivated A horizon thickness is typically 5–7 cm, A horizon thickness in cultivated areas varies from 5 cm (i.e., no thickening) to as much as 60 cm, with most in the range of 10–30 cm. The isolated position of the remnant Pleistocene surfaces (Figures 8-4 and 8-5) and the thinness of A horizons upslope of cultivated areas indicates that thickening of cultivated A horizons resulted from local redistribution of topsoil. No textural or mineralogical differences were found between uncultivated A horizons, cultivated A horizons, or recent-sediment deposits (Sandor 1983; Sandor et al. 1986a). Most A horizons are loams or sandy loams with about 18 percent clay.

Color and structure differences between uncultivated and cultivated A horizons suggest degradation of the fertility and physical condition of the cultivated soils. In contrast to the darker-colored uncultivated A horizons with granular structure, cultivated A horizons commonly are lighter in color and have a more blocky, nearly massive structure. These changes in soil morphology are indicators that cultivated A horizons lost organic matter and associated nutrients (e.g., N and P), and were compacted (Table 8-1; Sandor et al. 1986b).

Losses of organic matter (indicated by organic carbon content in Table 8-1) and N in the prehistorically cultivated A horizons amount to over 40 percent. Although organic matter losses decrease with depth, they continue into the upper Bt horizon, deeper than for any other soil property measured. Organic matter and N levels in the recent-sediment deposits are similar to those in the uncultivated A horizons, indicating that terraced soils prior to cultivation had at least as much organic matter as the natural soils. Similar losses of organic matter and N have been reported in many studies of soils under modern conventional cultivation (e.g., Stevenson 1982). The persistence of degradation in the prehistoric agricultural soils may partly relate to the vegetation changes and accelerated erosion.

Bulk density data indicate that cultivated A horizons are compacted relative to uncultivated A horizons and data from recent-sediment deposits suggest that the compaction resulted from cultivation rather than terracing (Table 8-1). This amount of compaction (about 9 percent) has been reported to decrease corn root growth and yields (see Sandor 1983:254). Compaction of the cultivated soils is probably best explained by the relationship of bulk density to organic matter content. The beneficial effects of organic matter in maintaining a porous, granular topsoil with relatively low bulk density are well known (Greenland 1977; Stevenson 1982). When soil organic matter decreases significantly, as is common under conventional cultivation, soils tend to compact and display structural degradation.

Phosphorus, another key soil-based nutrient, also shows a pattern of lower concentration in cultivated A and BAt horizons (Table 8-1; Sandor et al. 1986c). Phosphorus fractionation studies (Sandor et al. 1986c) reveal losses from the fraction most available to plants, in contrast to prehistorically cultivated soils in Wisconsin and Colombia analyzed by Eidt (1977). Differences in soil P fraction distribution between cultivated areas were detected but further study is required. Nutrient analyses suggest that these prehistoric farmers did not use fertilizers. In general, there is little evidence for the use of fertilizers by prehistoric farmers in the Southwest (Arrhenius 1963; Fish and Fish 1984). However, alternative means of maintaining sufficient nutrient levels, such as additions from runoff events (e.g., Nabhan 1979) or wide plant spacings, might have

TABLE 8-1

Properties of Soils Sampled in the Sapillo and Mimbres Valleys, New Mexico

Horizon	Sample	Bulk Density g cm⁻³	pH	Organic Carbon g kg⁻¹	Total Nitrogen	Total Phosphorus mg kg⁻¹	Moderately Available Phosphorus
Upper A (0–5 to 7 cm)	Cultivated	1.41 (0.12) a**	6.0 (0.4) a**	9.8 (3.7) a**	0.78 (0.30) a**	355 (50) a*	48 (11)
	Uncultivated	1.29 (0.08) b	5.8 (0.2) ab	18.0 (4.6) b	1.33 (0.33) b	417 (43) a	54 (19)
	Sediment	1.17 (0.09) b	5.6 (0.2) b	23.1 (8.1) b	1.44 (0.49) b	448 (58) b	76 (22)
A	Cultivated	1.42 (0.09) a**	6.0 (0.3) a*	9.8 (2.3) a**	0.79 (0.22) a**	343 (57) a**	32 (8) a**
	Uncultivated	1.30 (0.08) b	5.8 (0.2) b	17.9 (4.4) b	1.32 (0.34) b	417 (43) b	54 (19) ab
	Sediment	1.20 (0.11) b	5.8 (0.5) ab	21.4 (7.3) b	1.36 (0.47) b	444 (48) b	76 (22) b
BAt	Cultivated	1.44 (0.09)	5.9 (0.4)	9.6 (1.7)**	0.84 (0.20)**	330 (43)*	
	Uncultivated	1.40 (0.06)	5.9 (0.2)	15.6 (3.0)	1.32 (0.22)	401 (8)	
Upper Bt	Cultivated	1.60 (0.12)	6.0 (0.5)	6.5 (2.0)**	0.69 (0.09)	338 (46)	
	Uncultivated	1.66 (0.05)	6.4 (0.3)	9.6 (2.9)	0.87 (0.19)	341 (20)	
Bt	Cultivated	1.62 (0.15)	6.6 (0.4)	5.2 (2.3)			
	Uncultivated	1.62 (0.05)	6.8 (0.1)	7.5 (1.6)			

1. Soil sample groups: Cultivated = prehistoric agricultural soils, Uncultivated = uncultivated soils, Sediment = recent-sediment deposits.

2. Data are means with standard deviations in parentheses.

3. *, ** = Significant differences between sample groups at the 0.05 and 0.01 probability levels, respectively.

4. Means followed by different letters are significantly different at the 0.05 probability level using Bonferroni's inequality.

5. Moderately available P refers to P Fraction no. 1 in Sandor et al. (1986c) and Eidt (1977).

6. Table modified from Sandor et al. (1986b, 1986c). For details on sampling, laboratory methods, and statistical analysis, see those references.

compensated for the lack of fertilizer. The only nutrient found to have increased in cultivated soils is Mn (Sandor et al. 1986c). Similarly high Mn in the recent sediment deposits and in runoff suggests that Mn is relatively mobile during runoff events and accumulated in cultivated soils by entrapment in agricultural terraces.

A crop growth experiment was conducted to test whether observed differences between cultivated and uncultivated soils corresponded to actual changes in agricultural productivity and to further evaluate the fertility of the prehistoric agricultural soils. A traditional variety of corn (Chapalote variety, see Cordell 1984) was grown for 28 days in samples of uncultivated and cultivated soil under controlled conditions in a greenhouse (Sandor and Gersper 1988). Corn growth and N content in treatments without added fertilizer were greater in the uncultivated soil, which corresponds with the higher N content of the uncultivated soil (Table 8-1). However, P nutrition was better in corn grown in the cultivated soil, which contradicts data showing generally higher P in the uncultivated soil (Table 8-1; Sandor and Gersper 1988). With N and P fertilization, growth was similar in both soils and significantly greater than when the soils were not fertilized. This implies that during prehistoric farming, yields would have improved significantly with fertilization. Simultaneous testing with barley (a standard test plant) and comparison to similar greenhouse trials run previously with modern agricultural soils suggest that both uncultivated and prehistorically cultivated soils are potentially productive by modern standards, especially if fertilized with N.

STUDIES IN PERU

History of Terrace Agriculture

Agricultural terraces in the Colca Valley, Peru (Figure 8-7) provide an opportunity to investigate soils cultivated during the past 1500 years or more. Although many of the agricultural terraces are presently farmed, over half are abandoned, probably since the time of the Spanish conquest (Denevan 1987). Unlike the New Mexico case where selected geomorphic settings were used for runoff agriculture, nearly the entire Colca Valley was transformed into a terraced landscape with skillfully engineered series of rock walls up to 3 m high and a remarkable irrigation system (Figure 8-8; Denevan 1987; Treacy 1989a, 1989b). The long his-

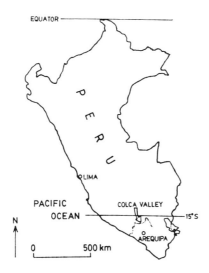

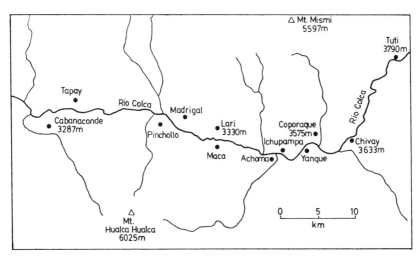

Figure 8-7. Location of the Colca Valley, Peru. Lower figure modified from Denevan (1987).

tory and continuity of terrace agriculture is substantiated by 17 radiocarbon ages from terraced soils and adjacent archaeological sites containing similar artifacts (Sandor 1987; Malpass 1987). Most of these ages fall between 1300 and 1700 yr B.P., suggesting that the main agricultural terrace and irrigation network of the Colca Valley was emplaced as a unified system during this time. Two older ages of 2500 and 3500 yr B.P.

Figure 8-8. Agricultural terraces in the Colca Valley, Peru. Abandoned agricultural terraces in foreground. Stratovolcanoes in background (Mt. Hualca Hualca on right, active Mt. Ampato on left).

were obtained from soil organic matter at the base of terraced A horizons. However, it is not yet known whether these older A horizons represent earlier agricultural soils or natural A horizons buried by later agricultural terracing (Sandor 1987). Older walls within some present terraced walls (Malpass 1987), and younger radiocarbon ages and stratification in a few excavated terraces, show that more work is needed to understand the evolution and modification of the agricultural terraces.

Physical Environment and Soil Formation

Information about the physical environment of the Colca Valley is essential to understanding the development of agriculture and soils there. Certain climatic and geomorphic factors especially influence crop ecology and the distribution of soil properties that affect agricultural productivity. The valley is situated on the semiarid western side of the Andes in southern Peru. Because of its location at a high altitude (about 3350 m for the valley floor in the main study area) in the tropics, temperatures are cool (e.g., annual mean temperature of 10°C at about 3600 m) and daily temperature fluctuations greatly exceed seasonal temperature differences

(ONERN 1973). With the high topographic relief (total elevation range is about 3000 to 6000 m, agricultural terraces occur from about 3000 to 4000 m) and temperature gradients, crops are stratified by elevation and topographic position. For example, corn is grown up to about 3400 m, preferably on steeper terraced slopes with cold air drainage that are not as prone to killing frosts (Treacy 1989b). The valley receives about 75 percent of its 400 mm average annual precipitation during the summer. Research by Thompson et al. (1985) on the Quelccaya Ice Cap in southern Peru suggests a generally similar climate over the past 1500 years, with episodic drier and moister periods. The rather sparse natural vegetation consists mainly of perennial grasses, hardy shrubs, and cacti.

Volcanism has been a dominant geologic factor in the region from the late Cretaceous and Tertiary periods through the Quaternary (ONERN 1973; Sébrier et al. 1985). Andesite is the major rock type but rhyolitic tuff and other volcanics, including unweathered volcanic ash, also occur. Soil parent materials are primarily alluvium and colluvium derived from these volcanic rocks (Sandor 1987). Volcanic activity during the period of prehistoric agriculture is shown by the apparent burial of agricultural terraces by lava flows in the nearby Andahua Valley (Shippee 1932). Mt. Ampato, a nearby stratovolcano (Figure 8-8) shows signs of present activity. Sébrier et al. (1985) documented normal faults of Pleistocene and Holocene age in the Colca Valley that are associated with volcanism. Extensive landslides in areas of the Colca Valley may be partly caused by earthquakes (Sandor 1987).

The Andes have been subject to major glaciations for at least 3.5 Ma (Clapperton 1983). Present glaciers are above about 5000 m near the Colca Valley and advanced to about 4000 m in altitude during the Pleistocene. Glaciers have generally been confined to the altiplano (Figures 8-8, 8-9, and 8-10) and the Colca Valley was formed principally by fluvial processes.

The Colca Valley contains at least seven major stepped alluvial surfaces separated by steep slopes (Figures 8-9 and 8-10). The valley drains large previously glaciated areas, and several of these surfaces are Pleistocene outwash terraces underlain by as much as 250 m of volcanic alluvium and other sediments. Middle to late Pleistocene ages (64,000 ± 14,000 and 172,000 years ± 14,000 years, K/Ar dating at the Institute of Human Origins Geochronology Center, Berkeley, California, and the University of Arizona Laboratory of Isotope Geochemistry) were determined for andesitic lava flows overlying alluvium in the valley (Figure

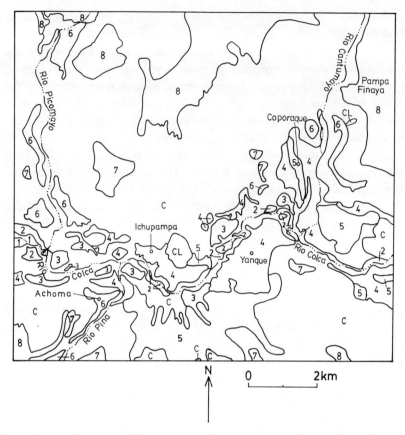

Figure 8-9.   Preliminary surficial geology and general soil map of part of the Colca Valley.

LEGEND

Alluvial Surfaces and Deposits

Qal$_1$ *Channel and floodplain surfaces* of the Rio Colca underlain by interbedded gravel (primarily well-rounded, up to boulder size), sand, and silt. Bedrock outcrops in some areas. Soils include various Entisols.

Qal$_{2-5}$ *Low to intermediate alluvial terrace and fan surfaces* of the Rio Colca and large tributaries. Primarily constructional surfaces graded from <5 to about 100 m above the present valley floor, underlain by interbedded gravel (primarily well-rounded, up to boulder size), fine-grained sediments, and buried soils. Volcanic ash and cinder deposits and carbonate layers present in some areas. Colluvium containing more angular gravel inter-tongues with alluvium in some areas. Soils primarily Mollisols, some with well-developed argillic horizons on Qal$_{4-5}$.

8-9, lava flows are associated with map unit Qal₅). The oldest, highest surfaces are commonly erosional, with a few meters of sediment over bedrock.

The degree of soil development in the valley relates closely to geomorphic setting and age (Figures 8-9 and 8-10; Sandor 1987). Soil properties resulting from pedogenesis in the valley affect agricultural productivity by influencing slope stability, water retention and movement, root behavior, and fertility (Sandor 1987; Eash 1989). Younger soils without clay accumulation occur on lower valley surfaces, while strongly developed soils with argillic horizons, Bk or calcic horizons, and duripans are associated with older surfaces. The degree of soil development in this region is notable given the high altitude environment (Sandor 1987; Wilcox et al. 1988). Many soils on steep slopes (e.g., 40–60 percent slopes) are also well-developed, suggesting unusual stability for terrain normally considered highly erodible. The stability of ancient agricultural terraces on these steep slopes is partly attributed to the argillic horizons and duripans into which terrace walls are anchored. Even with the variation in subsoil development, most natural soils are Mollisols. Further study of natural soil genesis and distribution is being

---

Qal$_{6-7}$ *High alluvial terrace and fan surfaces* of the Rio Colca and large tributaries. Both constructional surfaces (primarily Qal$_6$; underlain by fills up to about 150 m thick) and erosion surfaces (primarily Qal$_7$; underlain by thin fills < about 5 m thick) are present. Surfaces graded from about 150–400 m above the present valley floor, underlain by materials similar to those described for Qal$_{2-5}$. Soils are primarily Mollisols, some with well-developed argillic and calcic horizons, and Duripans.

QT$_8$ *High plateau (altiplano) surfaces* >400–600 m above the present valley floor. Deposits not examined.

Colluvium, Bedrock, and Other Materials

C *Steeply sloping erosional surfaces, undifferentiated;* underlain by colluvium, alluvium and bedrock. Slopes primarily >20%. Includes mountains, hillslopes, drainageways, and scarps of dissected alluvial terraces and fans.

CL Landslides.

Symbols

1-8 Qal$_{1-7}$ and QT$_8$, respectively. Qal$_{6-7}$ assumed to be Quaternary in age. QT$_8$ assumed to be Quaternary to Tertiary in age.

Map base is approximately 1 : 50,000 aerial photo (photo no. 14720, July 15, 1955) obtained from Peru (Servicia Aerofotografico Nacional).

Figure 8-10. Geomorphic surfaces of the Colca Valley. Numbers correspond to those used in Figure 8-9. Photo by Robert Benfer.

conducted, as is an attempt to develop a chronology of geomorphic surfaces and soil formation.

Soil and Crop Management Practices

Before presenting data on cultivated soils, traditional crop and soil management practices are discussed because they significantly influence observed soil properties. Information about traditional agricultural methods is available from farmers in the Colca Valley who have a direct cultural and agricultural connection to the ancient terraced fields. The favorable condition of much of the land indicates that these people have a wealth of agricultural knowledge that is potentially applicable to other areas. For example, they have a soil classification system oriented toward agricultural management (Guillet et al. 1989).

Several crop management practices help maintain soil productivity in the valley. One practice involves various types of intercropping, where two or more crops are grown in the same field simultaneously. A wide variety of native (e.g., corn, quinoa, potatoes, and other tubers) and introduced (e.g., barley, fava beans, alfalfa) crops are grown (Denevan 1987; Treacy 1986b). Crop rotations involving nitrogen-fixing legumes and fallowing are also used. The farmers are well aware of the need for such practices to maintain soil productivity.

Several soil management practices have had significant long-term effects on soil properties and productivity. The most visible of these practices is terracing. The rock walls of the agricultural terraces have foundations set well into B horizons and commonly project 1.5 to 2 m above the ground surface. Most of these terrace walls are intact except where they have been destroyed by livestock or landslides (Sandor 1987). Tillage is mainly done with a chisel-like plow. In terms of effect on soil, this low-impact tillage is similar to conservation tillage in current U.S. agriculture, recommended because it minimizes structural damage and helps maintain organic matter levels and good tilth (Stinner and House 1989). Fertilization is a traditional practice in the Andes (Donkin 1979). Manure from livestock and ashes from hearths and burned vegetation are carefully collected and applied to soils in the Colca Valley. Lastly, most agricultural terraces are irrigated from canals that originate several kilometers away near mountain glaciers. Chemical analyses of two irrigation streams indicate low salt content, with small amounts of nutrients such as Ca, Mg, and K, as well as Na. These soils are not subject to salinity problems that some other ancient agriculturalists using irrigation contended with (e.g., see Douglass 1984).

Soils in Agricultural Terraces

Long-term agricultural use has substantially altered natural soils in the Colca Valley. Soil changes are most evident in A horizons and include thickening, distinctive soil structure and pores, irregular depth distribution of organic matter, enrichment in N and P, and pH decrease. These terraced soils are similar to anthropogenic soils especially well-documented in Europe, which were altered during centuries of land use (e.g., Groenman-van Waateringe and Robinson 1988; Sandor 1983:24–31). General types of these anthropogenic horizons include plaggen epipedons, anthropic epipedons, and agric horizons (Soil Survey Staff 1975). Features of all these horizons were detected in agricultural soils in the Colca Valley.

The most visible of the changes in morphological and physical properties of the Peruvian terraced soils is increased A horizon thickness. Terracing commonly has thickened A horizons by 0.3–1.3 m through accumulation of soil material upslope of terrace walls. Agricultural terraces were primarily filled by hand from the back to front of each terrace, although some were at least partly filled by local sediment transport along slopes (Treacy 1989b). The composition of terraced soils indicates local fill sources (Sandor 1987). The terraced fill geometry is similar to the wedge-shaped form observed in the New Mexico agricultural terraces (Figures 8-2 and 8-11). Terraced soils are commonly loams or sandy loams but have slightly more silt and less sand than natural A horizons (Eash 1989). Other distinctive physical characteristics of terraced A horizons include friable consistence, stable granular to subangular blocky structure, numerous macropores, and evidence of earthworm activity in presently farmed soils (Figure 8-11; Sandor 1987). Unlike many modern agricultural soils and the New Mexico terraced soils, these A horizons show no evidence of compaction. The relatively low bulk density (Table 8-2) is attributed mainly to the traditional management practices that maintain sufficient soil organic matter levels. The observed physical properties are favorable for agriculture in providing a deep, easily penetrable root medium with fairly high available water capacity. Buried organic matter–enriched horizons are also common in terraced soils and may represent original A horizons buried by terraced fills,

Figure 8-11. A horizons in presently cultivated agricultural terrace. Note buried A horizon (31–36 cm depth, radiocarbon age of 610 ± 60 B.P.).

TABLE 8-2

Properties of A Horizons in the Colca Valley, Peru Study Area

Sample	Bulk Density	pH	Organic C	Total N	NO$_3$-N	Total P	Available P
	g cm^{-3}		———— g kg^{-1} ————			—— mg kg^{-1} ——	
Presently Cultivated Soils	1.33 (0.10)	6.3 (0.2)	17.5 (2.3)	1.72 (0.22)	20 (14)	910 (97)	15 (4)
Abandoned Agricultural Soils	1.35 (0.10)	6.7 (0.4)	15.8 (5.1)	1.57 (0.51)	5 (1)	1313 (244)	44 (11)
Uncultivated Soils	1.38 (0.09)	7.2 (0.5)	13.5 (4.0)	1.17 (0.30)	7 (3)	773 (86)	12 (8)
LSD$_{0.05}$	0.05	0.2	2.0	0.18	4	81	4

Notes:

1. Data are means with standard deviations in parentheses.
2. Samples from two cultivated (n = 34) and abandoned (n = 34) agricultural terrace transects, and three uncultivated (n = 30) area transects, are combined in this table. Within transects, samples from upper A horizons (0–15 cm depth) were taken at 5-m intervals (Eash 1989).
3. LSD$_{0.05}$ = Least significant difference at the 0.05 level.
4. For details on sampling, laboratory methods, and statistical analyses, see Eash (1989) and Sandor (1987).

buried A horizons within terraced fills (implying multiple fills perhaps associated with terrace reconstruction activity), or additions of organic amendments by farmers (Sandor 1987). The buried A horizon shown in Figure 8-11, radiocarbon dated at 610 ± 60 yr B.P. and very rich in P, is interpreted as soil which received a large addition of fertilizing material.

Cultivated soils in some areas of the Colca Valley have distinctive chemical properties and generally elevated fertility status relative to uncultivated soils (Table 8-2; Sandor 1987). Both presently cultivated and abandoned terraced A horizons have significantly greater total N and organic matter levels than their uncultivated counterparts. Levels of available N in the form of nitrate are relatively high in presently cultivated A horizons, but are relatively low in uncultivated and abandoned A horizons. Nearly all A horizons examined have pH in the optimal range (slightly acid to neutral) for nutrient availability to plants (Tisdale et al. 1985). The lower pH in terraced A horizons is associated with the higher organic matter content. Terraced A horizons are also enriched in P, and have available P levels (Olsen extract) considered more than sufficient for several types of crops (Olsen and Sommers 1982). The high amounts of P in terraced A horizons reflect residual accumulation from centuries of fertilization. The highest P amounts occur in abandoned A horizons, suggesting that P accumulated over the long prehistoric period has been partly depleted in the historic period, perhaps presently. High levels of P in the abandoned soils may be partly associated with the former use of guano as a fertilizer (Julien 1985; Eash 1989). Phosphorus, originating from fertilization or cultural activity, has moved from near the surface possibly more than one meter into calcareous B horizons (Sandor 1987). Significant movement of P is notable because P is usually considered relatively immobile in soil within the time span of agricultural land use (Smeck 1973; Eidt 1977; Tisdale et al. 1985).

CONCLUSIONS

Studies of soils at prehistoric agricultural sites can lead to a greater understanding of past and present interaction between agriculture and its physical environment. The two examples of prehistoric agriculture presented illustrate a wide range of possible effects of cultivation on soils, depending on a number of cultural and environmental factors.

In the Mimbres, New Mexico area, prehistorically cultivated soils remain partly degraded nearly 900 years after agriculture ceased. The soils and landscape used were sensitive to disturbance and have not recovered to their natural condition. Much can be learned from the sites and their environmental settings about prehistoric agricultural strategies, especially about water use in arid regions. The runoff agriculture techniques employed at these sites have potential value for modern arid land agriculture (Office of Technology Assessment 1983), but the erosion problems noted in this case reiterate the need for careful soil and water management.

In the Colca Valley, Peru, the favorable condition of many of the terraced soils after more than 1500 years of cultivation indicates a carefully constructed agricultural system well-adapted to its mountainous environment. This case demonstrates that traditional agricultural management practices such as crop rotation, terracing, minimum tillage, and organic matter management can help conserve soils over long periods of agricultural use. These management practices originated during prehistoric times in locations such as the Colca Valley, and are recommended in present efforts to develop sustainable agricultural systems.

These studies indicate the long-lasting imprint that agriculture can have on soils and landscapes. The knowledge that can be gained by studying the past at prehistoric agricultural sites should be useful in predicting the future effects of current agriculture on soil resources.

ACKNOWLEDGMENTS

I am grateful to many people who have shared in the research on ancient agricultural soils in New Mexico and Peru. Here, I thank John Hawley, Neal Eash, the late John Treacy, and William Denevan for their help. Thanks also to Vance Holliday for organizing the 1988 Fryxell Symposium and the publication that followed. The anonymous reviewers provided constructive criticism helpful in improving the essay. Support of this research by the National Science Foundation and The Charles A. Lindbergh Fund, Inc., is much appreciated.

REFERENCES

Anyon, R., P. A. Gilman, and S. A. LeBlanc
    1981   A Reevaluation of the Mogollon-Mimbres Archaeological Sequence. *The Kiva* 46:253–277.

Arrhenius, O.
1963   Investigation of Soil From Old Indian Sites. *Ethnos* 2:122–136.

Butzer, K. W.
1982   *Archaeology as Human Ecology: Method and Theory for a Contextual Approach.* Cambridge University Press.

Clapperton, C. M.
1983   The Glaciation of the Andes. *Quaternary Science Reviews* 2:83–155.

Cordell, L. S.
1984   *Prehistory of the Southwest.* Academic Press, New York.

Denevan, W. M.
1987   Terrace Abandonment in the Colca Valley, Peru. In *Pre-Hispanic Agricultural Terraces in the Andean Region*, edited by W. M. Denevan, K. Mathewson, and G. Knapp, pp. 1–43. British Archaeological Reports, International Series 359(l), Oxford.

Donkin, R.
1979   *Agricultural Terracing in the Aboriginal New World.* University of Arizona Press, Tucson.

Doolittle, W. E.
1985   The Use of Check Dams for Protecting Downstream Agricultural Lands in the Prehistoric Southwest: A Contextual Analysis. *Journal Anthropological Research* 41:279–305.

Douglass, G. K. (editor)
1984   *Agricultural Sustainability in a Changing World Order.* Westview Press, Boulder, Colorado.

Eash, N. S.
1989   Natural and Ancient Agricultural Soils in the Colca Valley, Peru. Unpublished M.S. thesis, Agronomy Department, Iowa State University, Ames.

Eidt, R. C.
1977   Detection and Examination of Anthrosols by Phosphate Analysis. *Science* 197:1322–1333.

Euler, R. C., G. J. Gumerman, T. N. V. Karlstrom, J. S. Dean, and R. H. Hevly
1979   The Colorado Plateaus: Cultural Dynamics and Paleoenvironment. *Science* 205:1089–1101.

Evenari, M., L. Shanan, and N. Tadmor
1982   *The Negev: The Challenge of the Desert.* 2d rev. ed. Harvard University Press, Cambridge, Massachusetts.

Fish, S. K., and P. R. Fish (editors)
1984   *Prehistoric Agricultural Strategies in the Southwest.* Anthropological Research Papers No. 33, Arizona State University

Greenland, D. J.
    1977   Soil Damage by Intensive Arable Cultivation: Temporary or Permanent? *Philos. Trans. R. Soc. London B* 281:193–208.

Groenman-van Waateringe, C. W., and M. Robinson (editors)
    1988   *Man-made Soils.* British Archaeological Reports, International Series 410, Oxford.

Guillet, D. W., L. Furbee, J. A. Sandor, and R. A. Benfer
    1989   *Cognitive and Behavioral Studies of Soil Management in the Colca Valley, Peru.* Technical report to the National Science Foundation, Washington, DC.

Hack, J. T.
    1942   *The Changing Physical Environment of the Hopi Indians of Arizona.* Reports of the Awatovi Expedition. Peabody Museum, Harvard University, No. 1. Harvard University Press, Cambridge, Massachusetts.

Herbel, C. H., and L. H. Gile
    1973   Field Moisture Regimes and Morphology of Some Arid-land Soils in New Mexico. In *Field Soil Water Regime*, edited by R. R. Bruce, pp. 119–152. Spec. Pub. 5. Soil Sci. Soc. Am., Madison, Wisconsin.

Hubbell, D. S., and J. L. Gardner
    1944   Some Edaphic and Ecological Effects of Water Spreading on Rangelands. *Ecology* 25:27–44.

Julien, C. J.
    1985   Guano and Resource Control in Sixteenth-century Arequipa. In *Andean Ecology and Civilization*, edited by S. Masuda, I. Shimada, and C. Morris, pp. 185–231. University of Tokyo Press.

Leopold, L. B., and W. B. Bull
    1979   Base Level, Aggradation, and Grade. *Proc. of the American Philosophical Society* 123:168–202.

Malpass, M. A.
    1987   Prehistoric Agricultural Terracing at Chijra in the Colca Valley, Peru: Preliminary Report II. In *Pre-Hispanic Agricultural Terraces in the Andean Region*, edited by W. M. Denevan, K. Mathewson, and G. Knapp, pp. 45–66. British Archaeological Reports, International Series 359(l), Oxford.

Minnis, P. E.
    1985   *Social Adaptation to Food Stress: A Prehistoric Southwestern Example.* University of Chicago Press.

Nabhan, G. P.
    1979   The Ecology of Floodwater Farming in Arid Southwestern North America. *Agro-Ecosystems* 5:245–255.

Office of Technology Assessment
    1983   *Water-Related Technologies for Sustainable Agriculture in U.S. Arid/Semiarid Lands.* U.S. Congress, Washington, D.C.

Olsen, S. R., and L. E. Sommers
  1982   Phosphorus. In *Methods of Soil Analysis*, Part 2, 2d ed., Agronomy 9:403–430,
         edited by A. L. Page et al., American Society of Agronomy, Madison,
         Wisconsin.

ONERN
  1973   *Inventario, Evaluación, y Uso Racional de los Recursos Naturales de la Costa: Cuen-
         ca del Río Camaná-Majes*, 2 vols. Oficina Nacional de Evaluación de Recursos
         Naturales, Lima, Peru.

Osborn, H. B., and K. G. Renard
  1970   Thunderstorm Runoff on the Walnut Gulch Experimental Watershed, Ari-
         zona, USA. *Proc. IASH-UNESCO Symposium on Results of Research on Repre-
         sentative and Experimental Basins.* Victoria University of Wellington, New
         Zealand. IASH 96:455–464.

Sandor, J. A.
  1983   *Soils at Prehistoric Agricultural Terracing Sites in New Mexico.* Ph.D. disserta-
         tion. Univ. of California, Berkeley. University Microfilms, Ann Arbor,
         Michigan.
  1987   Initial Investigation of Soils in Agricultural Terraces in the Colca Valley,
         Peru. In *Pre-Hispanic Agricultural Terraces in the Andean Region*, edited by W.
         M. Denevan, K. Mathewson, and G. Knapp, pp. 163–192. British Archae-
         ological Reports, International Series 359(l), Oxford.

Sandor, J. A., and P. L. Gersper
  1988   Evaluation of Soil Fertility in Some Prehistoric Agricultural Terraces in New
         Mexico. *Agronomy J.* 80:846–850.

Sandor, J. A., P. L. Gersper, and J. W. Hawley
  1986a Soils at Prehistoric Agricultural Terracing Sites in New Mexico: l. Site Place-
         ment, Soil Morphology, and Classification. *Soil Sci. Soc. Am. J.* 50:166–173.
  1986b Soils at Prehistoric Agricultural Terracing Sites in New Mexico: II. Organic
         Matter and Bulk Density Changes. *Soil Sci. Soc. Am. J.* 50:173–177.
  1986c Soils at Prehistoric Agricultural Terracing Sites in New Mexico: III. Phos-
         phorus, Selected Micronutrients, and pH. *Soil Sci. Soc. Am. J.* 50:177–180.

Sébrier, M., J. L. Mercier, F. Mégard, G. Laubacher, and E. Carey-Gailhardus
  1985   Quaternary Normal and Reverse Faulting and the State of Stress in the
         Central Andes of Southern Peru. *Tectonics* 4:739–780.

Shippee, R.
  1932   Lost Valleys of Peru: Results of the Shippee-Johnson Peruvian Expedition.
         Geographical Review 22:562–581.

Smeck, N. E.
  1973   Phosphorus: An Indicator of Pedogenetic Weathering Processes. *Soil Science*
         115:199–206.

Soil Survey Staff
  1975   *Soil Taxonomy.* USDA-SCS Agricultural Handbook 436. U.S. Government
         Printing Office, Washington, DC.

Stevenson, F. J.
  1982   *Humus Chemistry: Genesis, Composition, Reactions.* John Wiley and Sons, New
          York.

Stewart, G. R., and M. Donnelly
  1943   Soil and Water Economy in the Pueblo Southwest. *Scientific Monthly* 56:31–
          44, 134–144.

Stinner, B. R., and G. J. House
  1989   The Search for Sustainable Agroecosystems. *J. of Soil and Water Conservation*
          44:111–115.

Thompson, L. G., E. Mosley Thompson, J. F. Bolzan, and B. R. Koci
  1985   A 1500-year Record of Tropical Precipitation in Ice Cores From the Quelc-
          caya Ice Cap, Peru. *Science* 229:971–973.

Tisdale, S. L., W. L. Nelson, and J. D. Beaton
  1985   *Soil Fertility and Fertilizers.* 4th ed. MacMillan Publishing Co., New York.

Treacy, J.
  1989a   Agricultural Terraces in Peru's Colca Valley: Promises and Problems of an
          Ancient Technology. In *Fragile Lands in South America: The Search for Sustain-
          able Uses,* edited by J. O. Browder, pp. 209–229. Westview Press, Boulder,
          Colorado.
  1989b   *The Fields of Coporaque: Agricultural Terracing and Water Management in the Col-
          ca Valley, Arequipa, Peru.* Ph.D. Dissertation, Department of Geography,
          University of Wisconsin, Madison, Wisconsin.

Wilcox, B. P., B. L. Allen, and F. C. Bryant
  1988.   Description and Classification of Soils of the High-Elevation Grasslands of
          Central Peru. *Geoderma* 42:79–94.

Wilson, A. M., and D. D. Briske
  1979   Seminal and Adventitious Root Growth of Blue Grama Seedlings on the
          Central Plains. *J. Range Manage.* 32:209–213.

245

VANCE T. HOLLIDAY AND
PAUL GOLDBERG

Glossary of Selected Soil
Science Terms

This glossary is intended to be a reference for soil science terms, largely from pedology, that are used in this volume. As such, the glossary is also intended to be an initial source of information for the more commonly used terms in pedology that are likely to be encountered in archaeological research. The emphasis is on soil horizon nomenclature and soil classification following the terminology of the U.S. Department of Agriculture (Soil Survey Staff 1975, 1981, 1990) with some modifications as noted. Also included are some terms basic to soil micromorphology and several miscellaneous terms commonly used among Quaternary soil stratigraphers, soil geomorphologists, and geoarchaeologists.

GENERAL DEFINITIONS OF SOIL HORIZONS

The following symbols are used for describing soils in the field. For more complete definitions see Buol et al. (1989), Birkeland (1984), Soil Survey Staff (1975, 1990), or Soil Science Society of America (1987).

Master Horizons

O   Surface horizon dominated by organic material and very dark.

A   Mineral horizon that forms at the surface or below an O horizon characterized by accumulation of organic matter mixed with mineral matter, but not like an E or B horizon, typically darker than underlying horizons.

E   Mineral horizon typically below an A or O and characterized by loss of clay, iron and/or aluminum and concentration of more resistant materials and usually lighter in color than underlying horizons due to the losses.

B   Mineral horizon usually underlying an O, A, or E horizon with little or no evidence of original rock or sediment structure, typically redder than underlying or overlying horizons and characterized by: accumulation of carbonates, gypsum, clay, iron, or aluminum or any combination of these; leaching of carbonates; development of blocky or prismatic structure; or any combination of these characteristics.

C   Any mineral horizon, except R, lacking the characteristics of the O, E, A, or B; representing essentially unaltered or slightly altered parent material.

R   Hard bedrock.

K   A mineral horizon impregnated by carbonate such that the carbonate dominates its morphology; generally well-cemented. Not officially recognized by the Soil Conservation Service; see Gile et al. (1965).

Selected Subordinate Horizons

These are suffixes to the Master Horizon symbols (e.g., Ab, Btk). For a full list see Guthrie and Witty (1982) or Wilding et al. (1983:385–386). Any given master/subordinate horizon symbol can be subdivided using letters (e.g., Bw1, Bw2).

b   Buried mineral horizon. Added to all horizons or buried soils (e.g., A-Bw-Ab-Btb-Bkb-Cb). If multiple buried soils are present the b can be numbered (e.g., A-Bw-Ab1-Btb1-Ab2-Cb2).

g   Strong gleying; iron has been reduced; colors are typically olive, yellow, or neutral and often mottled.

h   B horizon with an accumulation of organic matter; usually associated with an E horizon.

s   B horizon with accumulation of iron and/or aluminum; usually associated with an E horizon.

n   Accumulation of exchangeable sodium.

k   B horizon (sometimes C horizon) with a zone of visible accumulation of calcium carbonate.

p   plow zone, usually A horizon.
t   B horizon with accumulation of clay.
w   B horizon with color and/or structural development, but no accumu-
    lation of other material (weakly developed B).
y   B or C horizon with accumulation of gypsum.
z   B or C horizon with accumulation of salts more soluble than gyp-
    sum.

GENERAL CONCEPTS FOR SELECTED DIAGNOSTIC HORIZONS IN *SOIL TAXONOMY*

The following are very general definitions of terms used in the soil classification system of the U.S. Department of Agriculture. Considerable field
and laboratory data are necessary to determine diagnostic horizons. For a
complete list and criteria see *Soil Taxonomy* (Soil Survey Staff 1975, 1990).
Diagnostic horizons are not exact equivalents of field designations (e.g.,
not all Bt horizons are argillic horizons), although there is a general
relationship. Some probable field equivalents are given in parentheses.

Epipedons (Diagnostic Surface Horizons)

Anthropic   Mollic epipedon high in phosphorous content (A).
Histic   Surface horizon very high in organic matter (O).
Mollic   Deep, dark, humus–rich surface horizon with abundant cations
    (A, A&B).
Ochric   Surface horizon that does not meet the qualifications of any
    other epipedon (A).
Plaggen   An artificially made surface layer produced by long-continued
    manuring.

Diagnostic Subsurface Horizons

Albic   Light-colored horizon with significant loss of clay and free iron
    oxides (E).
Argillic   Horizon of significant clay accumulation (Bt).
Calcic   Horizon of significant accumulation of calcium carbonate (Bk).
Cambic   Some reddening and/or structural development; re-
    organization of carbonates if originally present (Bw).
Natric   Argillic horizon high in sodium (Btn).
Oxic   Horizon virtually depleted of all weatherable primary minerals
    and very low in bases.

Petrocalcic   Calcic horizon strongly cemented by calcium carbonate (K).

Spodic   Horizon of significant accumulation of aluminum and organic matter with or without iron (Bh, Bs, Bhs).

GENERAL CONCEPTS OF THE SOIL ORDERS IN *SOIL TAXONOMY*

To properly classify a soil one must follow the guidelines and criteria for diagnostic horizons and classification in *Soil Taxonomy*. The principal characteristics of the soil orders are presented below.

Alfisols   Soils with argillic horizon, but no mollic and are lower in bases than Mollisols (A-Bt). Typically found in humid, temperate regions.

Aridisols   Soils formed in desert conditions (Entisols can also be found in deserts) or under other conditions restricting moisture availability to plants (high salt content; soils on slopes); with or without argillic horizon, but commonly with calcic, gypsic or salic horizons (A-Bw-Bk; A-Bt-K; A-By).

Entisols   Soils with little evidence of pedogenesis (A-C, A-R); very few diagnostic horizons.

Histosols   Organic soils, such as peats.

Inceptisols   Soils exhibiting more pedogenic development than Entisols with appearance of diagnostic surface and subsurface horizons that are not as well developed as in most other orders (A-Bw).

Mollisols   Soils with a mollic epipedon and high in bases throughout; typical of continental grasslands.

Oxisols   Soils with an oxic horizon; found in tropical regions and include many soils formerly termed Laterites and Latosols.

Spodosols   Soils with spodic horizons (O-A-E-Bh/Bs/Bhs); typical in cool, humid climates under coniferous forests.

Ultisols   Highly weathered soils with argillic horizons and very low in bases (A-Bt); typically found on older landscapes in warm, humid climates.

Vertisols   Soils high in clay content that shrink and swell markedly.

SELECTED MICROMORPHOLOGICAL TERMS

For more complete definitions and listings of terms see Jongerius and Rutherford (1979) and Bullock et al. (1985).

Argillans   Coatings of clay on natural surfaces (e.g., pores, crack, peds, sand grains) of soils.

B(Birefringence)-fabric Fabric of fine material viewed under cross-polarized light.

Fabric The spatial arrangement of constituents of the soil, including solid, liquid, and gaseous components.

Gefuric Related Distribution Coarser particles are linked by bridges of finer material and are not in contact with each other.

Groundmass Fine and coarse material constituting the base of the material seen in thin section.

Hypocoating Accumulation of material (e.g., calcite or sesquioxides) within the groundmass, adjacent to or below the surface of a grain or void.

Microcontrasted Particles Discrete particles less than 30 μm which are set off from others because of their opacity, for example.

Papules Fragments of clay, typically laminated, with external sharp boundaries in comparison to surrounding material.

Porphyric Related Distribution Coarser particles are found in a groundmass of finer material.

MISCELLANEOUS TERMS

Anthrosol Soils "whose native traits have been significantly altered by human activities" (Eidt 1984:23). Eidt (1984:23) further subdivides anthrosols into "anthropogenic" soils, which have been intentionally altered, and "anthropic" soils, which have been unintentionally altered (not to be confused with the same term used in *Soil Taxonomy*). Anthropogenic soils would include the plaggen epipedon of *Soil Taxonomy* (see above and Groenman-van Waateringe and Robinson 1988).

Biosequence A sequence of related soils that differ primarily because of differences in plants and soil organisms (Jenny 1980:201–206; Soil Science Society of America 1987).

Catena A sequence of related soils along a slope that vary due to variations in relief and drainage; a kind of "toposequence" (see below) (Birkeland 1984:238–254; Soil Science Society of America 1987).

Chronosequence A sequence of related soils that differ primarily because of age differences between the soils (Jenny 1980:201–206; Soil Science Society of America 1987).

Climosequence A sequence of related soils that differ primarily because of climatic differences between the soils (Jenny 1980:201–206).

Eluviation Removal of soil material from one horizon to another; usually from an upper to a lower horizon in the soil profile (Soil Science Society of America 1987; Buol et al. 1989:128–119).

Illuviation Accumulation of soil material removed from one horizon to another; usually from an upper to a lower horizon in the soil profile (Soil Science Society of America 1987).

Lithosequence A sequence of related soils that differ primarily because of differences in parent material among the soils (Jenny 1980:201–206; Soil Science Society of America 1987).

Paleosol A term widely used in archaeology and other Quaternary studies, but poorly defined (Fenwick 1985). Definitions include: soils of obvious antiquity (Morrison 1967:10); ancient soils (Butzer 1971:170); soils formed on a landscape of the past (Ruhe 1965:755; Yaalon 1971:29) or under an environment of the past (Yaalon 1983); or soils formed under conditions generally different from those of to-day (Plaisance and Cailleux 1981:702). Specific types of paleosols include buried soils, which are soils that have been covered by sediment, relict soils, which are soils formed on pre-existing land-scapes and never buried, and exhumed soils, which are soils that were buried and subsequently re-exposed (Ruhe 1965; Valentine and Dalrymple 1976). In these definitions, specifics concerning pre-existing or past landscapes or past environments or how old the soil has to be is never defined.

Pedoturbation Mixing of sediments and soils by flora or fauna (includ-ing humans) (Buol et al. 1989:120–121).

Profile A vertical section of the soil through all of its horizons and ex-tending into the C horizon (Soil Science Society of America 1987).

Solum The upper and most weathered part of the soil profile; the A, E, and B horizons (Soil Science Society of America 1987)

Tilth The physical condition of the soil with respect to plant growth, e.g., ease of tillage, fitness as a seedbed, impedance to seedling emer-gence and root penetration (Soil Science Society of America 1987).

Toposequence A sequence of related soils that differ primarily because of differences in position on the landscape; a "catena" (see above) is a kind of toposequence (Jenny 1980:201–206; Soil Science Society of America 1987).

REFERENCES

Birkeland, P. W.
  1984   *Soils and Geomorphology.* Oxford University Press, New York.

Bullock, P., N. Fedoroff, A. Jongerius, G. Stoops, and T. Tursina
  1985   *Handbook for Soil Thin Section Description.* Waine Research Publications, Wolverhampton, England.

Buol, S. W., F. D. Hole, and R. J. McCracken
  1989   *Soil Genesis and Classification,* 3d ed. The Iowa State University Press, Ames.

Butzer, K. W.
  1971   *Environment and Archaeology,* 2d ed. Aldine, Chicago.

Eidt, R. C.
1984   *Advances in Abandoned Settlement Analysis: Application to Prehistoric Anthrosols in Columbia, South America.* The Center for Latin America, University of Wisconsin-Milwaukee.

Fenwick, I. M.
1985   Paleosols: Problems of Recognition and Interpretation. In *Soils and Quaternary Landscape Evolution*, edited by J. Boardman, pp. 3–21. John Wiley & Sons, Chichester, United Kingdom.

Gile, L. H., F. F. Peterson, and R. B. Grossman
1965   The K Horizon—a Master Soil Horizon of Carbonate Accumulation. *Soil Science* 99:74–82.

Groenman-van Waateringe, W., and M. Robinson (editors)
1988   *Man-Made Soils.* BAR International Series 410, Osney Mead, England.

Guthrie, R. L., and J. E. Witty
1982   New Designations for Soil Horizons and Layers and the New Soil Survey Manual. *Soil Science Society of America Journal* 46:443–444.

Jenny, H.
1980   *The Soil Resource: Origin and Behavior.* Springer-Verlag, New York.

Jongerius, A., and G. K. Rutherford (editors)
1979   *Glossary of Soil Micromorphology.* Pudoc, Wageningen, The Netherlands.

Morrison, R. B.
1967   Principals of Quaternary Soil Stratigraphy. In *Quaternary Soils*, edited by R. B. Morrison and H. E. Wright, pp. 1–69. Desert Research Institute, University of Nevada, Reno.

Plaisance, G., and A. Cailleux
1981   *Dictionary of Soils.* Amerind Publishing Co., New Delhi.

Ruhe, R. V.
1965   Quaternary Paleopedology. In *The Quaternary of the United States*, edited by H. E. Wright, Jr., and D. G. Frey, pp. 755–764. Princeton University Press, Princeton, New Jersey.

Soil Science Society of America
1987   *Glossary of Soil Science Terms.* Soil Science Society of America, Madison, Wisconsin.

Soil Survey Staff
1975   *Soil Taxonomy.* U.S. Department of Agriculture, Agriculture Handbook 436.
1981   *Soil Survey Manual* (working draft, 430-V). U. S. Department of Agriculture.
1990   *Keys to Soil Taxonomy*, 4th ed. SMSS Technical Monograph 19. Blacksburg, Virginia.

Valentine, K. W. G., and J. B. Dalrymple
  1976   Quaternary Buried Paleosols: A Critical Review. *Quaternary Research* 6:209–222.

Wilding, L. P., N. E. Smeck, and G. F. Hall
  1983   Glossary of Horizon Designations. In *Pedogenesis and Soil Taxonomy, part 2, The Soil Orders*, edited by L. P. Wilding, N. Smeck, and G. F. Hall, pp. 383–387. Elsevier, Developments in Soil Science 11B, Amsterdam.

Yaalon, D. H.
  1971   Soil-forming Processes in Time and Space. In *Paleopedology*, edited by D. H. Yaalon, pp. 29–40. University of Israel Press, Jerusalem.
  1983   Climate, Time and Soil Development. In *Pedogenesis and Soil Taxonomy, part 1, Concepts and Interactions* edited by L. P. Wilding, N. E. Smeck, and G. F. Hall, pp. 233–251. Elsevier, Developments in Soil Science 11A, Amsterdam.